PENGI

THE NIN
AND C

MARTIN LUTHER (1483–1546), Christian professor and pastor at the University of Wittenberg (Saxony, Germany), lived and worked during an epoch of tumultuous social, political, and religious turmoil—the fall of late medieval Christendom and the rise of the modern West. In the early sixteenth century, he identified key features of the biblical message—preeminently the gospel of salvation focused on Jesus Christ. However, when he proposed that the Roman Catholic Church reform its teaching and practice to emphasize this message, the papacy rejected his interpretations as heretical—excommunicating him and his followers as "Lutherans." The controversy surrounding Luther prompted various protest movements throughout Europe to express their grievances—often differing radically from Luther's reform—and contributing to the upheaval of the age and what became known as the Protestant Reformation(s).

WILLIAM R. RUSSELL, pastor and scholar, serves Augustana Lutheran Church, Minneapolis, Minnesota, where he investigates the life and work of Martin Luther. With a Ph.D. from the University of Iowa and an M.Div. from Luther Seminary, Russell has authored/edited eight books and dozens of articles. A sought-after speaker, he has addressed audiences from Canada to Brazil, Malaysia to Puerto Rico, Oslo to Cape Town. He currently serves as president of the American Academy of Religion, Upper Midwest Region. Married to Ann Svennungsen, he has three grown children and two grandchildren.

MARTIN LUTHER

The Ninety-Five Theses and Other Writings

Translated and Edited with an Introduction by WILLIAM R. RUSSELL

PENGUIN BOOKS

PENGUIN BOOKS

An imprint of Penguin Random House LLC
375 Hudson Street
New York, New York 10014
penguin.com

Library of Congress Cataloging-in-Publication Data

Names: Luther, Martin, 1483–1546, author. | Russell, William R., 1954– translator, editor. |
Luther, Martin, 1483–1546. Disputatio pro declaratione virtutis indulgentiarum. English.
Title: The Ninety-five theses and other writings / Martin Luther ;
translated and edited with an introduction by William R. Russell.
Description: New York : Penguin Books, 2017. | Includes bibliographical references.
Identifiers: LCCN 2017021273 | ISBN 9780143107583 (paperback)
Subjects: LCSH: Theology—Early works to 1800. | BISAC: RELIGION /
Christianity / History. | RELIGION / Christianity / Lutheran. | HISTORY / Europe / Western.
Classification: LCC BR331 .E5 2017c | DDC 230/.41—dc23
LC record available at https://lccn.loc.gov/2017021273

Printed in the United States of America

For Mary Elizabeth Russell Koslig

Contents

THE NINETY-FIVE THESES
AND OTHER WRITINGS

Preface

When I stepped into the work on this book in the summer of 2012, I welcomed the expected set of moves it would provide—a steadying pace from home to office to library. A dance of sorts, with a rhythm I knew well. I could use some of that—a little predictability with a normal tempo. John, our twenty-eight-year-old son, had been diagnosed with leukemia the previous fall. His illness had floored us and we were struggling to regain our footing. We stumbled through those early, chaotic months of his chemo and crises, but were beginning to stand again—staggering toward a world of realistic expectations. John's Down syndrome had complicated his treatment. It also helped him, characteristically, to find his own way. His oncologists, a group not known for irrational exuberance, would pronounce him cured in June 2014.

The expected then twisted into the unimaginable. By January 2015, John's leukemia had returned—with no medical cure in sight. Recurrence for him meant death. We staggered with him as we tried to help him die well. On the morning of May 2, he convulsed a bit and his beautiful heart stopped. He seemed scared, even with his dear sister at his right side and his strong mom at his left. They spoke soft words of encouragement; whispered a Bible camp song into his ears. I cradled his bony legs and prayed. John's earthly dance was over.

As we made our way in that darkness, so many partners supported us. In those years and since, church, family, and friends, physicians, nurses, and therapists have held us upright and helped us put one foot in front of the other. Support beyond measure for a loss beyond calculation. In John's last months with us, however, one companion surprised me: Martin Luther. Perhaps he shouldn't have. I've been studying Luther closely for thirty-five years. I know the "Luther canon." I know his public, earth-shaking, epoch-defining deeds. And because of the way he lived and the kinds of writings he left us, I know he encountered grief and despair—offering pastoral care to others and struggling with his own limitations and losses.

I admit that during this work, I wasn't always looking at Luther for support and wisdom, I was looking at his grammar and syntax. I welcomed the breaks from the sacred work of accompanying John—translating, contextualizing, interpreting a passage could take me away from the painful and chaotic dizziness of it all. After such respites, I could better reposition myself next to John (as well as my wife and daughters). That alone would have been helpful enough.

The Reformer, though, would not stay a purely intellectual pursuit. No mere distraction or object of historical curiosity, the sixteenth-century Luther led me toward comfort and strength while giving voice to my pain and weakness. His five-hundred-year-old words and profound insights began to touch me deeply. He exemplifies the truth of poet-philosopher David Whyte's claim that "the past is never just the past."[1]

Despite (or, perhaps, because of) eyes blurred with grief, I saw in a new way how the Reformer moved amid the epic changes in his world. I could see him improvise through his own dizzying chaos and buckle under loads he did not choose and could not carry; how he leaned on others amid his darkest of struggles. My perspective revealed aspects of Luther I hadn't seen before—specifically, how he tended to his core insight, "The First and Chief Article."[2] I saw how, through it all, he wanted his life and work to express authentically what he'd learned about God and humanity, life and death, law and gospel. The profound encouragement and strength all of that provided, I must admit, surprised me.

My family, in different ways, continues to surprise me. For all those surprises, great and small, I would simply say thanks to: Ann, John (of blessed memory), daughters Sarah and Mary, sons-in-law Dan and Geoff, grandkids John and Annika. The incalculable ways you find to love and care for one another (including me) and so many others are wonderful—loving, laughing, learning, believing, serving with you is a blessing indeed. Thank you, dear ones.

I'm grateful also for trusted friends and colleagues, some for their professional expertise, some for their personal support: Carolyn Carlson (senior Penguin editor who first approached me with this project), Brice Eichlersmith (profound at praying), Tom Greenspon (weaver of wisdom), Robert Kolb (amiable dean of U.S. Luther researchers), Jack Leveille (Renaissance handball player), Rick Lischer (too young to be retired), Leipzigers Johannes Markert and Helge Voigt (who made this an international project), Jim May (Latinist extraordinaire), Paul Rogers (encourager and Germanophile), John Roth (bishop-scholar of the ELCA), Elda Rotor (patient vice president and publisher, Penguin Classics), Phil Ruge-Jones (Heidelberg Disputation expert), Pamela Stalheim Lane (esteemed pastoral colleague), Gary Simpson (longtime theological conversation partner), Eric Trozzo (interpreter of Luther in Southeast Asia), Tim Wengert (wise Luther wonk), and Steve and Mary Wilkins Peterson (generous providers of friendship and welcome).

In addition, numerous institutions have given much-needed support for this work. Preeminently, I'm thankful for Augustana Lutheran Church in Minneapolis. To serve as your pastor is an exciting privilege. As a group, you support and challenge one another and me in ways that Martin Luther would applaud. I've had you in mind consistently as I tried to make Luther speak English. Every page is a response to this question: "How will this play at Augustana?"

Further, thanks to the American Academy of Religion's "Martin Luther and Global Lutheranism Group" (where I first made the case for a fresh Luther translation to commemorate the five-hundredth anniversary of the 95 Theses), the AAR's Upper Midwest Region (where my duties as president are way too much fun), Luther Seminary in St. Paul, Minnesota (particularly the Library—congenial staff, wonderful resources, renewers of books, etc.), the Minneapolis Area Synod (ELCA) and its enlightened Peer Group program (I'm looking at you, "Old Dogs"), the North American Forum on Luther Research (with its tradition of research sharing), the Lutheran Studies Centre at Sabah Theological Seminary in Malaysia (for the space and time to work, for students with non-Western eyes, for wonderful conversations, for great hospitality), and, finally, Penguin Books (with its dynamic commitment to publish great works of great thinkers).

In closing, I would be remiss if I did not acknowledge my debt, along with my gratitude and respect, to the editors and translators of the venerable American Edition of *Luther's Works*.[3] LW began to appear shortly after I was born, so your work has been the English voice of Luther in my head throughout my life. Although American edited English has clearly changed in the last sixty years, your work remains the starting point for anyone who would translate the Reformer into English. Similarities between the new translations in this volume and the translations of LW are gratefully acknowledged. Any improvements I've made are based on your work (indeed, when in doubt, I deferred to you). Any errors I've introduced are my responsibility.

One last prefatory word: note the "Glossary of Names." Luther mentions dozens of persons in these pages and to explain their significance in annotations would be distracting and cumbersome to the general reader.

WILLIAM R. RUSSELL

Introduction, with Luther's Foreword to the Complete Edition of His Latin Writings

Martin Luther talked his way into human history. From private conversations with Katie and their children[1] to public events of epoch-changing magnitude, he spoke. As a congenial host, he talked about matters great and small with the countless folks who enjoyed the hospitality of the Luthers' table.[2] As a stirring teacher, he talked about theological matters and their connections to church practice with students, colleagues, and church-types of all kinds. As a powerful preacher, he talked about the gospel with congregations of peasants and princes, saints and sinners. As an interpreter of the Bible, he talked with shop owners and household servants about how they described their lives—listening for the right words to translate the Scriptures into understandable German. As an Augustinian Brother, he talked about his sins with his father-confessor and he talked to God with his confreres.

All that talking got him into trouble. Big trouble. Charles V, the Holy Roman Emperor of the German Nation, ordered Luther to attend the Imperial Diet of April 1521—so the Reformer could publicly admit that he had misspoken and beg for His Majesty's pardon.[3] Luther knew his life hung in the balance, but he couldn't know that the future of Western civilization also depended on what happened next. On that spring day in the southwestern German city of Worms,[4] the gathered royalty of Christendom would demand that Luther stop talking—about the Bible, Jesus Christ, and the gospel. More than just a gag order, this was a demand that he take it all back—not only every reform-related word he'd spoken, but every published word he'd ever written. They stacked his books on the table in front of him. He was to retract it all and confess his colossal mistakes in front of God and everybody. Submit to the Emperor or suffer the consequences.

As if more tension were needed, every Saxon knew what had happened a century earlier to John Huss, a reform-minded priest from nearby Bohemia. In 1414, Huss, like Luther, was summoned to give an account of his teaching. For Huss, it was the Council of Constance. Huss, like Luther, had been granted a promise of safe-conduct to attend, without fear of retribution. At Constance, the assembly listened to Huss and condemned his teachings as blasphemous. For complicated reasons not related specifically to Huss, the council released the emperor from his oath to protect the Bohemian priest. Promises to heretics need not be kept. They then burned Huss at the stake in the summer of 1415.

With such a fate a distinct possibility for Luther, the pressure intensified excruciatingly. So he talked:

> Because your sublime majesty and your lordships seek a straight answer, I will provide it. . . . I need to be convinced by the testimony of the Scriptures or by obvious reason, because I do not trust the pope or councils in themselves. We know they have, all too frequently, made mistakes and contradicted themselves. I am bound by the Scriptures I have quoted. My conscience is captive to the Word of God. I cannot and I will not retract anything, since it is neither safe nor right to go against conscience. That's all I can do. God help me. Amen.[5]

His plea for God's intervention seemed to work, to the surprise of many. The emperor honored the safe-conduct, and Luther left Worms to return to Wittenberg. The diet condemned him in absentia and offered a bounty for his capture, dead or alive. However, under the protection of the princes of Saxony, Luther had benefactors so powerful that the emperor couldn't get to him. Luther lived to the in those days exceedingly advanced age of sixty-two—avoiding the empire's gallows and the pope's fire. Although he would never leave Saxony again, he kept talking: chatting with Katie and raising their children, conversing with guests at table, teaching his students, preaching the gospel, speaking at public events of all kinds, etc.

When he wasn't talking, it seems, he was writing. The critical edition of Luther's original Latin and German works is massive—121 encyclopedia-sized volumes and some eighty thousand pages. With an average spine width of three inches per volume, that's more than thirty running feet of books. Apparently, Luther "never had an unpublished thought."[6]

Toward the end of his life, he wrote a foreword to a collection of his works: an introductory piece for inquirers, for people who had heard about him and were now about to read some of his writings. In it, he reviews the formative events that brought him to public notice and shaped his life's work. Notably, he recalls how he came to know "the righteousness of God" and how God's righteousness came to bring him so much comfort and strength, when it had once brought him so much fear and helplessness.

> So, we begin this collection with Luther's own words, his description of the events that would lead him to reemphasize the gospel, redefine the church, and recast the Christian life. We let Luther introduce himself and tell his own story of what led to his excommunication, prompted the Roman Catholic Church to expel all Protestants, and ignited a firestorm of wars across Europe. *Foreword to the Complete Edition of Luther's Latin Writings.*[7]

From Martin Luther to the Dear Reader: Salvation Be with You, To be honest, I have been trying for a long time to stop those who would collect and publish my writings or, more precisely, my muddled ramblings. I do not want my works to lead earnest inquirers astray and I do not want to get in the way of the classics. Besides, by the grace of God, numerous books of theology have been written, preeminently Philip's *Loci communes*.[8] Such works can instruct theologians and bishops quite well—preparing them to proclaim well (i.e., with power) and to preach well the doctrine of living faith. This is especially true now that the Holy Scriptures have been translated into so many languages. But my books are rather crude and disorganized, even chaotic. I had to write them, after all, as the events of my life unfolded. And now, even I cannot easily place them in their proper order.

I hope everyone would forget my books. That way, there would be more space for better writings. My colleagues, it seems, came every day to nag me with their annoying audacity. They stuffed my ears with complaints that it will happen anyway. They contended that, if I do not allow them to publish my works while I am still alive, then others will certainly publish them and, because they are clueless about the causes and the timing of the events, their confusion will lead to even greater misunderstanding. Their impertinence won and so I allowed them to publish this collection. Even our most illustrious Prince-Elector, John Frederick, added his wish and command to their voices. By his command, the printers were not only compelled to publish these writings, they were to do it as soon as possible.

At the outset, then, I would make a plea to each faithful reader. I beg of you, for the sake of our Lord Jesus Christ, that you read these works cautiously and with great compassion. Keep in mind that I was once-upon-a-time, a monk and a crazy papist before I entered the struggle. I was so drunk, sloshed (you might say), with the pope's dogmas. With all my heart, I would have attacked everyone who would retract, even an iota, of their obedience to the pope. Indeed, I would have supported anyone who attacked them. I was like Saul—just like so many in our time. I was not a block of ice like John Eck and his dupes, whose defense of the pope was cold-hearted at best. I could see that they defended the pope more for themselves, rather than because they had any personal stake in the issues. As near as I can tell, they still mock the pope to this day, gaming the issues like a bunch of Epicureans. I cared deeply about the cause. I dreaded Christ's return, but still, in my heart of hearts, desired salvation.

You will see here how many significant ideas I obediently submitted to the pope in my earlier writings—ideas I later rejected, and continue to reject as terrible, wicked blasphemy and sacrilege. Faithful readers will write this error off to the time and my inexperience. The other side will slanderously claim that I'm contradicting myself. At first I was alone, so clumsy and inexperienced in such huge issues. I got into this brouhaha unintentionally and not because I wanted or planned to do so. God Almighty understands this.

When the indulgences of 1517 were being sold (or, better, were "hawked") in these regions for the most shameful profits, I was a preacher and a new doctor of theology.[9] Of course, I tried to persuade parishioners away from indulgences—urging them to ignore the clamors of the indulgence peddlers. People of faith certainly had more important things to do. And I took it for granted the pope would support me and I assumed I could trust him. The pope, after all, had so strongly criticized the over-the-top antics of those "officers of the pope" (as we called those preachers of indulgences back then).

I soon wrote two letters: one to Archbishop Albert of Mainz, who received half of the money from the indulgences (by the way, something I did not know then, was that the other half went to the pope). The other letter I wrote to Bishop Jerome of Brandenburg. I begged them both to stop the barefaced blasphemy of the peddlers.

But they didn't take the poor little brother seriously. Though ignored, I published the theses and, in German, *The Sermon on Indulgences*. Then I published *The Explanations to the 95 Theses*—where, in honor of the pope, I worked out the notion that indulgences are not to be condemned, but rather simply that good and loving actions are preferable to buying indulgences.

As it turned out, this was tantamount to destroying heaven and consuming the earth with fire. The pope charged me and summoned me to Rome—and the whole papal system came after me. All this took place in 1518, the year Emperor Maximilian convoked the Diet at Augsburg, where Cardinal Cajetan served as the pope's representative. The Eminence Duke of Saxony, Elector Prince Frederick, contacted him on my behalf and they agreed not to force me to go to Rome. Rather, Cajetan would summon me to Augsburg and examine me there to deal with the matter. Not long after that, the diet adjourned.[10]

Meanwhile, the Germans were no longer willing to endure the pillaging, marketing, and constant posing of the rascals from Rome. It was as if they were all waiting with bated breath to see what would happen in my case. Apparently, the issue had not been brought up before. No theologian or bishop had had the temerity to take it on. That did not matter. What was important is the winds of popular support were in my favor. The papists had swathed the entire world with their rituals and observances. Their "Romanisms" had worn us out. We detested those antics.

Then, with provisions and protections supplied by Prince Frederick, I went to the Diet at Augsburg. My hosts were most gracious and, after a few days, I went to see the cardinal.[11] Apparently, he was quoting me every day, even though he had not read my writings himself. My excellent hosts would not allow me to go to the cardinal without a letter of safe-conduct from the emperor himself. The cardinal's representative was peculiarly problematic, urging that if I would only recant what I'd said and written, then everything would be all right!

As they say, the greater the wrong, the longer the path to fix it.

Finally, on the third day, he demanded to know why I did not come to the cardinal, who was waiting for me with the greatest benevolence. I responded that the gentlemen, whom Prince Frederick sent to accompany me, had advised me to wait for my audience with the cardinal until the emperor's protection arrived. I am compelled, therefore, to take their advice. Once I receive the official safe-conduct, I will come immediately (as the Imperial Diet would have to act on it). At this point he exploded: "What?!" he said, "Do you really expect Prince Frederick to defend you by force?" I said, "I'm not looking for that." He asked, "And where will you live?" I replied, "Under heaven." Then he asked me, "If you had the pope and the cardinals in your power, what would you do?" "I would," said I, "show them all respect and honor." With that, he wagged his finger and cleared his throat at me like Italians do, and left. He did not return.

On that day, the Imperial Diet informed the cardinal that the emperor's protection (i.e., safe-conduct) had been granted me and admonished him that he should not design anything too severe against me. He is said to have replied, "It is well. I shall nevertheless do whatever my duty demands." These things were the start of that tumult. The rest can be learned from the accounts included later.

Prince Frederick brought Master Philipp Melanchthon to Wittenberg that same year to teach Greek and I gained a coworker in our common theological labors. The Lord has done so much through Philipp, not only in the study of languages, but also in theology. It drives Satan and all his bloodsuckers crazy.[12]

Maximilian died, early the following year, in February 1519, and Prince Frederick served as a sort of "interim emperor." With that, the ruckus settled down a bit. That is, until the despicable excommunication, the papal thunderbolt, landed. Eck and the Papal Legate, Caraccioli, brought Rome's official condemnation of Luther to Germany and began to promote it in our lands—Eck in this area and Caraccioli outside of Saxony. The latter even snuck up on Duke Frederick during mass in Cologne, on the Sunday after the investiture of Charles V as Emperor. Frederick stood up to that papal pup, with several princes looking on—displaying great courage and chastising him because of the whole ruckus Eck and he had caused in his territories (as well as in the lands of his brother John). The prince caught them completely off guard and they shamefully backed down in disgrace. The prince, in his great wisdom, had deciphered the Roman Hierarchy's methods and he knew how to handle them. His good sense allowed him to stay ahead of them so often and so strategically that those Romanists could not keep up.

Therefore, they were not much of a test for him. He showed no interest in the Golden Rose that Pope Leo X sent him that year. In fact, he disrespected it.[13] So the Romanists were forced to despair of their attempts to deceive so great a prince. The gospel advanced happily under the shadow of that prince and was widely propagated. His authority influenced so many, for because he was so wise and a most keen-sighted prince, he could incur the suspicion only among the hateful that he wanted to nourish and protect heresy and heretics. This did the papacy great harm.

That same year, Eck challenged Karlstadt and me to a disputation at the University of Leipzig. I was unable to participate directly in the disputation, because Duke George would not grant me safe-conduct (despite all my letters). I still went to Leipzig, but not as a lead disputant. Rather, I went as a member of Karlstadt's team and the safe-conduct granted to him covered all of us. I am still not sure who blocked my safe-conduct. Until then, Duke George had not been against me—of that, I'm certain.

At some point, Eck heard that I was refusing to dispute with him, so he visited me. I said, "How can I participate, if I do not have a safe-conduct from Duke George?" And he said, "Karlstadt is not the one I want. I have come here because of you. What if I get safe-conduct for you? Would you then join in the disputation with me?" I responded, "Obtain it and I will be there." Not long after he left, safe-conduct for me arrived and with it, the chance to debate.

Eck did this because he saw the victory set before him. I denied that the pope was the head of the church by divine right. Well, that opened the floodgates for him to flatter the pope and, by pouring praises on him, he could earn the pope's approval. On the other hand, he could bring me down with his spiteful suspicions. That's what he did so vehemently throughout the debate. Even though, he could neither prove his point nor refute mine. At one of the breakfasts, Duke George said to Eck and me, "If the pope is pope by human or divine right, then the pope remains the pope." He would never have said this had he not been influenced by the disputation. He would have simply approved of Eck's position.

With this situation, note how difficult it is to fight with, and prevail over, mistaken practices that have engrained themselves by their use throughout the world. How by force of habit, they almost seemed natural. Those old sayings contain a note of truth: "It's hard to let go of customs," and, "Custom is second nature." [14] And Augustine knew it, too: "A custom becomes a necessity, if you don't resist it." [15] I had then already read and taught the sacred Scriptures most diligently for seven years, privately and publicly, so that I knew them nearly all by memory. [16] I had also acquired the beginning of the knowledge of Christ and faith in him, i.e., not by works but by faith in Christ are we made righteous and saved. Finally, regarding that of which I speak, I had already defended the proposition publicly that the pope is not the head of the church by divine right. Nevertheless, I did not draw the conclusion, namely, that the pope must be of the devil. For what is not of God must be of the devil.

As mentioned above, I was completely overwhelmed by the status and the title of the sacred church (and by my own achievements). I allowed the pope so much power by human right that, even if it were rooted in the authority of God, it would be a devilish lie. We obey parents and magistrates because God wills it, not because they command it. [17] That is why I can tolerate, without too much ill will, the folks who continue to hold on to the papacy so intensely—especially those who have not studied Scripture (or other writings, for that matter). I had studied Holy Scripture so persistently for all those years and I had continued to hold so obstinately on to the papacy.

As I mentioned already, in 1519, Leo X dispatched Karl von Miltitz to present the Papal Rose to Prince Frederick. And when he did so, he turned up the pressure on the prince to send me to Rome. Along with the Rose, he brought apostolic letters citing me to appear—so many briefs that he could cover some 70 different cities with them. That is, if the prince wanted to hand me over to Rome.

Karl, though, exposed his true heart to me when we met:

Martin, I figured you were just an old scholar, warming himself by the stove, talking to himself. But I can see that you still possess youth and vitality. If I had 25,000 soldiers, I'm not sure I could take you to Rome. I've questioned folks throughout my journey, wanting to get their opinions of you. To my surprise, where one person took the pope's side, three took yours against him.

His survey sample, it turns out, was skewed. He included maids and virgins from local establishments in his informal poll about "the Roman chair."[18] They didn't understand the phrase and assumed he was asking about regular household chairs. All they could figure out was, "What do we know about chairs in Rome, are they stone or wooden?"

Anyway, he suggested that I provide a sort of peace-offering and he would try his best to convince the pope (or at least) to respond in kind. I promised to do my best, within the bounds of a clear conscience and the truth. I craved peace also. I was dragged into these conflicts and driven by necessity. I did what I could. Do not blame me.

After that, he summoned John Tetzel to meet with him. The Dominican was the one most directly responsible for the debacle and apparently, Miltitz threatened him with such severe papal condemnations that Tetzel broke down with fear. That was the beginning of Tetzel's decline. Now the one who had fearlessly terrified others, was himself terrified. In the end, apparently, the sickness of his own soul consumed him. When I found out, I sent him a supportive note. I wrote it with compassion, asking him to take comfort and not to concern himself with what I had said about him. Nevertheless, he seems to have succumbed to his own conscience and the wrath of the pope.

Karl's reprimand seems to have been too little, too late. Besides, in my estimation, the fault lies with the man from Mainz.[19] He didn't stifle Tetzel's rantings at the beginning, when I appealed for him to do so. Had he done it, the situation would not have gotten so out of control. Similarly, if the pope had taken this advice and dealt with the matter early on, like Karl did (granted, it was too late), the matter would not have escalated. And he could have done that before he judged me, without even listening to my case. He preferred, rather, to rant and rave as he condemned me.

The man from Mainz, in my humble opinion, is the real culprit. He was so smart and clever that he fooled himself. He tried to keep his profits from indulgences by attacking my theology. And now neither counsel nor councils can fix it. They would now be too little, too late. The Lord rises to bring judgment to the people. Though they possess the power to kill us, they want more than their small arms. We, however, live secure. Some of them, the ones who have not completely lost their senses, can easily sense it.

That was the year I lectured on the Psalms for the second time. In between, I had lectured on St. Paul's letters to the Churches of Rome and Galatia, and the one to the Hebrews. The experience I gained in those courses gave me more confidence as an interpreter. Along the way, I became completely taken with St. Paul— particularly his Letter to the Romans. But something stood in my way. It was not ". . . the cold curdling blood about my heart"[20] that was the matter. Rather, it was a specific phrase in chapter 1:17, ". . . the righteousness of God is revealed," blocked my path. I had grown to hate that phrase, "righteousness of God," because I had only learned how to interpret it philosophically, as "proper" or "active" righteousness. That is, that God is righteous and condemns sinners (that is, those who are unrighteous). All teachers approached the text that way.

Even though, as a monk, my life was blameless, I knew that I was a sinner in God's eyes—and my conscience was horribly conflicted. I was not able to trust that God was satisfied with my efforts. Indeed, I did not love the God of righteousness, but hated this God who punishes sinners. And secretly, and probably blasphemously, my murmurings were massive.[21] I was angry with God and I complained: "All right! As if it is not enough that wretched sinners are damned for all time because of original sin, they are squashed by every misfortune because of the law in the Ten Commandments. We do not need God to increase our pain by the gospel, particularly when the gospel threatens us with God's righteousness and wrath!" I ranted in my angry and anxious conscience. All the while, I kept hammering at that place in St. Paul. I could not have wanted anything more than to know what he meant.

Finally, thanks to God's mercy, while I meditated on it around the clock, I noticed the larger context of the words, "For in it the righteousness of God is revealed, as it is written, 'The one who through faith is righteous shall live.'" I then began to see that the righteousness of God is indeed God's gift. It is the righteousness by which the righteous person lives; that is, by faith. This means that the righteousness of God is revealed by the gospel. In other words, it is the passive righteousness by which the God of mercy justifies us by faith. As it is written, "The one who through faith is righteous shall live." At that point, I felt that I had been completely reborn, that heaven had flung its gates wide open and I was allowed in! All of Scripture took on a completely new demeanor to me. So, I ran through the Scriptures from memory. I discovered similar terms and phrases: the work of God is the work that God does in us; the power of God is how God empowers us; the wisdom of God, with which God makes us wise; the strength of God; the salvation of God; the glory of God.

And I savored this sweetest of words with a love as great as the hatred with which I had previously detested them: "the righteousness of God." Therefore, that place in Paul became for me the door to paradise. I later re-read Augustine's *Spirit and the Letter* and, hoping against hope, I found that he also understood the righteousness of God in a similar way—that is, the righteousness with which God justifies (or clothes) us. Even though he had expressed this imprecisely and did not clearly or completely explicate imputed righteousness. Still, I was happy enough that he taught God's righteousness as that which justifies us. Increasingly empowered with such ideas, I started to interpret the Psalms for a second time. That work would have become a commentary of some size, if I hadn't again been forced to abandon that project early on, when Emperor Charles V set the Imperial Diet to meet at Worms the following spring.

If you do read these ill-conceived works, I want you to know, faithful reader, and do remember: at the time, I was the only one writing things like this. I gained knowledge by writing and teaching (as Augustine put it). I did not appear from out of nowhere to take the lead position, as others have done. They are a bunch of blowhards. They have not struggled. They have not faced temptation. Their inexperience and superficial knowledge of Scripture leaves them with little substance.

Indulgences were the big issue through 1521. After that, the "sacramentarians" and the "Anabaptists" arose. I will write a foreword about them in succeeding volumes, if I live that long.

Good-bye, my Reader in the Lord—pray that God's Word continues to overtake its enemy, Satan. The devil is both powerful and evil—at this moment, more fierce and terrible than ever. He knows his days are numbered and his pope's reign is at risk.

May God bring to completion the work begun in us, to the glory of the Almighty. Amen.

March 5, 1545

For some time, Luther's colleagues had been after him to let them collect his Latin writings and publish them as a set. Eventually, they cajoled him into compliance. Their success, perhaps, shows his age. Young Luther was famously undeterrable from his chosen public path. Now, a year before his death, he gives in. They wanted his permission and his endorsement. Maybe they wore the old codger down. Maybe they outfoxed him—going over his head, to their prince, John Frederick. They asked his Majesty "to encourage" Luther's cooperation. A royal letter finds the Reformer; he obeys, signs off on the planned collection, and writes this foreword.

Luther did not have to write such an amazing piece. He could've simply dashed something off to fulfill the royal request. This foreword provides a precious retelling of his early attempts at reform and how he endured through the backlash—multifaceted, tumultuous, unpredictable, precarious. More than the ruminations of a senior citizen spouting tales of how difficult he had it when he was young, the stories woven together here provide a backdrop to Luther's understanding of how his life and work unfolded, how God's grace found him, and how the good news of the gospel engendered a response that changed his life. These stories provide the basic narrative that energized Luther's vocation—prompting him to seek the reformation of the church and her witness, with that good news at the center.

Eleven months after he wrote this, the old man's prayer was answered. He died on February 18, 1546, believing that God was indeed completing the work begun in him the day he was born, November 10, 1483. Martin was born in the wee hours that day and once the sun came up, Papa Hans took his son to the City Church of Eisleben to have him baptized into the Christian faith. It was the feast of St. Martin, so the boy was christened accordingly.

Luther's foreword is a sort of overture. It introduces us to the formative events of the early Reformation and indicates how we might interpret his life's work. First and foremost: listen for the themes and recurring rhythms of Luther's thought and theological priorities. Hear them in the improvisations and in the refrain to which he so consistently returns.

His most enduring contribution, if it were up to him, would be how his reformation efforts are variations on a single theme: God's mercy and grace. We can hear his wide-ranging, ongoing appeal—how the Reformer's insight can benefit anyone who struggles with life's ultimate questions. No *Star Wars* character, content to live "a long time ago in a galaxy far, far away," his voice continues to resonate far beyond its sixteenth-century German origins.

Indeed, the reach of Luther's voice today would astound him—beyond what he would have imagined as the ends of the earth. A student at Sabah Seminary, on the Malaysian coast of Borneo, expressed this so clearly to me in the spring of 2016: "It is as if Martin Luther is writing down my thoughts." How can this be? How can Martin Luther's work, after five hundred years, find resonance on an island in the South China Sea? He could hardly have known a place like Malaysia existed. And most citizens of that wonderfully diverse place have never heard of him—although that is likely to change as students like this, who "get" Luther, amplify his voice in Southeast Asia.[22]

Well beyond this singular anecdote, Luther is enhancing conversations in surprising ways and in surprising places around the world—particularly in the so-called "global South," where churches are growing. In Africa, for example, the Lutheran churches in Namibia and Tanzania have been among the most dynamic churches in the Lutheran World Federation.[23] And Luther can help the churches of the "global North" move beyond their perceived establishment status to proclaim the gospel and serve their neighbors in new ways.

One aspect of Luther's appeal is his consistent commitment to the distinction between "Law and Gospel." He begins with "the law," a faithful and authentic description of the realities facing every human being. Death, meaninglessness, and guilt threaten all people, regardless of their location.[24] Luther's realism can surprise us: Asian seminarians who are reading Luther for the first time, Namibians who live where Lutherans make up half their country's population, and scholars from the United States who've been reading Luther for many years. He would remind us that we do not (in fact, cannot) explain away loss and suffering—as if pain would not hurt us if we could only interpret it as part of some larger (even divine?) plan. Luther would speak the truth. He testifies to the inexplicable absurdity of suffering and death. His achingly accurate description of our human situation and our participation in its painful realities beats at the heart of his most important insight. He called this "the Law."

This law, says Luther, is not simply a moral code of conduct we should follow (though it does include issues of righteous living). Luther draws his understanding of the law from the New Testament. He picks up on the Apostle Paul's notion of "God's wrath," from which arises the pervasive human sense of dread, that something is wrong with the world and our participation in it. The law, among other things, always points out the depth of human need. The law threatens us with its continual accusations. Take an honest look around. In our heart of hearts, we know we are going to die like everyone else. We question deeply whether our lives mean anything (or not). On top of that, truth be told, we are not nearly as morally upright as we hope others think we are.

In the context of these harsh realities, Luther would speak

about the gospel of hope, forgiveness, and life. The gospel eclipses, by far, the importance of the law (as important as the law is). At the heart of his understanding of the Scriptures is this gospel: God in Jesus Christ has acted to rescue humankind and the whole world from the painful realities exposed by the Law. Luther called this grace and mercy of Christ "the Good News" (the root meaning of the German *Evangelium* and *Evangelisch* and the Old English *God spell*). For Luther, this Good News needs a church to proclaim it and the church of his day did not do that—thus it needed reformation.

This Gospel Word animates Luther's theology in vital ways, as he embraces the mysteries and paradoxes of the faith. The doctrine of the Holy Trinity emphasizes God's intention and power to repair what humankind has broken. The Sacraments (only two, for Luther: Baptism and the Lord's Supper) are means of grace. The hierarchy and organizational structures of the church are important insofar as they help folks to hear the gospel and assist believers in their vocations in everyday life. The church is identified and unified by the presence of the Word and the Sacraments.

Next, the documents collected here are entire writings, complete in themselves. As such, each follows the arc of its argument to its conclusion. Certainly, it is tempting to clean up Luther, to edit out the parts that may seem too irreverent or irrelevant for modern sensibilities. However, part of Luther's power as a communicator emanates from his willingness to engage the great issues of his day honestly, with an eye on the practical, down-to-earth impact of his ideas.

That said, he writes with a sense of personal urgency, as he draws on language and metaphors from the everyday lives of his audiences. This immediacy can disarm, even offend, modern sensibilities. Luther's audiences and their circumstances, though, would determine his choice of speech. Even when he writes for academics, he has lay folks and their issues in mind (particularly the parishioners of Wittenberg). When he needs to, he uses the gritty language of peasants in the market, the fields, and the pubs—intending consistently to connect the gospel with folks' realities.

Third, note how he rejects pious superficiality. Religious

platitudes and overreaching intellectual systems, what he called "theologies of glory," do not play well with him. He takes the Christian faith too seriously to let such talk remain unchallenged. Luther's earthy faith allowed him to believe boldly, even as he could not fully articulate the deeper realities of that belief. He would speak truth about Jesus, the One who claimed, "I am the Truth" (John 14:6). To do that with humility, for Luther, means to recognize the mysterious character of that assertion. If Christ is God incarnate, the second person of the Holy Trinity, then human speech cannot fully explain how that is the case. As he puts it in a sermon for Trinity Sunday, "It is certainly not good German, and it doesn't sound right, to describe God with the word, 'Three-fold-ness' [*Dreifaeltigkeit*] (and the Latin word *Trinitas* is no better). But, because that's all we've got, we must do the best we can. As I have said, this article of faith is so high above our understanding and language, that God must accept us like a Father accepts the blathering and blabbering of his children. We speak the best we can, while believing what is right and true."[25]

Interestingly, Luther's recognition of the limits of human language to explain the Incarnation of Christ did not keep him from speaking about him. What else would explain his huge literary output? Luther was convinced that a sort of "logic of faith" was at work beyond a "logic of reason." That is, God, out of Divine goodness and mercy" did what sinful humankind could not do—in the mystery of the cross and resurrection.

The good news of the gospel means that, by God's grace, Christ has redeemed those who have been enslaved, liberated those who have been held captive, forgiven those who deserved punishment. This salvation was, for Luther, the heart of the Christian matter. And, when he was at his best, he stuck to that basic insight. Indeed, much of his genius lay in his ability not to claim too much, but to articulate the truth of the gospel (and its corollaries) throughout his career.

And he did so to such a wide range of audiences that, as readers shall see here, he provides numerous ways for readers to "hear" his voice—addressing earnest parishioners, debating pompous academics, teaching illiterate children (and their equally illiterate parents), confronting the combined papal and imperial powers of Christendom. Through it all, he remains faithfully authentic—offering strength and comfort to all who suffer and struggle with events beyond their control. Need a supportive, tender word? Check. Need someone to get in your face? He'll do that, too. From the opening of the *Ninety-Five Theses* (". . . The entire life of the Christian is one of repentance . . .") to the apex of the Heidelberg Disputation (". . . a theologian of the cross calls a thing what it is . . ."), and then to the sermon at Leipzig's Pleissenburg, when illness overtook him ("I cannot go on . . ."), his voice is *real*.

So one may certainly sample Luther's writings here—find the ones that speak to you most readily, then move to others. If you are acquainted with philosophy and theology, then the disputations and confessional writings are good places to start. If history and biography move you, then a straightforward reading of the text makes sense. The sermons, with their creative uses of metaphor and rhetoric, may provide ready access for those who have not read much Luther or sources like this before. If you like reading other people's mail, start with the letters.

While this book allows for picking and choosing, I note that a large number of decisions have already been made. The only document the Penguin Classics folks insisted be included in this volume is the *Ninety-Five Theses*. The others are my choices (in conversation, certainly, with other scholars). It's a daunting task, I must say—with more than 99 percent of Luther's works left out. So, a word or two about what is not here.

First, Luther's infamous anti-Jewish writings[26] do not fit. They have certainly played an ugly role in Western history;[27] however, they are on the margin of the Reformer's own life and work, reflective of his flawed assumptions and limitations as a late-medieval person. To include these tracts in a book like this would make them seem more important to Luther's primary work and intentions than they were.

Furthermore, they have been officially disavowed by Lutherans worldwide.[28] Although some eighty million believers around the world identify, in some way, with the name "Lutheran," this does not mean they accept everything the Reformer said as authoritative. Luther is hardly understood as one akin to the Oracle of Delphi belching forth prophecies. The Lutheran Confessional Writings (preeminently the Ecumenical Creeds, Augsburg Confession, and the "Small Catechism," the latter included here) summarize Lutheran approaches to the Bible and critique Luther himself.

Second, there is simply not room in a volume like this for either Luther's "Reformation Treatises" of 1520 (*The Freedom of a Christian, Address to the Christian Nobility of the German Nation,* and *The Babylonian Captivity of the Church*) or his 1525 opus *The Bondage of the Will.* These evocative works are simply too large to be accommodated here. Further, they are all readily available in separate editions.

WILLIAM R. RUSSELL

Abbreviations

BC	*The Book of Concord: The Confessions of the Evangelical Lutheran Church*, edited by Robert Kolb and Timothy Wengert (Minneapolis: Fortress Press, 2000).
LC	Large Catechism (in BC)
LW	*Luther's Works* (American Edition), 55 volumes, edited by Jaroslav Pelikan and Helmut Lehmann (St. Louis and Minneapolis: Concordia and Fortress Press, 1955–80).
SA	"Smalcald Articles" by Martin Luther (in BC).
SC	"Small Catechism" by Martin Luther (in BC).
WA	*D. Martin Luthers Werke: Kritische Gesamtausgabe* (Weimar: H. Böhlaus Nachfolger, 1883–). Published in four parts:

    1. *Tischreden* (table talk), 6 volumes (abbreviation: WATR)

    2. *Deutsche Bibel* (The German Bible), 15 volumes (abbreviation: WADB)

    3. *Briefwechsel* (correspondence), 18 volumes (abbreviation: WABR)

    4. *Schriften* (writings), 72 volumes (abbreviation: WA)

The Ninety-Five Theses
and Other Writings

The Ninety-Five Theses:
A Disputation to Clarify the Power
of Indulgences (1517)[1]

October 31, 1517: Martin Luther, a junior professor at the University of Wittenberg, dutifully mails a letter to his Archbishop and changes the world—just following custom, an act of academic due diligence. He bundled the letter with a couple of other items: a copy of ninety-five statements (aka "theses") on "indulgences" to be debated publicly at the university and an essay he'd written on the topic. It could easily have gone unnoticed. Someone could have mishandled it on its three-hundred-mile journey from Wittenberg. The archbishop's bureaucracy could have tossed it on the stack of similar mailings—an administrative matter, a nonurgent notice about an upcoming scholarly exercise at one of the universities on lands of the archdiocese. Luther's act was due diligence, expected from academics who proposed disputations in their field of expertise. He could not imagine he was about to alter the course of history. Yet that simple act, performed at the University of Wittenberg, a backwater town at the edge of the Holy Roman Empire, would lead to the dissolution of Christendom and place an agenda for reform before the Roman Catholic Church that the mother church would reject—expelling Luther and his ilk. Thus, Luther's *Ninety-Five Theses* signaled the end of medieval Europe and the beginning of the modern period—and more (which is considerable).

Ironically, as earth-shaking and profound as his action was, almost no one at the time noticed, and subsequent generations have struggled to describe it. Despite the current popular depictions on stage, screen, and canvas, Luther's post that day was not a public event or rebellious act. Although there is scant evidence that he actually posted the *Ninety-Five Theses*, placard-style, on a local church door in Wittenberg, the materials he sent to Albert, archbishop of Mainz, still exist.

Scott Hendrix, eminent scholar of Luther's life and work, puts it this way:

> Pictures of a defiant Luther with hammer in hand as if he were starting a popular revolt are pure make-believe. Such pictures turned up for the first time in the nineteenth century. If the ninety-five theses were posted on the eve of All Saints, it was merely an invitation to qualified debaters, not a call to arms.[2]

That's it?! An open invitation from a junior professor to a debate at a medieval university. Really? Not much drama at a debate, especially when the debaters are qualified. Spectacle, however entertaining, does not always equal substance. That's what Protestants commemorate and Roman Catholics bemoan every October 31?

If they only knew.

Not much drama, but huge historical consequence. Luther's invitation to debate signaled the sunset of medieval Christendom and the dawn of modernity. Although we cannot be sure whether he "nailed" or "mailed" the theses (or both) and this disputation never actually occurred, the issues raised here would touch a nerve that convulsed Europe. Indeed, the issues in this document (and the way it frames those issues) led to contentious debates of the issues facing Medieval Christendom. Politicians and wealthy land owners took positions on various sides of the issues. The conflict eventuated into what later became known as the Protestant Reformation—or, better, "the Reformations."[3]

So, what were "indulgences"? They were promises, made by the church to penitent believers, that the punishments required by their sins before entering paradise had been satisfied. They had been forgiven by God's grace; their salvation and heavenly destination were secure. Yet, satisfaction for their sins was still in order. Indulgences were like "promissory notes" from the church (specifically the pope) that could be obtained by believers to reduce the punishments that awaited them in purgatory. Penitents could obtain indulgences by performing pious actions: go on pilgrimage, venerate relics, observe feast days, and the like. Eventually, the church came to accept monetary contributions as satisfaction for the punishment of sinners.

The evolution of indulgences in the theology and practice of the church had not allowed for a full and open conversation about them. As a dutiful professor of theology, Luther wanted to have that conversation. Little did he know that these Theses would change the world. And they would soon catapult him out of his quiet classroom and monastery into the chaos of shifting epochs and clashing cultures.

For the love of truth and a desire to elucidate it, the following theses shall be debated in Wittenberg, with the Reverend Father Martin Luther, MA, STM, Professor of Theology, presiding. He requests written responses from those unable to attend and debate with us in person.

In the Name of Our Lord, Jesus Christ, Amen.

1. When our Lord and Teacher Jesus Christ said, "Repent, etc.,"[4] he meant that the entire life of believers be a life of repentance.

2. Jesus' saying does not refer to the sacrament of penance (that is, confession and satisfaction as administered by priests).

3. And it does not mean inner repentance only—mere internal repentance is useless if it does not produce external self-control of one's selfish desires.

4. Therefore, the penalty for sin endures so long as the hatred of self lasts (which is true internal repentance) until we enter the Kingdom of Heaven.[5]

5.   The pope does not intend to reduce (and cannot reduce) any penalties—except those under his authority or authorized by canon law.[6]

6.   The pope cannot reduce any guilt. He can only clarify and announce that such guilt is reduced by God. The pope, however, may certainly lessen penalties in cases under his jurisdiction. Therefore, if the pope's authority to forgive debt in those cases under his jurisdiction were disregarded, that debt would certainly remain.

7.   God reduces no one's guilt without, at the same time, humbling them in all things and making them submit to the priest as the vicar of God.

8.   The penitential canons apply to the living only, and, as the canons themselves state, they do not apply to the dead.

9.   The Holy Spirit, therefore, is kind to us through the pope—insofar as the pope in his decrees always makes an exception in the case of death and emergencies.

10. Priests act ignorantly and wickedly when they commute canonical penalties of the dying to purgatory.

11. Those weeds of commuting canonical penalties to purgatory were evidently planted while the bishops slept.[7]

12. Earlier, canonical penalties were imposed before, not after, absolution—as tests of true contrition.

13. Death releases the dying from the penalties of canon law—and the dead have a right to be released from them.

14. Imperfect piety or love on the part of the dying necessarily brings with it great fear—the smaller the love, the greater the fear.

15. This fear or terror is so close to the terror of despair that, in and of itself, it matches the penalty of purgatory—not to mention the other sorts of punishment.

16. The differences between hell, purgatory, and heaven are akin to the differences between despair, fear, and the assurance of salvation.

17. It appears, for the people in purgatory, love should increase and fear should decrease—necessarily.

18. Furthermore, neither reason nor Scripture prove that souls in purgatory are outside the state of merit—that is, they are unable to grow in love.

19. Nor does it seem proved that souls in purgatory, at least not all of them, are certain and assured of their own salvation, even if we ourselves may be entirely certain of our salvation.

20. Therefore, when the pope talks about "plenary remission of all penalties," he does not actually mean "all penalties," but only those he has imposed.

21. Thus, indulgence preachers falsely claim that one is freed from all punishment and is saved by the indulgences of the pope.

22. Indeed, the pope cannot reduce the penalties of souls in purgatory that canon law says they should have paid in this life.

23. If remission of all penalties whatsoever could be granted to anyone at all, certainly it would be granted only to the most perfect, that is, to very few.

24. For this reason most people are necessarily deceived by that indiscriminate and high-sounding promise of release from penalty.

25. That power that the pope has generally over purgatory corresponds to the power that bishops or pastors have specifically over their own dioceses or parishes.

26. The pope does a good thing when he forgives those who are in purgatory, not by the power of the keys, which he does not have; but by praying for them.

27. The chant, "When the coin in the coffer rings, the soul from purgatory springs," is simply a human doctrine.

28. It is certain that when money clinks in the money chest, greed and avarice can be increased; but when the church intercedes, the result is in the hands of God alone.

29. Who knows whether all souls in purgatory wish to be redeemed, because we have exceptions in the legends of St. Severinus and St. Paschal.

30. No one is sure of the integrity of one's own contrition, much less can one be sure of having received plenary forgiveness.

31. The one who buys indulgences honestly is as rare as the one who is honestly contrite—indeed, such a person is exceedingly rare.

32. Those who believe that they can be certain of their salvation because they have indulgence letters will be eternally damned, together with their teachers.

33. We must especially be on our guard against those who say that the pope's pardons are the inestimable gift of God by which we are reconciled to God.

34. The graces of indulgences are concerned only with the penalties of sacramental satisfaction established by human beings.

35. They who teach that contrition is not necessary on the part of those who intend to buy souls out of purgatory or to buy confessional privileges preach unchristian doctrine.

36. Any truly contrite Christian has a right to full remission of punishment and guilt, apart from a letter of indulgence.

37. All true Christians, whether living or dead, participate in all the blessings of Christ and the church; and this is granted to them by God, even without indulgence letters.

38. Still, we do not ignore papal remission and blessing at all, because they are the proclamation of Divine remission (as mentioned above).[8]

39. Even theologians of the highest rank find it exceedingly difficult to tell people that indulgences are useful, while also maintaining the need for true contrition.

40. Truly contrite believers seek out and love their punishments; indulgences, however, relax penalties and cause contrite persons to hate them—at least it provides the conditions for hating them.

41. Papal indulgences must be preached with caution, lest people erroneously think that they are preferable to other good works of love.

42. Christians are to be taught that the pope does not intend that the buying of indulgences should in any way be compared with works of mercy.

43. Christians are to be taught that the one who gives to the poor or lends to the needy does a better deed than the one who buys indulgences.

44. Because love grows by works of love, a person thereby becomes better. A person does not, however, become

better by means of indulgences but is merely freed from penalties.

45. Christians are to be taught that those who see a needy person and pass by, yet give their money for indulgences, do not buy papal indulgences but God's wrath.

46. Christians are to be taught that, unless they have more than they need, they must reserve enough for their family needs and by no means squander it on indulgences.

47. Christians are to be taught that the buying of indulgences is a matter of free choice, not commanded.

48. Christians are to be taught that the pope, in granting indulgences, needs and thus desires their devout prayer more than their money.

49. Christians are to be taught that papal indulgences are useful, only if they do not put their trust in them, but very harmful if they lose their fear of God because of them.

50. Christians are to be taught that if the pope knew the exactions of the indulgence preachers, then he would prefer that St. Peter's Basilica were burned to ashes than constructed with the flesh and bones of his sheep.

51. We should teach Christians that the pope would and should wish to give of his own money, even selling the basilica of St. Peter if he had to, to repay so many from whom the indulgence-hawkers cajoled money.

52. It is vain to trust in salvation by indulgence letters, even though the indulgence hawker, or even the pope, were to offer his soul as security.

53. The enemies of Christ and the pope prohibit the preaching of the Word of God in some churches so that indulgences can be preached in others.

54. Whoever devotes an equal amount or more time to indulgences than to the Word in a single sermon infringes upon the Word of God.

55. It is certainly the pope's sentiment that if indulgences, which are a very insignificant thing, are celebrated with one bell, one procession, and one ceremony, then the gospel, which is the very greatest thing, should be preached with a hundred bells, a hundred processions, a hundred ceremonies.

56. The treasures of the church, out of which the pope distributes indulgences, are not sufficiently discussed or known among the people of Christ.

57. That indulgences are not temporal treasures is certainly clear, for many [indulgence] preachers do not distribute them freely but only gather them.

58. Nor are they the merits of Christ and the saints, for, even without the pope, the latter always work grace for the inner person—and the cross, death, and hell for the outer person.

59. St. Laurence said that the poor of the church were the treasures of the church, but he used "treasure" in the context of his time and place.

60. We have cause to say that the keys of the church, given by the merits of Christ, are that treasure;

61. Because clearly the pope's power applies only to the remission of church-related penalties and legal cases under his jurisdiction.

62. The church's true treasure is the most holy gospel of God's glory and grace.

63. But this treasure is naturally most odious, for it makes the first to be last.[9]

64. On the other hand, the treasure of indulgences is naturally most acceptable, for it makes the last to be first.

65. Therefore the treasures of the gospel are nets with which one formerly fished for people of wealth.

66. The treasures of indulgences are nets with which one now fishes for the wealth of people.

67. Manipulators claim that indulgences are the greatest graces, but they interpret them as such only to promote gain.

68. They are nevertheless in truth the most insignificant graces when compared with the grace of God and the piety of the cross.

69. Bishops and clerics must welcome the representatives of papal indulgences with all due reverence.

70. But they need to be more watchful and listen carefully, so that these people do not preach their own dreams instead of misrepresentations of what the pope has commissioned.

71. Let the one who speaks against the truth concerning papal indulgences be anathema and accursed;

72. But let the one who guards against the lust and license of the indulgence preachers be blessed;

73. Just as the pope justly thunders against those who by any means whatsoever contrive harm to the sale of indulgences.

74. But much more does he intend to thunder against those who use indulgences as a pretext to contrive harm to holy love and truth.

75. To consider papal indulgences so great that they could absolve a person, even if they had done the impossible and had violated the mother of God, is madness.

76. We say on the contrary that papal indulgences cannot remove the very least of venial sins as far as guilt is concerned.

77. To say that even St. Peter, if he were now pope, could not grant greater graces is blasphemy against St. Peter and the pope.

78. We say on the contrary that even the present pope, or any pope whatsoever, has greater graces at his disposal, that is, the gospel, spiritual powers, gifts of healing, etc., as it is written in 1 Corinthians 12[:28].

79. To say that the cross emblazoned with the papal coat of arms, and set up by the indulgence preachers, is equal in worth to the cross of Christ is blasphemy.

80. The bishops, pastors, and theologians who permit such talk to be spread among the people must be held accountable for it.

81. This unbridled preaching of indulgences makes it difficult even for the learned to rescue the reverence which is due the pope from slander or from the shrewd questions of the laity,

82. Such as: "Why does not the pope empty purgatory for the sake of holy love and the dire need of the souls that are there if he redeems an infinite number of souls for the sake of miserable money with which to build a church? The former reasons would be most just; the latter is most trivial."

83. Again, "Why are funeral and anniversary masses for the dead continued and why does he not return or permit the

withdrawal of the endowments founded for them, because it is wrong to pray for the redeemed?"

84. Again, "What is this new piety of God and the pope that for a consideration of money they permit a person who is impious and their enemy to buy out of purgatory the pious soul of a friend of God and do not rather, because of the need of that pious and beloved soul, free it for pure love's sake?"

85. Again, "Why are the penitential canons, long since abrogated and dead in fact and through disuse, now satisfied by the granting of indulgences as though they were still alive and in force?"

86. Again, "Why does not the pope, whose wealth is today greater than the wealth of the richest Crassus,[10] build this one basilica of St. Peter with his own money rather than with the money of poor believers?"

87. Again, "What does the pope reduce or grant to those who by perfect contrition already have a right to full remission and blessings?"

88. Again, "What greater blessing could come to the church than if the pope were to bestow these remissions and blessings on every believer a hundred times a day, as he now does but once?"

89. "Because the pope seeks the salvation of souls rather than money by his indulgences, why does he suspend the indulgences and pardons previously granted when they have equal efficacy?"

90. To repress these very sharp arguments of the laity by force alone, and not to resolve them by giving reasons, is to expose the church and the pope to the ridicule of their enemies and to make Christians unhappy.

91. If, therefore, indulgences were preached in accordance with the spirit and intention of the pope, all these doubts would be readily resolved. Indeed, they would not exist.

92. Away then with all those prophets who say to the people of Christ, "Peace, peace," and there is no peace![11]

93. Blessed be all those prophets who say to the people of Christ, "Cross, cross," and there is no cross!

94. Christians should be exhorted to be diligent in following Christ, their head, through penalties, death, and hell;

95. And thus be confident of entering into heaven through many tribulations rather than through the false security of peace.[12]

The Heidelberg Disputation (1518)[1]

April–May 1518: The German Augustinians convene in Heidelberg for their triennial assembly—to conduct the order's business, to hear speeches, to be inspired, etc. The date and place were set long before. The keynoter and topic were set when the ruckus caused by the *Ninety-Five Theses* thrust Luther into the spotlight. The brothers would want, and need, to hear about this so-called Wittenberg theology. So John Staupitz, the head of the order in Germany, tabbed Luther. The venerable Staupitz (coincidentally, dean of the University of Wittenberg), who knew and supported Luther, instructed him to avoid the controversial topic of indulgences and stick to more central theological ideas. Luther obeyed, but actually moved in an even more radical direction. His theme, the "Theology of the Cross," focuses on traditional theological topics: God's law and human works, sin and forgiveness, free will and grace. But he deals with them in a new way. Luther no longer proposes to reform only the content of the church's teaching on topics like indulgences. Here he proposes a new method, a new way, of theological reflection—calling "theologians of the cross" to wrestle honestly with the paradoxes of the faith.

Brother Martin Luther, Master of Theology, will chair the proceedings as Brother Leonhard Beier, Master of Philosophy, defends the following theses at the May meeting of Augustinians at the usual place in the famous city of Heidelberg.

REGARDING THEOLOGY

The Spirit teaches us in Proverbs 3:5, ". . . do not rely on your own insight." Therefore, we do not trust our abilities and we respectfully submit these theological paradoxes to those of us who gather at Heidelberg. In this way, we might plainly see if they do or do not actually stem from the Apostle Paul (that chosen vessel and instrument of Christ) and from St. Augustine (the Apostle's most faithful interpreter).[2]

God's Law is the best teaching by which to live. The law, however, cannot help human beings become righteous before God.[3] The Law, rather, actually stands in the way of that goal.[4]

    The Apostle Paul clarifies this in Romans 3:21: "But now, apart from law, the righteousness of God has been disclosed. . . ." St. Augustine puts it thus in his book *The Spirit and the Letter*: "Without the law, that is, without its support." In Romans 5:20 the Apostle states, "But law came in, with the result that the trespass multiplied," and in Romans 7:9 he adds, "I was once alive apart from the law, but when the commandment came, sin revived." For this reason, in Romans 8:2 Paul describes the law as "the law of sin and of death." And, in 2 Corinthians 3:6 he writes, "The letter kills." Throughout his book *The Spirit and the Letter*, St. Augustine then applies this to every law, including God's most holy law.

Human works, even with the help of natural principles and repeated effort, are even less able to assist people toward that goal.

    God gives people the divine law (which is holy and spotless, true, righteous, etc.), to assist them beyond their human capacities—to show them that which is good and motivate them toward it. Yet the reverse happens and they do Evil instead. How can they, with only their own power and without this kind of help, do good deeds? If people do not do what's right with external assistance like this, then they will do even less on their own. As the Apostle puts it,

"All people are corrupt and worthless—there is no one who has understanding, there is no one who seeks God. All have turned aside."[5]

Human works always look nice and appear to be good. However, they are all probably still mortal sins.

Human works may look nice from the outside, but on the inside they are unclean (as Christ says about the Pharisees in Matthew 23:27). These works may seem good and beautiful, but God does not judge externals only. Rather, God searches "the minds and hearts."[6] Without grace and faith it is impossible to have a pure heart. "He cleansed their hearts by faith."[7]

Here's the evidence for this thesis: First, if the works of righteous folks are sins (see thesis seven below), then even more are the works of unrighteous folks. Yet, the righteous talk about their works in this way: "Do not enter into judgment with your servant, Lord, because no one living is righteous before you."[8]

Second, the Apostle Paul says in Galatians 3:10, "All who rely on the works of the law are under the curse." Now, because human works are the works of the law and venial sins do not warrant the curse, then they are actually mortal sins.

Third, Romans 2:21 states, "You who teach others not to steal, do you steal?" St. Augustine interprets this to mean that people are thieves according to their guilty consciences even if they publicly judge or reprimand other thieves.

God's works always look unattractive and appear to be bad. However, they are true everlasting merits.

Isaiah 53:2 clearly states that the works of God are unattractive: "He had no form of comeliness." In 1 Samuel 2:6, "The Lord kills and brings to life; the Lord brings down to Sheol and raises up." This means the Lord humbles and terrifies us by the law and our sins. That way, we appear to the eyes of others, as in our own, as nothing, foolish, and wicked—because we are. We acknowledge and confess that no form or beauty belongs to us. Our lives are hidden in God, with only naked confidence in God's mercy. We find in ourselves nothing but sin, foolishness, death, and hell. As the Apostle writes, "As sorrowful, yet always rejoicing; as dying, and behold we live."⁹ Isaiah calls this "the alien work of God" (28:21)—that God works in us (that is, the Lord humbles us thoroughly, making us despair, so that we may be lifted up in Divine mercy, giving us hope). Habakkuk 3:2 alludes to this: "In wrath remember mercy." Such people are, therefore, displeased with all their works; see no beauty, but only their unattractiveness. Indeed, they also do those things which appear foolish and disgusting to others.

We become aware of this, either when God punishes us or when we accuse ourselves, as 1 Corinthians 11:31 says, "If we judged ourselves truly, we should not be judged" by the Lord. Deuteronomy 32:36 also states, "The Lord will vindicate God's people and have compassion on the Lord's servants." Therefore, the "unsightly works" which God does in us, those works which are humble and devout, are really immortal. Humility and fear of God are our entire merit.¹⁰

These human works—those works that appear to be good, but are actually mortal sins—are not necessarily crimes.

Crimes are those misdeeds which can be adjudicated before a court: adultery, theft, homicide, slander, etc. Mortal sins, however, are works that seem nice, but actually grow like fruit from an evil tree with evil roots. Augustine describes this in *Against Julian*, book IV.

God's works, the works that God accomplishes through human beings, do not accumulate merit for those folks, as if they were not still sinners.

In Ecclesiastes 7:20, we read, "Surely there is no one on earth so righteous as to do good without ever sinning." Some people maintain that, although righteous persons indeed sin, they do not sin when they are doing what is right.

We would respond: If that is what this passage intends to say, then why so much useless verbiage? Does the Holy Spirit enjoy such rambling jibber-jabber? This meaning could be more straightforwardly said: "There is no one on earth so righteous as to act without ever sinning." Why does the Spirit add ". . . as to do good," as if another person were righteous who did evil? Because no one except a righteous person does good. And when the Spirit speaks of sins outside the realm of good works the Spirit speaks like this: "Though the righteous fall seven times, they will rise again."[11] The Spirit does not say, "Righteous people fall seven times when they do good."

A metaphor comes to mind: if someone chops with a corroded and dull hatchet, even though the worker is a good craftsperson, the tool leaves bad, rough, and ugly gashes. So it is when God works through us.

People who perform righteous works commit mortal sins unless they are concerned, out of a pious fear of God, that they are committing mortal sins.[12]

First, Thesis Four clarifies this: Those who put their faith in their good works ought to do so with dread. It is just plain wrong to take honor from God and bestow it on oneself—to please oneself, to admire one's own accomplishments, to worship oneself as an idol. Those with such overconfidence in themselves do not stand in awe before God. If they were afraid, they would not be so self-satisfied. They would not be so pleased with themselves. Rather, they would be pleased with God.

Second, the Psalmist writes: "Enter not into judgment with your servant."[13] And Psalm 32:5, "I said, 'I will confess my transgressions to the Lord'," etc. These are clearly not venial sins because confession and repentance are not necessary for venial sins. If, therefore, they are mortal sins and all the saints intercede for them, as it is stated in the same place, then the works of the saints are mortal sins. But the works of the saints are good works, wherefore they are meritorious for them only through the fear of their humble confession.

Third, note the request of the Lord's Prayer, "Forgive us our debts."[14] Because this is the Saints' prayer, those debts for which they pray are actually good works. Yet, according to Matthew 6:15, they are in fact mortal sins: "if you

do not forgive others, neither will your Father forgive."
Even the saints must pray this prayer sincerely and forgive
others. If they do not, then such unforgiven debts would
condemn them.

Fourth, Revelation 21:27 says, "Nothing unclean will
enter into [heaven]": Thus all barriers to someone's entry
into the kingdom of heaven are mortal sin (or it would be
necessary to interpret the concept of mortal sin in another
way). Venial sin, however, impedes entry by making the soul
unclean—and thus has no place in the kingdom of heaven.

And you all know the numerous other verses that prove
this. . . .

Human works are mortal sins when they are done without
pious fear and in overconfident, evil self-assurance.

This follows directly from Thesis Seven: when there is no
fear, there is no humility. A lack of humility leads to pride.
And where there is pride, there are the wrath and judgment
of God. God opposes the haughty. To be sure, if human
pride would come to an end, then sin would be no more.

To assert that works without Christ are dead, but not mortal
sin, would seem to reject the fear of God—which is dangerous.

If we do not fear God, we take the risk of becoming self-
satisfied and proud. When we do that, we inevitably glorify
created things when we ought to glorify the Creator. When
that happens, we should immediately strive to redirect our
glory to God. As Scripture advises us: "Do not delay to
turn back to the Lord. . . ."[15] If one offends God by denying the glory God deserves, how much more does that person offend the Almighty when he or she shamelessly
behaves like this? Be that as it may, we all know that the
one who is not in Christ or who withdraws from the Lord,
withholds glory from God.

It is definitely difficult to understand how a work can be both
dead and yet not a harmful, mortal sin.

Here's my proof: Scripture does not speak of dead things
like this: stating that something is not mortal and yet is

dead. Neither does grammar, which says that "dead" is a stronger term than "mortal." Grammarians call a mortal work one that kills. A dead work is not one that has been killed, but one that is not alive. God, however, despises what is not alive, as is written in Proverbs 15:8, "The sacrifice of the wicked is an abomination to the Lord."

Also, the will must do something with respect to such a dead work, namely, either love or hate it. The will cannot hate dead works because the will is evil. Consequently the will loves dead works, and therefore it loves dead things. This very act itself is an evil work, a work against God whom the will should love and honor in this and in every deed.

We cannot evade pride and receive authentic hope—that is, unless we are afraid that all our works might be judged and condemned.

This is derived from Thesis Four: We cannot hope in God unless we have despaired in all creatures and know that no created thing can help us without God. Because we do not hope purely (as said above) and because we still place confidence in something created, we must, because of the impurity in all things, fear the judgment of God. In this way, we can avoid pride, not only in our works, but in our inclination toward such arrogance. That way, it will not please us to have confidence in that which is created.

From God's perspective, sins are truly venial when we fear that they are mortal.

What's been said above clarifies this: as much as we accuse ourselves, so much God pardons us, according to Isaiah 43:26, "Confess your misdeed so that you will be justified" and Psalm 141:4, "Do not turn my heart to any evil, to busy myself with wicked deeds."

Free will, after the fall, exists in name only; and if it "does what it is capable of," then it commits a mortal sin.[16]

The first part is clear: the will is captive and subject to sin. Not that the will is nothing—but it is only "free" to do evil. As John 8:34 and 36 put it: "Everyone who commits sin is a slave to sin" . . . and, "if the Son makes you free, you will be free indeed." And St. Augustine says in *The Spirit and the Letter,* "Free will without grace has the power to do nothing but sin"; and in *Against Julian,* book II, "You call the will free, but in fact it is an enslaved will," and in many other places.

The second part is clear from what has been said above, from Hosea 13:9 ("Israel, you are bringing misfortune upon yourself, because your salvation is alone with me"), and from similar passages.

Free will, after the fall, can only perform good works passively, but it can always do bad works actively.

Here's an example: As dead people can only take action about their lives in a passive way, so can dead people only take action about their death while they live. Free will, however, is dead, as demonstrated by the dead whom the Lord has raised up, as the teachers of holiness say—and especially St. Augustine proves this thesis in his various writings against the Pelagians.

Nor could free will maintain itself in a state of innocence, much less choose good deeds, in an active capacity. Rather, it could only behave passively.

The Master of the Sentences[17] quotes Augustine regarding this "active capacity": "These testimonies obviously demonstrate that humans received a righteous nature and a good will when they were created, and also the help by means of which they could prevail. Otherwise it would appear as though they had not fallen because of their own fault." He speaks of the active capacity, which is obviously contrary to Augustine's opinion in his book *Concerning Reprimand and Grace,* where the Bishop of Hippo puts it in this way: "He received the ability to act, if he so willed, but he did not have the will by means of which he could act." By "ability to act" he understands the passive capacity, and by "the will by means of which he could," the active capacity.

The second part, regarding the "passive capacity," the Master clarifies in the same distinction.

Those who believe that they can obtain grace by doing what is in them add sin to sin—and they multiply their guilt.

Based on the above, this much is clear: When persons do what is in themselves, they sin and seek themselves in all they do. But if they should suppose that through sin they might become worthy of or prepared for grace, they would add prideful self-satisfaction to their sin—as if they do not believe that sin is sin and evil is evil, which is an extreme sin. As Jeremiah 2:13 says, "For my people have committed two evils: they have forsaken me, the fountain of living waters, and hewed out cisterns for themselves, broken cisterns, that can hold no water"; that is, through sin they are far from me and yet they presume to do good by their own ability.

Now you might ask, "What are we supposed to do now? Shall we give up because we can do nothing but sin?" I would say, "By no means! But fall down and pray for grace. Hope in Christ who is our salvation, life, and resurrection." This is why the law teaches us like this: the law shows us our sin so that, having recognized our sin, we may seek and receive grace. Indeed, God "gives grace to the humble,"[18] and "whoever humbles themselves will be exalted."[19] The law humbles, grace exalts. The law effects fear and wrath, grace effects hope and mercy. "Through the law comes knowledge of sin,"[20] through knowledge of sin, however, comes humility, and through humility grace comes to us. Thus actions that are alien to God's nature result in deeds that do in fact belong to the nature of God. The Lord makes us sinners, but only so that sinners like us may be made righteous.

This kind of speech is no occasion for despair. Rather, it prompts the desire to humble ourselves and to seek the grace of Christ.

This follows from what has already been written: According to the Second Gospel, the kingdom of heaven comes to children and humble people—and Christ loves them.[21] Humble people are those of us who know we deserve to go to hell and that our sin stinks to high heaven—that is, only the law shows us our sin.

This proclamation, which tells us we are sinners, leads us from despair to hope. Such preaching concerning sin prepares us for grace; or, put another way, we recognize sin and faith in this sort of preaching. Desire for grace arises from recognition of sin. Sick persons seek a physician when they see how serious their illness is. Therefore, one does not give cause for despair or death by telling sick persons about the danger of their illness. In effect, however, one urges them to seek medical treatment. To say that we are nothing and to say that we constantly sin when we "do the best we can" does not cause people to lapse into despair (unless they are fools). Rather, we would make them concerned about the grace of our Lord Jesus Christ.

Surely persons must completely despair of their personal abilities before they are ready to receive the grace of Christ.

The law intends that humans despair of their own capabilities. The law leads them into hell and makes them poor—showing them that they are sinners in all their works. As the Apostle writes in Romans, chapters two and three, where he says, "I have already charged that all are under the power of sin." However, those who are "doing what is within themselves" and believe that they are doing something good, do not see that their deeds are worthless, nor do they despair of their own strength. They are so presumptuous that they strive for grace while relying on their own strength.

One is not worthy to be called a theologian who would look at the invisible dimensions of God as if they could be perceived through what has been made.[22]

The Apostle Paul exemplified this in Romans 1:22, when he identifies such folks as fools. Besides, the invisible dimensions of God are virtue, godliness, wisdom, justice, goodness, etc. Knowledge of these things makes one neither worthy or nor wise.

A theologian, rather, would look at the visible backside[23] of God as seen through suffering and the cross.

The backside and visible attributes of God are things such as humanity, weakness, foolishness—and these are the opposite of the invisible dimensions of divinity. The Apostle Paul, in 1 Corinthians 1:25, calls these attributes the weakness and foolishness of God. Because humans misused the knowledge of God through works, God wished again to be made known in suffering—to judge the wisdom of invisible things with the wisdom of visible things. That way, those who did not worship the God made known in the Divine works should worship the God hidden in suffering. As the Apostle says in 1 Corinthians 1:21: "For since, in the wisdom of God, the world did not know God through wisdom, God decided, through the foolishness of our proclamation, to save those who believe." Now it is not enough for anyone, and it does no good to recognize God in Divine glory and majesty, unless one recognizes God in the humiliation and disgrace of the cross. In this way, God destroys the wisdom of the wise, as Isaiah 45:15 puts it, "Truly, you are a God who hides."

We see this also in John 14:8, where Philip spoke as a theologian of glory: "Show us the Father." Christ immediately set aside this volatile thought about seeking God elsewhere and said, "Philip, the one who has seen me has seen the Father."[24] Because of this authentic theology, the recognition of God is in the crucified Christ. It is also stated in John 10 (John 14:6), "No one comes to the Father, but by me." "I am the door" [John 10:9], etc.

A theologian of glory calls a bad thing good and a good thing bad. A theologian of the cross calls a thing what it is.

Those who do not know Christ do not know God hidden in suffering. For that reason, they prefer works to suffering, glory to the cross, power to frailty, wisdom to foolishness. In general, they prefer good to bad. St. Paul calls these folks "enemies of the cross of Christ" in Philippians 3:18. They hate the cross and suffering, but they love their works and their glory. These folks call the good of the cross "evil." And the evil of a deed, they call "good."

God, on the other hand, can only be found in suffering and the cross, as mentioned above. The friends of the cross say the cross is good and works are evil. The cross, however, destroys works and crucifies the old Adam or Eve within us (who is particularly captivated by works). As human beings, we cannot help but overinflate our accomplishments—that is, until suffering and evil deflate and destroy them. Then we know that they are worthless and that our works are not ours, but God's.

The sort of wisdom that would look at the invisible attributes of God and interpret them through created things is prideful, blind, and stubborn.

We mentioned this above. Because they are ignorant of the cross and hate it, they instinctively love its opposites: wisdom, glory, strength, and so on. Therefore, this love both blinds them and makes them more obstinate—because an obsessive love cannot be satisfied by the thing that drives its obsession. For example, as the love of money grows with the more wealth one accumulates, so does this sort of spiritual edema demand ever more with ever less satisfaction. As the poet says, "The more water they drink, the more they thirst for it." The same thought is expressed in Ecclesiastes 1:8: "The eye is not satisfied with seeing or the ear filled with hearing." All such desires function like this.

So it is impossible to satisfy such an obsession by the acquisition of knowledge, because it always demands more. Likewise, fame does not extinguish the desire for glory; power does not extinguish the desire to rule, nor does praise satisfy praise, etc. As Christ says in John 4:13: "Everyone who drinks of this water will thirst again."

To cure this desire: don't give in to it, put an end to it. In other words, those who wish to become wise do not seek wisdom by progressing toward it—they become fools and pursue foolishness. Likewise, those who want to have great power, honor, pleasure, and contentment—they need to flee rather than seek power, honor, pleasure, and satisfaction in all things. This wisdom is foolish to the world.

The law enacts God's wrath—killing, accusing, indicting, judging, and punishing whatever is not in Christ.[25]

Thus Galatians 3:13 states, "Christ redeemed us from the curse of the law"; and, in the same chapter: "For all who rely on works of the law are under the curse," Galatians 3:10; Romans 4:15: "For the law brings wrath"; and Romans 7:10: "The very commandment which promised life proved to be the death of me"; Romans 2:12: "All who have sinned apart from the law will also perish apart from the law, and all who have sinned under the law will be judged by the law." Therefore, those who brag that they are wise and learned in the law are bragging about their confusion, their damnation, the wrath of God, and death. And Romans 2:23: "You that boast in the law . . ."

This sort of wisdom is not a bad thing and we should not flee from the law. That said, human beings apart from the theology of the cross misuse the best in the worst way.

Romans 7:12 and 1 Timothy 4:4: The Law is holy, all the gifts of God are good, and every created thing is very good.[26] But, as we said above, those who have not been brought low and reduced to nothing through the cross and suffering take credit for works and wisdom and do not acknowledge God. Such folks misuse and disgrace the gifts of God.

However, those who have been crushed by suffering know that they do not handle it on their own, but that God accomplishes everything in them. Because of this, they view their good works (or lack of good works) from the same perspective. They do not brag if they do good works. They are not upset if God does not do good works through them. They understand that it is enough to suffer and be crushed by the cross, so that they might be annihilated all the more. Christ says this in John 3:7, "You must be born from above." To be born anew, one must first die and then be raised up with Christ. Indeed, to die means to accept the presence of death.

The one who does much is not righteous—but rather, the one who (apart from work) believes much in Christ.[27]

We do not obtain the righteousness of God through oft-repeated actions (as Aristotle taught)—but by faith, because "The one who through faith is righteous shall live,"[28] and "A person believes with the heart and so is justified."[29] Therefore, I wish to have the words "apart from work" understood in the following manner: It is not that righteous folks do nothing—it is just that their works do not make them righteous. In fact, their righteousness produces works. Because grace and faith are given without our works, after they have been bestowed, works follow. Romans 3:20 states it this way, "No human being will be justified in God's sight by works of the law," and, "For we hold that a person is justified by faith apart from works of law."[30]

Put another way: works contribute nothing to one's justification before God. Therefore, a person knows that works done by faith are not one's own but God's. Because of this, one does not seek to become justified or glorified through works, but seeks God. One's justification by faith in Christ is sufficient. Christ is such a person's wisdom, righteousness, etc.,[31] so that we may be both Christ's works and tools.

The law says, "Do this," and it is never done. Grace says, "Believe in this," and everything is already done.

The first statement is evident in many places throughout the works of the Apostle Paul and his interpreter, St. Augustine. And it has been stated often enough above that the law works wrath and keeps all humans under the curse. The second part is clear from the same sources, because faith justifies. As St. Augustine writes, "The law orders what faith obtains"—because through faith Christ is in us, indeed, one with us. Christ is righteous and has fulfilled every command of God. Therefore, we also fulfill everything through the Lord, because, through faith, Christ has become ours.

Christ's work is accurately called "a primary work" and our work "a secondary work." That is, this secondary work pleases God because of the grace of the primary work.

Because Christ lives in us through faith, the Lord motivates us to do good works through faith in that primary work. Indeed, the works of Christ fulfill the commands of God given to us through faith. When we look at such works, we are moved to do likewise. For this reason, the Apostle Paul says, "Therefore be imitators of God, as beloved children."[32] Deeds of mercy are aroused by the works through which Christ has saved us, as St. Gregory says: "Every deed of Christ instructs and motivates us." If Christ's action is in us, then it lives in us through faith, because, according to the verse, it is extremely attractive: "Draw me after you, let us make haste"[33] toward the fragrance "of your anointing oils," that is, "your works."[34]

God's love does not discover, but creates, that which pleases it. Human love comes about by the object that pleases it.

The second part is clear and all philosophers and theologians accept it: the object of love is its own cause. This assumes, with Aristotle, that all power of the soul is passive and material—able to act only in a receptive way. Further, this shows how Aristotle's philosophy contradicts theology, how it continually seeks what is its own and how it receives, rather than gives, good things.

The first part is clear because God's love, which lives in human beings, loves sinful, evil, foolish, and weak people—so that it might make us righteous, good, wise, and strong. Rather than seek its own good, the love of God moves outward and gives good. Sinners, therefore, are attractive because they are loved; they are not loved because they are attractive.

Human love would avoid sinners and evil persons. Christ, however, says: "I did not come to call the righteous, but sinners."[35]

Such is the love of the cross. Born from the cross, this love does not move toward goodness so it might enjoy what's already there. Rather, it moves toward wicked and needy persons, in order to give goodness to them. The Apostle Paul says, "It is more blessed to give than to receive."[36] And for this reason, Psalm 41:1 says, "Happy are those who consider the needy and the poor." By our natural intellect, we are not able to conceive of something that does not yet exist, such as the potential in poor and needy folk. We can only see things that do exist, such as the True and the Good. Therefore the intellect evaluates appearances, is a respecter of persons, and judges according to that which can be seen, etc. [37]

Letter to Philipp Melanchthon: "Believe More Boldly than You Sin," from the Wartburg Castle (August 1, 1521)[1]

Summer 1521: Luther is in hiding from imperial forces at one of Prince Frederick III's castles (the Wartburg, near Eisenach, 165 miles southwest of Wittenberg); Frederick the Wise and Luther want to avoid the implementation of the Edict of Worms, the previous April—condemning him as a traitor, declaring him an enemy of the empire, and offering a reward for his capture (dead or alive). Away from Wittenberg, Luther exchanges letters with Philipp Melanchthon, his young colleague and a new addition to the faculty at the university. The outspoken Martin seeks to encourage and advise the quiet Philipp, who was unprepared to lead in Luther's absence. Melanchthon's anxieties compounded his predicament as he fretted over possible unintended and problematic consequences of their reform proposal—particularly the kinds of reforms being instituted in Wittenberg by their colleague Andreas Bodenstein von Karlstadt. Luther offers here some supportive advice, often misquoted outside of its original pastoral context, and misused to caricature Luther's theology as morally lax.

The controversy with Karlstadt would continue until Luther returned to Wittenberg the following spring to preach the famous "Eight Sermons in Lent," the next piece in our collection.

. . . . .

Dear Philipp,

. . . I am indeed happy that you have returned to the pattern of Christ's institution.[2] I intended to work specifically toward this, when I got home. Because we now recognize this tyranny and can resist it, we are no longer forced to receive only "one kind." And I will never say another private mass until the end of time. I beg of you: Pray to the Lord that Christ would hurry up and give us more of the Spirit, because I sense that the Lord will soon descend upon Germany—just as its unfaithfulness, its lack of piety, and its rejection of the gospel deserve. We will certainly receive the blame for this plague, because we heretics have so aggravated God. We will be ridiculed and despised by all people.[3] Our opponents, on the other hand, will find excuses for their sins, and will justify themselves. Yet, God will then show that wicked people cannot be made good. Neither kindness nor wrath will work, and many will be tempted to do evil. The Lord's will be done.[4] Amen.

If you are a preacher of grace, then preach real and not fake grace. If grace is true, then you must bear true and not false sin. God does not save those who are only fake sinners. Be a sinner—believing and rejoicing in Christ more boldly than you sin. And do so because Christ has overcome sin, death, and the world. If we are in this world, then we cannot help but sin. Our existence is not the dwelling place of righteousness. As Peter says, we look for new heavens and a new earth in which righteousness dwells.[5]

It is enough that by the bounteous glory of God, we have come to know the Lamb who takes away the sin of the world. No sin will separate us from the Lamb, even though we commit adultery and murder a thousand times a day. Do you think that the purchase price that was paid for the redemption of our sins by so great a Lamb is too small?

Pray boldly—you are also a huge sinner.

Eight Sermons in Lent (1522)[1]

March 9–16: Luther preaches this series of sermons, one a day for eight days. He had, since the Edict of Worms the previous spring, been in hiding at one of Frederick III's castles. When he found out that Andreas von Karlstadt (his faculty colleague) had begun to incite Wittenbergers to institute reforms by force, he came home. Mob rule was lurching toward chaos—attacking priests at mass, forcing nuns to marry, driving monks from the monastery, destroying paintings and statues in the town church. Luther chose his timing carefully: the liturgical season of Lent had just begun. Its many traditions and pious practices would be a catalyst for conflict. So Luther, wearing his monk's robe and haircut (the tonsure, a round, shaved patch on the top of the head), ascends the pulpit and starts to preach. His homiletical skill, amazing. The result, astounding. He would not replace one form of churchly legalism with another, nor would he enforce conformity over nonessential practices. He calms the storm. Order returns to Wittenberg. And, along the way, he demonstrates both the content and the method of the Reformation he envisioned.

THE FIRST SERMON: SUNDAY, MARCH 9, 1522 (THE FIRST SUNDAY IN LENT OR "INVOCAVIT SUNDAY")[2]

We all must die; and no one can die in place of another. Each person struggles with death in their own way. We can certainly cry out to others, but at the time of death, we must be prepared for the actual moment we die: because I cannot accompany you beyond the moment of your death—and you cannot accompany me. At this point, we take on the most important things of life as Christians—understanding and equipping ourselves with what you, Beloved, have heard from me many days ago.

First: we need to know that we are "children of wrath" and all our work, senses, and thoughts are, precisely, nothing. Because of this, we need a clear and powerful passage to undergird such a point—like the text from St. Paul in his letter to the Ephesians (actually, the Bible contains many passages like this, but I do not wish to overwhelm you with too many): "We are all children of wrath."[3] So you cannot claim: "I have built an altar, endowed masses," and the like.

Second, we need to know that God has sent the only begotten Son for us to believe in.[4] And whoever believes in Christ is set free from sin and becomes a child of God. John says this in his first chapter, ". . . Christ gave power to become children of God—to all those who believe in his name."[5] Precisely at this point, we should all be well acquainted with the Bible and repel the Devil with many passages. In these two matters, I still see nothing deficient or false. They have been preached to you clearly—and it would worry me if this were not the case. Indeed, I see it quite plainly, and, if I might even say so, you know more about this than I do. And there are not only a few of you, but many, who see this and understand it.

Third, we also need love. Through faith, let us love one another[6] as God has loved us. Without love, faith is nothing.[7] St. Paul writes in 1 Corinthians 13:1–2: "If I speak in the tongues of angels, but do not have love, I am nothing." To reinforce this, dear friends, isn't this what is so lacking around here? I sense little or no love and I can almost gauge that you have not been grateful to God for such a precious treasure and gift.

Let's make sure that Wittenberg does not become another Capernaum.[8] I see well that you know how to speak about doctrine, faith, and love—as they have been preached to you. No wonder, there. If a donkey can chant the lessons (more or less), then shouldn't you be able to recite dogma or recite some slogans? Dear friends, the kingdom of God (and it is here among us) does not consist in talk or words,[9] but in actions—in deeds, works, and practices. God does not want hearers and memorizers, but followers and doers.[10] This is faith active in love. Faith without love does not cut it—in fact it is not faith, only the appearance of faith. A face in a mirror is not a real face, but merely its reflection.[11]

Fourth, we need endurance. Because faithful people trust God and love their neighbors through daily acts of service, they are always subject to persecution. The devil never sleeps—giving him plenty of time to be creative. And endurance produces and brings hope.[12] And this hope freely submits to God and thus grows wiser. Faith absorbs these assaults and attacks—even growing stronger each day. Such a heart, content with being useful, neither rests nor takes stock of itself. Rather, this heart serves the needs and flourishing of its brothers and sisters, just as God has served it.

Precisely here, my friends, we must not act, simply because we have a right to do so. Instead, let us look at what our brothers and sisters need and what would be helpful to them. Paul puts it this way, *"Omnia mihi licent, sed non omnia expedient"* ("All things are lawful for me, but all things are not beneficial").[13] We are not all equally strong in faith—and many of you have a stronger faith than I. Therefore, we must not look at ourselves or focus on our rights, but to our neighbor.

As God spoke through Moses: ". . . I have carried you like a mother carries her child. . . ."[14] What does a mother do with her baby? First she gives milk, then cereal, then eggs and some soft food. If at the outset, she inverted this order and gave her baby solid food, it would do the child no good.[15] Therefore, let us deal with our brothers and sisters like this: endure with them for a sufficient amount of time—carrying their weaknesses and helping them to bear them. We should also give them milk like we received,[16] until they also grow strong. We don't travel toward paradise by ourselves. We bring our sisters and brothers with us—even if they are not yet our friends. If mothers were to abandon their children, where would we be? Dear brothers and sisters, when you have finished nursing, do not then keep your sibling from being fed as you were.

If I had been here, I would have preferred that things not be pushed this far. The cause is certainly right, but the pace is too fast. There are sisters and brothers on both sides—folks under our care, whom we need to bring along with us.

It's a bit like this: The sun has two effects: light and heat. No Ruler has enough power to control the sun's light. It remains fixed in its place. On the other hand, heat may be turned and guided, and yet always remains around the sun. Similarly, faith remains absolutely secure in our hearts and does not weaken. However, love bends and turns so that our neighbor may grasp and follow it. There are some who can run, others can walk, and still others who can hardly crawl.[17] Therefore we must not look at our own abilities, but at the abilities of our sisters and brothers—so that the devil does not destroy those who are weak in faith, as the weak in faith struggle to keep up with the strong in faith.

So follow me, my brothers and sisters. I have not destroyed a thing.[18] God put me on this path first, but I do not run ahead. Rather, I stay as long as God permits. I was also the one to whom God first revealed that the Word of God should be preached to you—and I am now certain that you do in fact have the plain Word of God.

Let us, therefore, respect one another, humbly lay ourselves at one another's feet, join hands together, and help each other. I want to do what is mine to do—and care for you as I would care for my own soul. The struggle here is not just against pope or bishop, but against the evil one.[19] Do you think the devil sleeps? Well, he doesn't. And he knows that the true light is dawning, although his eyes are closed against it. He would like nothing more than to sneak up on us and sucker-punch us when we're not looking. I know Satan well and I hope, for God's sake, I understand this about him: if the devil gets a toehold, then he will soon take over—and then we will be stuck, wondering how to be rid of him.

This means that all those who attacked the mass were wrong to do so—as well as those who supported them (not that the idea to end the mass might not have been good). It was just not done according to good order. You say, "It was right, based on Scripture." I confess that with you.[20] But what about the process? That was a riot. It lacked order and offended neighbors. If beforehand you had formally petitioned the council and they had taken it on, then you could know that the initiative had come from God. I would have initiated a more organized process—a more well-ordered way to proceed. And if the mass were not so evil, I would want to reinstitute it.

As I've said, I'm not even sure how to defend your actions. To the papists and their goofy-heads,[21] I could try this: "How do you know whether it was done with good or bad intention? The work in itself was really a good deed." To the devil, on the other hand, I'm not sure what I'd say. The devil might wait to toy with folks on their deathbeds—using Bible passages like these against them: "Every plant that my heavenly Father has not planted will be uprooted."[22] And "I have not sent them, yet they ran" (Jeremiah. 23:21). How could such folks stand up to the devil? He will throw them into hell.

On the other hand, I have the only weapon I need to fend off his assault, a weapon that will drive him from this world: I know that, even though I did not want it, I was called here by the council to preach. I was, therefore, willing to accept you as you were willing to receive me. And I was not that far away. You could have contacted me in writing. For a long time, I received not even a note. You chose to do this and now am I supposed to shoulder responsibility for it? Well, I will not do it—the burden would be too much for me to carry.

Mark this well: you do not automatically have the Spirit, just because you have a lot of Scriptural knowledge. And note also that "must" and "free" are two different things. A "must" is something required by necessity and must never be compromised—as, for instance, the faith, which I shall never permit anyone to take away from me and must always keep in my heart and freely confess the faith before everyone. But "free" is that in which I have choice, and may use or not, yet in such a way that it serves my brother and not me. So do not make a "must" out of what is "free," as you have done. That way, you may not be called to account for those who were led astray by your unloving misuse of liberty. For example, suppose you cajole someone to eat meat on Friday and at the point of death, that action comes back to haunt them: "I'm a wretch because I ate that meat and I am damned!" God will hold you responsible for that soul.

I, too, would like to establish any number of new practices, but too few people would likely follow my lead. What would be the use of that? Because I'm fairly certain that, when push comes to shove, those who would begin such a thing would also not stay with it to the end. They would likely be the first to desert. It would be as if I brought folks to the brink of conflict, and even though I had incited them to act, I would then abandon the fight—too afraid to face death. What feckless frauds!

Therefore, we need to offer others the same milk that we received, until they become strong in faith. There are many people who would agree with us and who would also eventually accept this change. But they just do not understand it fully. In the meantime, we would them drive away. So, let's love our neighbors. If we don't do that, our efforts are useless. We need to be patient with them for a time and not abandon the weak in faith. Plus, we must be prepared to enact and abandon many other things, as long as love requires it, and it does no harm to our faith.

If we do not pray to God intensely and do the right thing in this situation, it appears to me that all the anguish we've begun to heap on the papists will fall upon us. This is why I couldn't stay away any longer: I had to come home. I had to say these things to you.

This is enough for now about the mass; tomorrow we want to talk about images.

THE SECOND SERMON:
MONDAY, MARCH 10, 1522

My dear friends, yesterday you heard about the quintessential qualities of the Christian person: faith and love. Faith toward God and love toward others (specifically one's neighbors). Christians love and serve one another generously, as we have received from God, apart from merit and work. So there are two things: the first is the one and only indispensable thing and must be done. Second, there are things that are matters of choice and not of necessity. They may be done or not done without endangering one's faith or condemning them.

In both situations, love needs to treat the neighbor as God treats us. Love has to walk the right path—neither falling on the left side nor falling on the right side. Even in those areas which are "musts" and are necessary, like believing in Christ, love still does not force or inappropriately constrain others.

Thus, the mass is evil and it displeases God, because it is held as if it were a sacrifice and a good work that merits reward. Therefore, it needs to be abolished. At this point, there can be no question or doubt, any more than you need to ask whether you should worship God. Here we are entirely agreed: private masses need to go. As I have already written,[23] I wish they would be abolished everywhere and we would keep only the regular evangelical mass.

But Christian love ought not to push the issue with force. We should preach and teach with tongue and pen that to hold mass in such a manner is sinful. That said, no one should be dragged away from it by their hair. We must leave it to God. We need to let the Word alone work—without our work or meddling. Why? Because I do not have the power or skill to form the hearts of others like a potter molds clay and form them to please me.[24] I can only reach their ears; their hearts I cannot reach. And because I cannot pour faith into their hearts, I cannot, and should not, force anyone to believe. Only God can cause faith to live in one's heart. We should, therefore, give free course to the Word and not add our works to it. We have the "right to speak," but not the "right to enforce." We should preach the Word, but the results must be left solely to God's good pleasure.

Now if I would swoop in to stop it by force, there are many who would be compelled to consent to it and yet not know where they truly stand—whether it is right or wrong. And they would say, "I do not know if it is right or wrong. I do not know where I am. I was compelled by force to submit to the majority."

Further, such compulsion and coercion only make a mockery of themselves: external showiness, monkeying around, human ordinances, false saints, and hypocrites. Because where the heart is not good, I care nothing at all for the work. We must first win the hearts of the people. But that is done when I teach only the Word of God, preach the gospel, and say, "Dear princes or pastors, abandon the mass. It's not right. You sin when you do it." I must tell you this.

Yet, I still would not make it mandatory for them, nor advocate for a universal law. Whoever would follow me could do so, and whoever would not accept the changes could remain outside. In the latter case the Word would sink into the heart and do

its work. In this way, they would become convinced and acknowledge their errors, and fall away from the mass. Tomorrow,
others would do likewise. Thus God would achieve more with
the Word than if you and I were to concentrate all our power in
one place. When you have won the heart, you have won the person. And in this way, it must finally fall under its own weight
and come to an end.

If the hearts and minds of all concerned agree and are of one
accord, then go ahead and get rid of it. But if everyone is not,
heart and soul, in favor of getting rid of it, then leave it in God's
hands, I beg of you! Otherwise, the end will not be positive. I am
not advocating that the mass be reestablished. I am leaving it, in
God's name. Faith must not be chained and imprisoned, nor
bound by an ordinance to any work. This is the principle by
which you must be governed. Because I am sure you will not be
able to carry out your plans. And if you should carry them out
with such general laws, then I will recant everything that I have
written and preached and I will not support you. This I am telling you now. What harm can it do you? You still have your faith
in God, pure and strong so that this thing cannot hurt you.

Love, therefore, demands that you have compassion for the
weak, as all the apostles had. For instance, when Paul came to
Athens,[25] a mighty city, he found in the temple many ancient altars, and he went from one to the other and looked at them all,
but he did not kick down a single one of them with his foot.
Rather he went to the center of the market and said they were
nothing but idols and begged the people to abandon them; but
he did not destroy one of them by force. When the Word took
hold of their hearts, they forsook them of their own accord, and
in consequence the thing fell of itself. Likewise, if I had seen
them holding mass, I would have preached to them and admonished them. Had they heeded my admonition, I would have won
them; if not, I would nevertheless not have torn them from it by
the hair or employed any force, but simply allowed the Word to
act and prayed for them. Because the Word created heaven and
earth and all things (Psalm 33:6) the Word must do this thing,
and not we poor sinners.

In short, I will preach it, teach it, write it, but I will constrain no
one by force, because faith must come freely—without coercion.

Take me as an example: I disagreed with indulgences and with all the papists, but never with force. All I did was preach, teach, and write about God's Word. Otherwise, I did nothing. And while I slept or drank Wittenberg beer with my friends Philipp and Amsdorf,[26] the Word hurt the papacy more than any prince or emperor ever had. I did nothing. The Word did everything. Had I desired to incite conflict, I certainly could have. I could've started such a blood sport in Germany that the emperor himself would have been at risk. But what sort of fool's play would that have been?

I did nothing. The Word did the work.

What do you suppose Satan thinks when folks begin with violence as a means to their ends? He sits back in hell and muses, "Oh, what a good game those stupid fools are up to now!" But if we only spread the Word and let it alone do the work, then it torments the devil. Because the Word is powerful, it takes over human hearts and then deeds will follow as a result of being so captured.

In the early church, for example, various groups of Christians disagreed over how to understand Moses' law about circumcising males. Some Jewish converts wanted to continue the practice. Some Gentile converts did not. St. Paul settled the matter when he wrote that circumcision may be observed or not because it is not a practice that touches the essence of the Christian faith. They were not to make a law regarding circumcision, neither requiring it nor prohibiting it. Rather, each individual could decide. To circumcise or not to circumcise was not an essential question.[27]

That is, until the time of Jerome, who wanted to make a "must" out of the situation—attempting to make it a rule and a law that would prohibit circumcision altogether. Then St. Augustine entered the picture. And he agreed with St. Paul that it might be kept or not, as one wished. St. Jerome was miles away from St. Paul. The two doctors bumped heads rather forcefully, but after St. Augustine's death, St. Jerome won and the practice was prohibited. Afterward, popes came along and also wanted to weigh in. So they, too, made laws. And from one prohibition grew a thousand laws. Now they have completely buried us under their laws. This is what will happen here also. One law will quickly make two, two will increase to three, and so forth.

That is enough at this time concerning the things that are necessary. Let's be on guard, so we don't lead those of weak conscience in the wrong direction.[28]

THE THIRD SERMON:
TUESDAY, MARCH 11, 1522

We have heard the things that are "musts"—those necessary things that must be done or things that are needed without exception: such as doing away with private or particular masses. Because all works and practices that are either commanded or forbidden by God and thus have been instituted by the Almighty are "musts."

Nevertheless, no one should be dragged to them or away from them by their hair, because I can neither drive someone to heaven nor beat them into heaven with a stick. I said this plainly enough; I believe you understand what I mean.

Now follow the things that are not absolutely necessary— matters for which God gives us the freedom to choose or reject, to do or not to do. For example, a person is free to marry (or not) and monks and nuns are free to leave the cloistered life (or not). Such matters of free choice are not to be forbidden or mandated by anyone. It is wrong to do so because it contradicts God's order.[29]

Approach an issue of freedom, such as being married or remaining single, like this: if your choice is not too burdensome, then stick with it. However, do not make your choice a universal law. Allow others their freedom. If you are a priest or monk, nun or sister, who cannot abstain, then you may take a spouse and be married. That way, your conscience can be relieved and you can stand before God and the world when you are assailed— especially when the devil attacks you at the hour of death. It is not enough to say, "So-and-so did it. I followed the crowd, according to the preaching of Dean Karlstadt or Gabriel (or Michael)."[30] No, you need to stand on your own two feet and prepare yourself to battle the devil. Take your stand on a strong and clear word of Scripture if you would prevail. If you can't do that, then the devil will pluck you like a dried leaf.

Therefore, the priests who have taken wives and the nuns who have taken husbands in order to save their consciences must stand squarely upon a clear Scriptural text—like this from St. Paul (and there are many more): "In later times some will depart from the faith by giving heed to deceitful spirits and doctrines of the devil (I think St. Paul is quite explicit at this point!) and will forbid marriage and the foods which God created."[31] The devil will not overthrow or devour this text. In fact, it will overthrow and devour him.

Any monks or nuns, therefore, who find they are too weak to remain chaste should examine themselves thoroughly. If their hearts and consciences are strong enough, then let them take a spouse. Would to God all monks and nuns could hear this sermon and properly understand this matter and all would leave their monastic houses. Then all the monasteries in the world would cease to exist. That's my wish.

At the moment, however, they have no understanding of the matter (because no one preaches it to them). They hear about others who've left the monastic life in other places. But those folks prepared well for their move. When they want to do likewise, they don't always prepare their consciences as well as they should—and they do not understand that this is a matter of free choice. This is bad, and yet it is better that the evil should be external rather than internal.

So I say, whatever God has left free shall remain free. If anyone, like the pope, the Antichrist, forbids such a thing, then you don't have to obey. Whoever can do so without harm and for love of neighbor may wear monastic garb or hairdos, because neither will hurt your faith. The robe will not strangle you, if you are wearing one at the moment.

My dear friends, I have therefore said it clearly enough, and I believe you've got it—do not make a free choice into a law. Don't say, "That priest has taken a wife, therefore all priests must marry." No way. Or, "this monk or that nun has left the monastic life, therefore they must all leave." No way. Or, "that individual has destroyed images in church and burned them, therefore all images must be burned." No way, my dear friends in Christ! And again, "if that priest has no wife, then no priest may marry." No way! Because those who cannot remain celibate should marry, and for others who can be celibate, it's good that they restrain themselves, as those who live in the Spirit and not in the flesh.[32] Neither should they worry too much about their vows, such as the monastic promises of obedience, chastity, and poverty (though they have more than enough). We cannot vow anything that is contrary to God's commands. God has made it a matter of free choice to marry or not to marry, and you, oh foolish one, would try to turn this liberty into a vow contrary to the ordinance of God!

You must, therefore, let this choice remain free and do not make a law out of it, because your vow is contrary to God's liberty. For example, if I vowed to punch my father in the face or to steal someone's possessions, do you believe such a vow would please God? As little as I ought to keep a vow to slug my father's mouth, so little ought I to abstain from marriage because I am bound by a vow of chastity. Because in both cases, God has ordered creation otherwise. God has ordered creation so that I am free to eat fish or meat. There ought to be no commandment concerning them. Therefore, all the Carthusians[33] and all monks and nuns depart from God's ordinance and liberty when they believe that if they eat meat they defile themselves.

Regarding Images[34]

But now let us look at images themselves: They are likewise not a necessity. And we're free to have them or not (even though we'd be much better off without them and I personally don't like them).

A huge conflict once raged between the papacy and the empire over the subject of images. The emperor concluded they had to go; the pope concluded they had to remain. Both were wrong. Much blood was shed. The pope won and the emperor lost.[35] What was the brouhaha all about? Each wanted to make a "must" out of something "free." God does not *tolerate* such a move.

Do you presume to do things differently from the way God Almighty has decreed? Certainly not—so let it alone. You read in the Law, "You shall not make for yourself an idol, whether in the form of anything that is in heaven above, or that is on the earth beneath, or that is in the water under the earth."[36] There you take your stand; that is your ground. Well, take a look! When our adversaries say: The meaning of the first commandment is that we should worship only one God and not any image, even as the next line states, "You shall not bow down to them or serve them,"[37] and when they say that it is the worship of images which is forbidden and not the making of them, they are shaking our foundation and making it uncertain. And if you reply: The text says, "You shall not make any images," then they say: It also says, "You shall not worship them." In the face of such uncertainty who would be so bold as to destroy the images? Not I.

Plus, we can even go further. They say: Did not Noah, Abraham, Jacob build altars?[38] And who will deny that? We must admit it. Also, Moses put up a bronze serpent, didn't he, as we read in Numbers 22)?[39] How then can you say that Moses prohibited images when he himself made one? It seems to me that such a serpent is an image, too. How shall we answer that? Also, don't we read that two birds were placed on the mercy seat (Exodus 37:7), the very place where God wanted worship to take place? Here we must admit that we may have images and make images, but we must not worship them, and if they are worshipped, they should be put away and destroyed, just as King Hezekiah broke in pieces the bronze serpent erected by Moses (2 Kings 18:4). And who will be so bold as to say, when challenged, that they worship the images? They will say, "Are you the one who dares to accuse us of worshipping them? Do not believe that they will acknowledge it. To be sure, it is true, but we cannot make them admit it. Just look how they acted when I condemned works without faith. They said: Do you believe that we have no faith, or that our works are performed without faith? Then I cannot press them any further, but must put my flute back in my pocket; for if they gain a hair's breadth, they make a hundred miles out of it.

It should have been preached, therefore, that images were nothing and that no service is done to God by placing them in a church; then they would have fallen of themselves. That is what I did; that is what Paul did in Athens, when he went into their churches and saw all their idols. He did not punch any of them in the mouth, but stood in the marketplace and said, "People of

Athens, you are all idolatrous" [Acts 17:16, 22]. He preached against their idols, but he overthrew none by force.

But you rush in, cause a ruckus, smash altars, and topple images! Do you really believe you can get rid of such altars in this way? No, you will only set them up more firmly. Even if you overthrew the images in this place, do you think you have overthrown those in Nuremberg and around the whole world? No way.

St. Paul, as we read in the Book of Acts [28:11], sat in a ship on whose prow were painted or carved the Twin Brothers [i.e., Castor and Pollux]. He went on board and did not bother about them at all. And he didn't dislodge them. Why did Luke describe the Twins at this point? Without doubt he wanted to show that outward things could do no harm to faith, if only the heart does not cleave to them or put its trust in them. This is what we must preach and teach, and let the Word alone do the work, as I said before. The Word must first capture our hearts and enlighten us; we will not be the ones to do it. The apostles emphasized their ministry and not the effectiveness of their ministry.

Let this be enough for today.

THE FOURTH SERMON:
WEDNESDAY, MARCH 12, 1522

Dear friends, we have now heard about matters that are "musts" (like when the mass is performed as a sacrifice). Next, we considered the things that are not necessary but free, such as marriage, the monastic life, and the removal of images.

We have discussed these four subjects, and have said that, no matter what, love is the captain. Regarding images in particular, we saw that they ought to be removed when they are worshipped; otherwise not—although because of the abuses they can cause, I wish they were everywhere abolished. This cannot be denied, because everyone who places an image in a church imagines they have performed a good service to God and they are doing a good work. And that, simply put, is idolatrous. But this, the greatest, foremost, and highest reason for abolishing images, you have passed by, and fastened on the least important reason of all. Because I suppose there is nobody, or certainly very few, who do not understand that the crucifix here is not my God. My God is in heaven and this is simply a sign.

The world, however, is full with that other abuse, because who would place a silver or wooden image in a church unless they thought they were serving God? Do you think that Prince Frederick, the bishop of Halle, and the others would have dragged so many silver images into the churches, if they thought they counted for nothing before God? No, they would not have bothered to do it. But this is not sufficient reason to abolish, destroy, and burn all images. Why? Because we must admit that there are still some people who hold no such wrong opinion of them, but to whom they may well be useful (although they are few in number). Nevertheless, we cannot and ought not to condemn a thing which may be any way useful to someone. You should rather have taught that images are nothing, that God cares nothing for them, and that God is not served nor pleased when we make images to appease the Almighty. Rather, we would do better to give a poor person a gold coin than to give God a gold image. God has forbidden the latter, but not the former. If they had heard this teaching that images count for nothing, they would have ceased of their own accord, and the images would have fallen without any uproar or tumult, as is already happening.

Therefore, we must be on our guard, because the devil, through his minions, is after us with all his craft and cunning. Even though it is true and no one can deny that the images are evil because they are abused, nevertheless we must not on that account reject them. We don't condemn anything because it is abused. The result would be complete confusion. God has commanded us in Deuteronomy 4[:19] not to lift up our eyes to the sun [and the moon and the stars], etc., that we may not worship them, for they are created to serve all nations. But there are many people who worship the sun and the stars. Therefore, we propose to rush in and pull the sun and stars from the skies. No, we had better let it be.

Likewise, wine and women bring many men to misery and make them into fools.[40] So, should we kill all the women and pour out all the wine? Also, gold and silver cause much evil. So, should we condemn them? Indeed, if we want to do away with our worst enemy, the one who hurts us the most, then we shall have to kill ourselves, because we have no greater enemy than our own heart (as the prophet Jeremiah 17[:9], says, "The human heart is crooked," or, as I take the meaning, "always curved to one side") And so on—what else would we not do?

Whoever messes with the devil needs good material, because the devil also dresses up and attends the consecrations. But I can trap him with this question, "Did you place the images in the churches because you think it's a special service to God?" And when he says, "yes" (as he must), we can deduce that he has turned something into idolatry that had been originally meant to serve God. He's misused those images and done something with them that God did not command. In fact, he has even not done something that God did command—that he should be helpful to his neighbor.

But I still haven't quite sprung the trap, even though (in reality) he's caught and won't admit it. So, he tries to get away by saying, "Yes, I help the poor, too; cannot I give to my neighbor and at the same time donate images?" This is just not the way it works. Because who wouldn't rather give a neighbor a gold piece than God a golden image? No, he would not bother with placing images in churches if he did not believe, as he actually does, that he was doing something for God.

Let me put it this way: images are neither here nor there, neither evil nor good. We may have them (or not), as we please. This trouble you've started, Mr. Devil, will not hit home with me, because I can't deny the possibility that images might potentially be used in a helpful way by some folks. And if I were asked about it, I would confess that none of these things offend anyone and if just one person were found on earth who used the images aright, the devil would soon point this out to me: "So, why do you condemn what may be used properly?" With that, he would have gone on offense and I would have to admit it.

He would not have gotten nearly so far if I had been here. He haughtily kept us apart, but he's done no harm to the Word of God. You wanted to mess with the devil, but you brought the wrong weapons. You must know the Scriptures well, if you want to fight the devil. Plus, be sure to use them at the right time.

About Fasting from, or Partaking in, Various Meats

Let's move on to talk about the eating of meats and what our attitude should be in this area. It is true that we are free to eat any kind of food, meats, fish, or butter. This no one can deny. It's simply the case that God's given us free choice about this. Nevertheless, we must know how to use our liberty, and in this matter treat the weaker brother or sister quite differently from those who are just plain stubborn.

Observe, then, how you ought to use this liberty:

First, if you cannot abstain from meat without harm to yourself, or if you are sick, you may eat whatever you like, and if anyone takes offense, let them be offended. Even if the entire world were offended by it, you are not committing a sin. God can approve it, in view of the liberty so graciously bestowed upon you and in view of your health needs that would be endangered by your abstinence.

Second, if you should be pressured to eat fish instead of meat on Friday, and to eat fish and abstain from eggs and butter during Lent, etc., as the pope has done with his fool's laws, then you must in no way allow yourself to be drawn away from the liberty in which God has placed you, but do just the contrary to spite him, and say: Because you forbid me to eat meat and presume to turn my liberty into law, I will eat meat in spite of you. And thus you must do in all other things that are matters of liberty. To give you an example: if the pope or anyone else were to force me to wear a cowl, just as he prescribes it, I would take off the cowl just to spite him. But because it is left to my own free choice, I wear it or take it off, according to my pleasure.

Third, there are some who are still weak in faith, who ought to be instructed, and who would gladly believe as we do. But their ignorance prevents them, and if this were preached to them, as it was to us, they would be one with us. We need to treat such well-meaning people rather differently from the way we treat stubborn people. We must bear patiently with these people and not use our liberty; because it brings no peril or harm to body or soul; in fact, it is rather salutary, and we are doing our brothers and sisters a great service besides. But if we use our liberty unnecessarily, and deliberately cause offense to our neighbor, we drive away the very one who in time would come to our faith.

Similarly, St. Paul circumcised Timothy because naive Jews had taken offense.[41] He reasoned like this: "What harm can it do? They are offended because they misunderstand." But when, in Antioch, they insisted that he ought and must circumcise Titus [Galatians 2:3], Paul resisted and, to spite them, refused to circumcise him [Galatians 2:11]. And he stood his ground.

And Paul did the same kind of thing when St. Peter, through his freedom, blew an evil thought into the hearts of some unsophisticated folks—Peter was eating pork and sausages with some Gentiles, but when some Jews arrived, he abstained from these foods and did not eat as he had previously—then the Gentile converts thought: "Whoa! We need to be like the Jews, eat no pork and follow the law of Moses." But when Paul learned that they were acting to the injury of evangelical freedom, he confronted Peter publicly and gave him an apostolic reprimand, saying, "If you, though a Jew, live like a Gentile, how can you compel the Gentiles to live like Jews?" [Galatians 2:14]. Thus we, too, should order our lives and use our liberty at the proper time, so that Christian liberty may suffer no injury, and no offense be given to our weak brothers and sisters who are still without the knowledge of this liberty.

THE FIFTH SERMON:
THURSDAY, MARCH 13, 1522

We have heard about things that are necessary, such as how the mass is not to be performed as a sacrifice. And we've heard about things that are not necessary, such as monks' leaving the monasteries, the marriage of priests, and images being kept in churches. We have seen how we need to handle such things—that no compulsion or statute ought to be enforced regarding them. And how no one should be compelled to perform such actions or prohibited from doing them by force. We must permit God's Word alone to do the work.

Now let us look at how to celebrate the Sublime Sacrament:

You have heard me preach against the ridiculous rules of the pope. And how I stood against them. For example, that no woman, even though she is a celibate nun, may wash the altar clothes on which Christ's body had rested, unless those linens had been previously cleaned by a celibate priest. And how, if a layperson touches the body of Christ, the priests rush over immediately to scrub those fingers (and there's a lot more of this sort of thing).

Yet, if a young woman were to sleep with a priest, the pope looks the other way and allows it to happen. And if she becomes pregnant and delivers a child, then the pope closes his eyes to that, too. He won't let them disturb the altar clothes and the sacrament, but if a priest latches on to it, in both kinds, then that's fine.

We've preached against these sorts of foolish laws and uncovered them to show that there is no sin connected to the pope's ridiculous rules and regulations—and that lay folks do not sin if they touch the cup or the body of Christ with their hands. You should give thanks to God that you have come to such clear knowledge, which many wonderful people have lacked.

But now you're acting just as foolish as the pope, if you think people *have to* hold the sacrament in their hands. If you want to show how good a Christian you are by touching the sacrament with your hands and you're using the sacrament (our most valuable treasure) in such a way, then it's a wonder you have not been struck to the ground by thunder and lightning. Of all the things God can tolerate, this he cannot allow, because you have made a requirement out of it. And if you don't quit it, the emperor (or any of his underlings) won't need to drive me out of here. I will go gladly. And I tell you, although my enemies have caused me so much great sorrow, none of them has hurt me as deeply as you have.

If you think you need to show off how good a Christian you are by handling the sacrament and bragging about it to the whole world, then Herod and Pilate are the top and best of all Christians. Because, to my eyes, they truly handled the body of Christ—when they nailed him to the cross and put him to death. My dear friends, God's reign is not in physical or outward objects, those things we are able to touch or sense, but in faith [Luke 17:20; Romans 14:17; 1 Corinthians 4:20].

Now, you could say, "We should live according to the Bible and that's what we're doing. God has instituted the Sacrament so that we must take it with our hands. After all, Christ did say, 'Take and eat. This is my body.'"[42]

I would respond like this: although I am completely convinced that the Lord's disciples took it with their hands, and although I admit that you may do the same without committing sin, I still cannot make it compulsory or defend doing so. My reason is that the devil, when he corners us, will argue, "Where have you read in the Scriptures that 'take' means 'grasping with the hands'?" How, then, are you going to prove or defend your practice? Indeed, how will you answer him when he cites from the Scriptures the very opposite, and proves that "take" does not mean to receive with the hands only, but also to convey to ourselves in other ways? "Listen to this, my good fellow," he will say, "is not the word 'take' used by three evangelists when they described the Lord's taking of gall and vinegar?[43] You must admit that the Lord did not touch or handle it with his hands, for his hands were nailed to the cross." This verse is a tough argument against me. And when he cites the passage: *Et accepit omnes timor*, "and fear took hold of them all,"[44] we have to admit that fear has no hands. With all of this, I am driven into a corner and have to give up. "To take" not only means to use one's hands, but to receive something in a number of different possible ways.

Dear friends, we must stand on solid ground, if we are to withstand the devil's attack [Ephesians 6:11]. Although I must acknowledge that you committed no sin when you touched the sacrament with your hands, nevertheless I must tell you that it was not a good work, because it caused offense everywhere— simply because the universal custom is to receive the Blessed Sacrament from the hands of the priest. Why will you not in this respect also serve those who are weak in faith and abstain from your liberty, particularly because it does not help you if you do it, nor harm you if you do not do it?

Therefore, no new practices should be introduced, unless the gospel has first been thoroughly preached and understood, as it has been among you. On this account, dear friends, let us deal soberly and wisely in the things that pertain to God, for God will not be mocked [Galatians 6:7]. The saints may endure mockery, but with God it is vastly different. Therefore, I beseech you, give up this practice.

Concerning Both Kinds in the Sacrament

Now let us speak of the two kinds. Although I hold that it is necessary that the sacrament should be received in both kinds, according to the institution of the Lord, nevertheless it must not be made compulsory nor a general law. We must rather promote and practice and preach the Word, and then afterward leave the result and execution of it entirely to the Word, giving everyone his freedom in this matter. Where this is not done, the sacrament becomes for me an outward work and a hypocrisy, which is just what the devil wants. But when the Word is given free course and is not bound to any external observance, it takes hold of one believer today and sinks into their heart. Tomorrow, it touches another and so on. Thus quietly and soberly it does its work, and no one will know how it all came about.

I was glad to know when someone wrote me, that some people here had begun to receive the sacrament in both kinds. You should have allowed it to remain thus and not forced it into a law. But now you go at it pell-mell and headlong force everyone to it. Dear friends, you will not succeed in that way. Because if you desire to be regarded as better Christians than others simply on account of taking the sacrament into your hands and also receiving it in both kinds, then you are bad Christians as far as I am concerned. In this way even a sow could be a Christian, for she has a big enough snout to receive the sacrament outwardly. We must deal soberly with such high things. Dear friends, this dare be no mockery, and if you are going to follow me, stop it. If you are not going to follow me, however, then no one need drive me away from you—I will leave you unasked, and I shall regret that I ever preached so much as one sermon in this place. The other things could be passed by, but this cannot be overlooked; for you have gone so far that people are saying: At Wittenberg there are very good Christians, for they take the sacrament in their hands and grasp the cup, and then they go to their brandy and swill themselves full. So the weak and well-meaning people, who would come to us if they had received as much instruction as we have, are driven away.

However, if there are people who are so smart that they must necessarily touch the sacrament with their hands, then let them have it delivered to their homes and there let them hold it too as long as they want. In public, though, let them stay away, because that won't hurt them and it won't offend our brothers, sisters, and neighbors—those who are so mad at us right now that they would kill us.

I would say again, that of all my enemies who have opposed me up to this time, none of them have hurt me as much as you.

This is enough for today; tomorrow we shall say more.

THE SIXTH SERMON:
FRIDAY, MARCH 14, 1522

In our conversation about the chief matter, we now come to the reception of the sacrament, which we have not yet finished. Today we shall see how to conduct ourselves here and who is worthy to receive the sacrament and who belongs there.

It is necessary here that your hearts and consciences be well instructed and that you make an important distinction between outward reception and internal, spiritual reception. Bodily and outward reception is that in which a person receives orally the body of Christ and his blood, and doubtless anyone can receive the sacrament in this way, without faith and love. But this does not make a person a Christian, for if it did, even a mouse would be a Christian, for it, too, can eat the bread and perchance even drink out of the cup. It is such a simple thing to do. But the true, inner, spiritual reception is a very different thing, for it consists in the right use of the sacrament and its fruits.

I would say in the first place that this reception occurs in faith and is inward and will have Christ. There is no external sign by which we Christians may be distinguished from others except this sacrament and baptism, but without faith outward reception is nothing. There must be faith to make the reception worthy and acceptable before God, otherwise it is nothing but sham and a mere external show, which is not Christianity at all.

Christianity consists solely in faith, and no outward work must be attached to it.

But faith (which we all must have, if we wish to go to the sacrament worthily) is a firm trust that Christ, the Son of God, stands in our place and has taken all our sins upon his shoulders and that he is the eternal satisfaction for our sin and reconciles us with God the Father. Those who have this kind of faith are the very ones who take preferred places at the sacrament. And neither devil nor hell nor sin can hurt them. Why? Because God is their protector and defender. And because I have this faith, I am certain that God is fighting for me. I am able to defy the devil, death, damnation, and degradation—and all the harm they threaten me. This is the great, inestimable treasure given us in Christ, which no one can describe or grasp in words. Only faith can take hold of the heart, and not everyone has such faith [2 Thessalonians 3:2].

Therefore, this sacrament must not be made into a law, as the Most Holy Father, the Pope, has done with his ridiculous command that every Christian needs to receive the Sacrament of the Altar at Easter time. And whoever does not commune then shall not be buried in a consecrated cemetery. How foolish is this papal law? We are not all the same and we do not all have the same amount of faith. The faith of one may be more robust than the faith of another. It is simply not possible to make a law out of the sacrament, and the greatest sins are committed at Easter solely on account of this unchristian command, whose purpose is to drive and force the people to the sacrament. And if robbery, usury, immorality, and all sins were cast upon one big heap, this sin would overtop all others, at the very time when they [who come to the sacrament] want to be most holy. Why? Because the pope can look into no one's heart to see whether or not there is faith in it.

However, if you believe that God steps in for you and gives everything for you, even the Divine blood, it's as if God were saying, "Follow me. Don't worry or hesitate and we'll see what can harm you. Let the devil, death, sin, hell, and all creation do their best. I will lead you and I will be your rear guard.[45] Trust me and boldly depend on me." The devil, damnation, depravity, and death cannot destroy those who believe. When God fights for you, then what can those things do to you?

Those who have such faith truly belong here and take the sacrament as a pledge or a guarantee, a sign that assures them of God's promise and grace. Of course, we do not all have such faith (would to God that one tenth of Christians had it!). You see, these kinds of precious, innumerable riches, which God's grace rains down on us,[46] are not for everybody in general. They are only for those of us who struggle, whether physically or spiritually—physically through persecution or spiritually through despair. This happens, externally or internally, when the devil weakens your heart, making it slow and sad. That way, you won't know where you stand in God's eyes, when the devil throws your sins in your face. And yet, God desires to dwell only in such scared and shaking hearts, as the prophet Isaiah says in chapter 66:2. Indeed, those who do not sense every day, within themselves, the torture of their sins would not want a shield, protector, or rear guard to stand with them. Such people are not ready for this food. This food comes to ". . . those who are hungry and desperate,"[47] because this food prefers to enter souls that are hungry, that struggle with their sins and would gladly release them.

Whoever is not prepared should abstain for a while from this sacrament, because this food will not enter a sated and full heart, and if it comes to such a heart, it is harmful.[48] Therefore, if we think upon and feel within us such distress of conscience and the fear of a timid heart, we shall come with all humbleness and reverence and not run to it brashly and hastily, without all fear and humility. So we do not always find that we are fit; today I have the grace and am fit for it, but not tomorrow. Indeed, it may be that for six months I may have no desire or fitness for it.

The ones, therefore, who are worthiest are the ones whom death and the devil so often attack. They are the ones to whom the sacrament gives the most comfort—so they might remember and firmly believe that nothing can harm them. With the sacrament, they receive him and nothing can snatch them away.[49] So death, the devil, and sin are not able to harm them.

This is what Christ did when he instituted the incomparable sacrament. He told his disciples he was about to depart, which would've horrified them so much that they would've embarrassed themselves. And when he went on to say, "One of you will betray me,"[50] it must have felt like a stab to the heart. Certainly, they would've heard that with such fear that they'd all have sat there, each one thinking he was God's betrayer. And when He saw them all shaken, terrified, and grief-stricken, etc., then Christ instituted immediately the incomparable sacrament as a way to comfort them. And comforting them again, because this bread is comfort for those who grieve, medicine for the sick, life for the dying, food for the hungry, and riches for the poor and needy—bringing life to those who are distressed on account of their sins and are daily tortured by them.

That is enough for now about how to partake of this sacrament. With this, I commend you to God.

THE SEVENTH SERMON:
SATURDAY, MARCH 15, 1522

You heard yesterday about how to partake of this holy and blessed sacrament and how it is given precisely to people who fear death, who have timid consciences, and who are despairing—those who are afraid of hell. These folks come prepared to receive this food for the strengthening of their weak faith and the comforting of their conscience. This is the true use and practice of this sacrament. However, those who do not find themselves in such a situation may abstain from coming until God stirs them and draws them through the Word.

We shall now speak of the fruit of this sacrament, which is love; that is, that we should treat our neighbor as God has treated us. Now we have received from God nothing but love and mercy. Because Christ has promised and gives us the righteousness of God and everything he has. Christ has poured out such great riches on us. No one can count them and no angel can understand or fathom them. God is a glowing bread oven full of love, whose aroma wafts its way from earth to heaven.

Love, I declare, is the sacrament's fruit. But this I do not yet perceive among you here in Wittenberg, even though you have had much preaching and, after all, you ought to have carried

this out in practice. This is the chief thing, which is the only
business of a Christian. But nobody wants to be in this, though
you want to practice all sorts of unnecessary things, which are
of no account. If you do not want to show yourselves Christians
by your love, then leave the other things undone, too, for St.
Paul says in 1 Corinthians 11 [1 Corinthians 13:1], "If I speak in
the tongues of mortals and of angels, but do not have love, I am
a noisy gong or a clanging cymbal." This is a terrible saying of
Paul: "And if I have prophetic powers, and understand all mysteries and all knowledge, and if I have all faith, so as to remove
mountains, but do not have love, I am nothing. If I give away all
my possessions, and if I hand over my body so that I may boast,
but do not have love, I gain nothing" [1 Corinthians 13:2–3].
Not yet have you come so far as this, though you have received
great and rich gifts from God, the highest of which is a knowledge of the Scriptures. It is true, you have the true gospel and the
pure Word of God, but no one as yet has given his goods to the
poor, no one has yet been burned, and even these things would
be nothing without love. You are willing to take all of God's
goods in the sacrament, but you are not willing to pour them out
again in love. Nobody extends a helping hand to another, nobody seriously considers the other person, but everyone looks
out for himself and his own gain, insists on his own way, and
lets everything else go hang. If anybody is helped, well and good;
but nobody looks after the poor to see how you might be able to
help them. This is a pity. You have heard many sermons about it
and all my books are full of it and have this one purpose, to urge
you to faith and love.

And if you will not love one another, God will send a great
plague upon you. Let this be a warning to you, for God will not
have his Word revealed and preached in vain. You are tempting
God too much, my friends; because if, in past generations, someone would have preached the Word to our forebears, they would
perhaps have acted differently. Or if it were preached even now
to the too-many poor children in the cloisters, they would receive it more joyfully than you. You are not heeding it at all and
you are playing around with all kinds of silliness that does not
matter.

I commend you to God.

THE EIGHTH SERMON: SUNDAY, MARCH 16, 1522 (THE SECOND SUNDAY OF LENT OR "REMINISCERE SUNDAY")

We have now heard about all the issues that need to be considered at this time, except confession. Let us speak of it now.

First, we find confession in the Bible. When people publicly committed sins or others knew about them, they were accused in front of the congregation. If they abandoned their sin, then the congregation would pray to God for them. But if they would not listen to their congregation, they were expelled, excluded from the community, and no one would have anything to do with them. This confession is commanded by God in Matthew 18, "If another member of the church sins against you, go and point out the fault when the two of you are alone. . . ." We no longer practice this kind of confession anymore and, at this point, we've abandoned the gospel text. Anybody able to reestablish it would accomplish a huge work.

Here is where you should have exerted yourselves—reestablishing this kind of confession and letting the other things go. No one would have been offended by this and everything would have gone smoothly and quietly. It could be done like this: When you see usurers, adulterers, thieves, drunks, etc., you should go to them privately, and urge them to stop their sinning. If they will not listen, then take two witnesses with you and admonish them again, as you would a sister or brother, to give up their sin. If they reject that, then tell the pastor in front of the whole congregation. Have your witnesses with you and make your case before the pastor in the presence of the people, saying: "Beloved pastor, this person has done this and that and would not take our loving admonition to stop this sin. I am officially charging them, together with my witnesses, who have heard this." If they will not give in and willingly acknowledge their guilt, then the pastor should exclude them from the assembly and impose the ban in the presence of the congregation. Do this for the sake of the whole community of faith, until they come to their senses and are received back again. This would be a Christian practice. But I cannot undertake to carry it out single-handedly.

Second, we confess when we go into a corner by ourselves and confess to God himself—spilling out before him all our burdens. Such confession is also commanded. From this comes the familiar word of Scripture: ". . . do righteousness and justice."[51] "To judge is to accuse and condemn ourselves; but to act righteously is to trust in the mercy of God."[52] As it is written, "Happy are those who observe justice, who do righteousness at all times."[53] Judgment is nothing else than our knowing and judging and condemning ourselves, and this is true humility and self-abasement. Righteousness is nothing else than our knowing ourselves and praying to God for the mercy and help through which God raises us up again. This is what David means when he says, "I have sinned; I will confess my transgressions to the Lord and you didst forgive the guilt of my sin; for this all your saints shall pray to you" [Psalm 32:5–6].

Third, there is also the kind of confession in which we meet with another person privately to share what troubles us. That way, we may hear words of comfort from someone else. This confession is commanded by the pope. It is this urging and forcing which I condemned when I wrote about confession. So, I refuse to go to confession simply because the pope commands and demands it. Because of this, I wish he'd leave the rite of confession alone—not compel or command us to do it, which he has not the power to do. I will, nevertheless, allow no one to take private confession away from me, and I would not give it up for all the treasures in the world, because I know what comfort and strength it has given me. No one knows what it can do for him except one who has struggled often and long with the devil. Yea, the devil would have slain me long ago, if the confession had not sustained me. For there are many doubtful matters which we cannot resolve or find the answer to on our own. We can, however, approach our sisters or brothers and tell them our troubles. What harm is there if we humble ourselves to our neighbors, put ourselves to shame, listen to their words of consolation, accept them, and believe them? It is as if we're listening to God's own words. That's what Matthew 18:19 says, "if two of you agree on earth about anything you ask, it will be done for you by my Father in heaven."

To be sure, we need numerous absolutions, so that we can strengthen our weak consciences and desperate hearts against the devil and before God. Therefore, one should neither prohibit nor withhold private confession. In fact, don't even encourage others to stay away from it. If folks, in the midst of wrestling with particular sins, want to deal with them and would like a word of hope they can count on, then let them confess to another person privately and hear the absolution, as if God's very self were speaking it through the mouth of the other. However, those who have a strong, solid faith that their sins are forgiven may let this kind of confession go. They can confess to God directly. That said, how many really have such a strong faith? So, as I have mentioned previously, I do not want to let private confession go and I do not want anybody forced to it. Leave it up to each person to decide as they will.

Because our God, the God we have, is not so stingy, so as to leave us with only one comfort or only one source of strength for our conscience—not just a single expression of forgiveness, but we have many absolutions in the gospel. We are richly showered with many absolutions. For instance, we have this in the gospel: ". . . If you forgive others their trespasses, your heavenly Father will also forgive you" [Matthew 6:14]. Another comfort we have in the Lord's Prayer: "Forgive us our debts," etc. [Matthew 6:12]. A third is our baptism, when I consider this: "See, my Lord, I have been baptized in your name so that I may be assured of your grace and mercy." And then we have private confession: when I go to receive an absolution so certain, it's as if God Almighty speaks it. That way, I can be assured that my sins are forgiven. Finally, I receive the Blessed Sacrament into myself, when I eat his body and drink his blood as a sign that I am rid of my sins. In this way, God frees me from all my frailties; and in order to make me certain of this, God gives me Christ's body to eat and blood to drink. All that, so I shall not and cannot doubt that I have a gracious God.

You can see, therefore, that confession must not be despised. It is a comforting practice—and we need to have multiple absolutions and assurances. Especially because we struggle with the devil, death, hell, and sin, we need all the weapons we can get.

So let us use the whole armor of God and all the implements that God provides for us to defend ourselves.[54]

You do not yet know how hard it is to fight with the devil and prevail. But I do. I know it well, because I've had to eat some of his lies. I know him well, and he knows me well, too.

If you had known the devil, then you would not have thrown confession away like this.

God bless. Amen.

Preface to St. Paul's Letter to the Romans (1522; 1546)[1]

February 18, 1546: Luther dies before this preface, in its final form, appears. Now connected with his last, revised translation of the Bible into German, it is a sort of personal testimony to his view of Scripture's vital, persistent, and dynamic core—the gospel of Jesus Christ. With a relatively few edits from the preface he published with the "September Testament" of 1522, the Reformer adds his expertise as a theologian to his talent as a translator—preparing his readers to engage a text that he had so brilliantly and carefully brought into German. The Reformer's insight into the mercy of God had come to him, he believed, as a gift. And it was a gift given amid his struggles to understand St. Paul's letter to the Christians at Rome. Those struggles, he freely admitted, were (at least in part) prompted by the same passage in Romans that eventually would (at least in part) bring him peace: Romans 1:17, "the just shall live by faith." Those words had, for a quarter of a century, summarized Luther's understanding of the Bible as the Word of God, the church as the community called into being by that Word, and the Christian life as "faith active in love." This biblical phrase, among others, brought Luther to know in his marrow the meaning of sin and righteousness, unbelief and faith, law and gospel. St. Paul had helped him understand the God of grace and mercy revealed in Jesus Christ. And in this preface, Luther wants his readers to understand God that way, too.

This letter is the chief part of the New Testament, and is truly the purest gospel. It is so valuable that every Christian should know it by heart, memorize each word, and use it every day, as if it were their soul's daily bread. We cannot read through it too often or meditate on it too much. The more we engage with it, the more precious it becomes and the sweeter it tastes.

I will do what I can, therefore, so far as God has given me power, to open a way into Romans through this preface, so that it may be better understood by everyone. Formerly, commentaries and all kinds of idle talk had obscured it from view, though in itself it is a bright light, almost sufficient to illuminate the entire Holy Scriptures.

To begin with we must have knowledge of its language and know what St. Paul means by the words: "law," "sin," "grace," "faith," "righteousness," "flesh," "spirit," and the like. Otherwise no reading of the book has any value.

The little word "law" you must not here take in human fashion as a teaching about what works are to be done or not done. That is the way with human laws; a law is fulfilled by works, even though one's heart is not in it. God, however, judges the depths of the heart. For this reason, the law of God also rules our innermost heart and our works cannot satisfy it. The law punishes as hypocrisy and lies the works not done from the bottom of the heart. Consequently, all people are called liars in [Psalm 116:11], because no one keeps or can keep God's law from the bottom of the heart. Because everyone, from a place deep within, finds no pleasure in what is good, but enjoys what is bad. If, now, there is no willing pleasure in the good, then the inmost heart is not set on the law of God. And such sin deserves God's wrath, even though externally one does many good deeds and leads an honorable life.

St. Paul concludes, therefore, in chapter 2[:13], that the Jews are all sinners, saying that only the doers of the law are righteous before God. He means by this that no one, in terms of his works, is a doer of the law. Rather, he speaks to them thus, "You teach one must not commit adultery, but you yourself commit adultery" [2:22]; and again, "In passing judgment upon another you condemn yourself, because you, the judge, are doing the very same things" [2:1]. This is as if to say, "You live a fine outward life in the works of the law, and you pass judgment on those who do not so live. You know how to teach everyone. You see the speck that is in the eye of another, but do not notice the log that is in your own eye" [Matthew 7:3].

Because even though you keep the law outwardly, with works—fearing punishment or loving reward—you are still doing all these things under duress. Such obedience without pleasure in and love for the law is forced and coerced. Because if the law were not there, and if it were up to you, you would act much rather act differently.

It follows from this that, in your heart of hearts, you hate the law. What would be the point then in your teaching others not to steal, if you yourself are a thief at heart, and would gladly be one outwardly if you dared? Though, to be sure, the outward work does not lag far behind among such hypocrites! So you teach others, but not yourself; nor do you yourself know what you are teaching—you have never yet understood the law correctly. Moreover, the law increases sin, as St. Paul says in chapter 5[:20], because the more the law demands what we cannot do, the more we hate the law. This is why Paul says, in chapter 7:14, that the law is spiritual.

So, what is this?: [2] If the law were about physical things, one might be able to fulfill it with the right amount of good works. However, because it is spiritual, the only way to fulfill it is with works done from the heart. And only God's Spirit gives this kind of heart to believers—molding them according to the law so that they receive a heartfelt desire for the law and so that they no longer act from fear and compulsion but from a willing heart. Therefore, the law is spiritual. It will be loved and fulfilled with this kind of a spiritual heart. It requires this kind of spirit. If that spirit is not in the heart, then sin, unhappiness with the law, and anger toward the law remains—even though the law itself is good and just and holy.

Learn this language of faith: that doing the works of the law and fulfilling the law are two very different things. The work of the law is everything that one does, or can do, toward keeping the law of one's own free will or powers. Because, however, in the midst of all these works and along with them, the heart continues to hate the law and must be compelled to obey it, these works are all wasted and are worth nothing. St. Paul indicates this in chapter 3, when he says, "For no human being will be justified in God's sight by deeds prescribed by the law."[3] So you see that the academic bickerers[4] and sophists misrepresent this when they teach people to prepare themselves for grace by means of works. How can one prepare for good with works, when good works are only done with revulsion and unwillingness in the heart? How can a work that stems from a defiant and disobedient heart please God?[5]

To fulfill the law, however, is to do its works with pleasure and love, to choose freely to live a godly and a good life, as if there were no penalties or duress. The Holy Spirit puts this delight and love for the law into our hearts, as St. Paul says in Romans 5:5. But the Holy Spirit is not given except in, with, and by faith in Jesus Christ, as St. Paul says in his introduction. And faith comes only through God's Word or gospel, which preaches Christ—saying that Christ is God's Son and truly human, has died and risen again for our sakes (as Paul says in 3:25, 4:25, and 10:9).

Thus, faith alone makes a person righteous and accomplishes all that the law requires. Based on Christ's merit, faith shows the Spirit. And the Spirit makes the heart glad and free, as the law requires. Good works stem from faith itself. That is what St. Paul means in chapter 3. After he rejects the works of the law, it sounds as if he would put an end to it with this faith. "Do we then overthrow the law by this faith? By no means! On the contrary, we uphold the law."[6] That is, we fulfill it by faith.

Sin, in Scripture, means more than external actions of one's body. Rather, sin includes all the motivations that prompt people to do such things; namely, its origin in the heart and all its powers. So the tiny words "to do" really mean that people have fallen and driven themselves completely into sin. Even the doing of external sinful deeds does not happen unless one has given in to it completely, body and soul. The Scriptures look especially into the heart, at the root and source of all sin: unbelief in the depths of the heart.

This is why faith alone justifies—bringing with it the spirit and the longing for good, external works. Similarly, unbelief alone commits sin—bringing the flesh and the longing for evil, external works (as it happened to Adam and Eve in the garden).[7]

Because of this, Christ calls unbelief sin. As he says in John

16:8–9, "The Spirit will convince the world because of sin . . . because they do not believe in me." For this reason, too, before good or bad works emerge (akin to the way good or bad fruit grows from a plant), there must first be in the heart either belief or unbelief. Unbelief is the root, the sap, and the chief power of all sin. In the Scriptures it is called the serpent's head and the head of the old dragon, which the seed of the woman, Christ, must trample underfoot, as was promised to Adam.[8]

The grace of God is different from the gift of God. Grace means, precisely, the favor or goodwill that God bears toward us, which flows from God to us—the divine inclination to give Christ, together with the Holy Spirit, along with the Spirit's gifts that God causes to flow into us (Romans 5: "the grace of God and the free gift in . . . Jesus Christ," etc.). Although the gifts and the Spirit grow in us every day, they are not yet completed in us because evil desires and sins remain and they continue to fight against the Spirit (Romans 7:5 and Galatians 5:17). Genesis 3 proclaims the conflict as between the woman's seed and the serpent's seed. Nevertheless, grace does so much that we become and we are completely righteous in God's sight—because God's grace is not divided or distributed piecemeal like the gifts. Rather, because of Christ, our Advocate and our Mediator, grace takes us completely into God's favor. And because of this, the gifts are begun in us.

In this sense, therefore, you can understand the seventh chapter, where St. Paul still calls himself a sinner. Yet he can say, in 8:1, that there is no condemnation for those who are in Christ and the incompleteness of the gifts or the Spirit does not change that. Because the flesh is not yet put to death, we remain sinners. But because we believe in Christ and have a beginning of the Spirit, God is so favorable and gracious to us that he will not count the sin against us or judge us because of it. Rather God deals with us according to our faith in Christ until sin is put to death.

Faith is not the human notion and dream that some people call faith. If they see that no improvement of life and no good works follow—although they can hear and say much about faith—then they fall into the error of saying, "Faith is not enough; one must do works in order to be righteous and be saved." This is due to the fact that when they hear the gospel, they get busy and by their own powers create an idea in their heart that says, "I believe"; they take this then to be a true faith. But, as it is a human figment and idea that never reaches the depths of the heart, nothing comes of it either, and no improvement follows.

Faith, however, is a divine work in us. It changes us and re-births us from God (John 1:12–13). It kills the old person within and makes us completely different people in heart and spirit and mind and powers; and it brings with it the Holy Spirit. Oh, it is a living, busy, active, mighty thing, this faith. It is impossible for it not to be doing good works incessantly. It does not ask whether good works are to be done, but before the question is asked, it has already done them, and is constantly doing them. Whoever does not do such works, however, is an unbeliever. He gropes and looks around for faith and good works, but knows neither what faith is nor what good works are. Yet he talks and talks, with many words, about faith and good works.

Faith is a vibrant courageous confidence in God's grace—so certain that faith would die for this grace a thousand times. This confidence in and understanding of God's grace makes us happy, gives us comfort, and brings us joy before God and all creatures. This is what the Holy Spirit does through faith. We all, there-fore, without being forced, become willing and happy to do Good and to serve others—even to endure all kinds of suffering, to love and praise God, the One who shows us this grace. We cannot, then, separate faith from works, any more than we can separate heat and light from fire. Beware, therefore, of your own wrong ideas and the good-for-nothing blabbermouths who think they are smart enough to disconnect faith from good works. They are fools. Ask God to work faith in you so you do not con-tinue without faith forever—no matter what you imagine and accomplish, no matter what you intend or are able to do.

Actually, such faith is righteousness. It is also called "the righ-teousness of God" or "that which is valid before God," because God gives it to us and counts it as righteousness for the sake of Christ our Mediator. And it even changes people, so that they give to others what they owe to them. With faith, they become free from sin and begin to find pleasure in God's commandments.

In this way, they honor God, and offer what they owe to God. So we serve our fellow human beings willingly, by whatever means we can, and thus pay our debt to everyone. Nature, free will, and our own strength cannot bring this righteousness into being. We cannot give faith to ourselves. We cannot take away our own unbelief. How can someone do away with a single sin, even the tiniest? On account of this, all that is done without faith, or in unbelief, is deceptive. It is hypocrisy and sin (Romans 14:23), no matter how impressive it is.

Flesh and spirit may not be properly understood here as if "flesh" refers only to sex, while "spirit" refers only to the heart or the inner person. Take Paul for example. He defines "flesh" the way Christ does in John 3:6: it is the entire human person, including body and soul, reason and all the senses—everything that is born of the flesh. So, learn to call "fleshy" those who think, teach, and talk a great deal about lofty spiritual matters, yet do so without grace. From the "works of the flesh" in Galatians, chapter 5, you can learn that Paul calls heresy and hatred "works of the flesh." Romans 8:3 says, "the law is weakened by the flesh," but this does not only refer to physical desires, but to all sins, and above all to unbelief, the most spiritual of all vices.

We should call those folks "spiritual" who engage the most external kind of works, as Christ did when he washed the disciples' feet or when Peter steered his boat and fished. "The flesh" refers to those who live and work, internally and externally, in the service of the flesh's gain and of this temporal life. "The spirit" refers to those who live and work, inwardly and outwardly, to serve the Spirit, with an eye on the future life.

Without such a grasp of these words, you will never understand this letter of St. Paul, nor will you understand any other book of Holy Scripture. Because of this, beware of all teachers who use these words in a different sense, no matter who they are, even Origen, Ambrose, Augustine, Jerome, and others like them or even above them.

And now we will take up the epistle:

It is right for a preacher of the gospel in the first place by revelation of the law and of sin to rebuke and to constitute as sin everything that is not the living fruit of the Spirit and of faith in Christ. People should be led to know themselves and their own wretchedness, and to become humble and ask for help. This is therefore what St. Paul does. He begins in chapter 1 to rebuke the gross sins and unbelief that are plainly evident. These were, and still are, the sins of the heathen who live without God's grace. He says: Through the gospel there shall be revealed the wrath of God from heaven against all because of their godless lives and their unrighteousness. For even though they know and daily recognize that there is a God, nevertheless nature itself, without grace, is so bad that it neither thanks nor honors God. Instead it blinds itself, and goes steadily from bad to worse until, after idolatry, it blatantly commits the most shameful sins, along with all the vices, and also allows others to commit them without reprimand.

In chapter 2 he extends his rebuke to include those who seem outwardly to be righteous and who commit their sins in secret. Such were the Jews and such are all the hypocrites who without desire or love for the law of God lead decent lives, but at heart hate God's law, and yet are quick to judge other people. This is the nature of all hypocrites—to think of themselves as pure, and yet to be full of covetousness, hatred, pride, and all uncleanness, Matthew 23[:25–28]. These are they who despise God's goodness, and in their hard-heartedness heap wrath upon themselves. Thus St. Paul, as a true interpreter of the law, leaves no one without sin, but proclaims the wrath of God upon all who would live well simply by nature or of their own volition. He makes them to be no better than the obvious sinners; indeed, he says they are stubborn and unrepentant.

In chapter 3 he throws them all together in a heap, and says that one is like the other: they are all sinners before God. Only, the Jews have had the word of God. Though not many have believed that word, this does not mean that the faith and truth of God are exhausted. He quotes incidentally a verse from Psalm 51[:4], that God remains justified in his words. Afterward he comes back to this again and proves also by Scripture that all are sinners. By the works of the law nobody is justified, but the law was given only that sin might be known.

Then he begins to teach the right way by which people must be justified and saved. He says: They are all sinners making no boast of God; but they must be justified without merit [of their own] through faith in Christ, who has merited this for us by his blood, and has become for us a mercy seat by God. God forgives all former sins to demonstrate that we are helped only by his righteousness, which he grants in faith, and which was revealed at that time through the gospel and was witnessed to beforehand by the law and the prophets. Thus the law is upheld by faith, though the works of the law are thereby put down, together with the boasting of them.

After the first three chapters, in which sin is revealed and faith's way to righteousness is taught, St. Paul begins in chapter 4 to meet certain protests and objections. First, he takes up the one that all people commonly make when they hear a faith justifies without works. They say, "Are we, then, to do no good works?" Therefore, he himself takes up the case of Abraham, and asks, "What did Abraham accomplish, then, with his good works? Were they all in vain? Were his works of no use?" He concludes that Abraham was justified by faith alone, even before the work of circumcision. But if the work of circumcision contributed nothing to his righteousness, though God had commanded it and it was a good work of obedience, then surely no other good work will contribute anything to righteousness. Rather, as Abraham's circumcision was an external sign by which he showed the righteousness that was already his in faith, so all good works are only external signs that follow out of faith; like good fruit. They demonstrate that a person is already inwardly righteous before God.

With this powerful illustration from the Scriptures, St. Paul confirms the doctrine of faith that he had set forth in chapter 3. He cites also another witness, David, who says in Psalm 32:1–2 that we are justified without works—although he does not remain without works when he has been justified. Then he gives the illustration a broader application, setting it over against all other works of the law. He concludes that the Jews cannot be Abraham's heirs merely because of their blood, still less because of the works of the law; they must inherit Abraham's faith, if they would be true heirs. For before the law—before the law of Moses and the law of circumcision—Abraham was justified by faith and called the father of all believers. Moreover, the law brings about wrath rather than grace, because no one keeps the law out of love for it and pleasure in it. The works of the law thus lead to disfavor rather than to grace. On account of this, faith alone must obtain the grace promised to Abraham, for these examples too were written for our sakes [Romans 15:4], that we too should believe.

In chapter 5 he comes to the fruits and works of faith: peace, joy, love to God and love to neighbor, as well as confidence, assurance, boldness, courage, and hope amid tribulation and suffering. For all this follows, if faith be true, because of the superabundant goodness that God shows us in Christ, causing Christ to die for us before we could ask it of him, indeed, while we were still enemies. Thus we have it that faith justifies without any works; and yet it does not follow that we are therefore to do no good works, but rather that the genuine works will not be lacking. Of these the work-righteous saints know nothing. They dream up works of their own in which there is no peace, joy, confidence, love, hope, boldness, or any of the qualities of true Christian work and faith.

After this, he digresses and makes a pleasant excursion. He tells whence come sin and righteousness, death and life—comparing Adam and Christ. He means to say that Christ had to come as a second Adam bequeathing his righteousness to us through a new spiritual birth in faith, just as the first Adam bequeathed sin to us through the old fleshly birth. Thus he declares and proves that no one by his own works can raise himself out of sin into righteousness, any more than he can prevent the birth of his own body. This is proved also by the fact that the divine law—which ought to assist toward righteousness, if anything can—has not only not helped, but has even increased sin. For the more the law forbids, the more our evil nature hates the law, and the more it wants to give in to its own lust. Thus the law makes Christ all the more necessary, and more grace is needed to help our nature.

In chapter 6 he takes up the special work of faith, the conflict of the spirit with the flesh for the complete slaying of the sin and lust that remain after we are justified. He teaches us that we are not by faith so freed from sin that we can be idle, slack, and careless, as though there were no longer any sin in us. Sin is present; but it is no longer reckoned for our condemnation, because of the faith that is struggling against it. On account of this, we have enough to do all our life long in taming the body, slaying its lusts, and compelling its members to obey the spirit and not the lusts. Thus we become like the death and resurrection of Christ, and complete our baptism—which signifies the death of sin and the new life of grace—until we are entirely purified and soon, and even harmed by his rise again with Christ in life forever.

This is true freedom from sin and the law (as he indicates toward the end of the chapter). Because this gift is free, we strive to do the Good joyfully and to live well without the law forcing us to do so. This spiritual freedom does not do away with the law, but gives what the law demands and along with that, it gives joy and love. It quiets the law and it does not allow the law to coerce us or force us to comply.

It is like a debt to a landlord that we cannot pay. There are two ways to get out of it: either the owner tears up the account and we pay nothing, or a benefactor pays the debt for us and satisfies the account. The latter way applies to Christ's work to free us from the law. This freedom, therefore, is no carefree carnal freedom with no need to act. Rather, our freedom performs many works of all kinds. It is free of the demands and obligations of the law.

Chapter 7 uses this analogy from married life to support this idea: When a husband dies, his widow is on her own. The one is set free from the other. The widow may or may not remarry. She is free to take another husband—something she could not do previously. Similarly, our conscience in our old sinful self is bound to the law. When that old person is slain by the Spirit, the conscience is liberated. The one is set free from the other. Yet the conscience must still act. Now, for the first time, it is truly free to hold fast to Christ, the new bridegroom—and to bear living fruit together.

Then he depicts more fully the nature of sin and of the law, how sin uses the law to stir things up and, thereby, become stronger. The old person comes to hate the law even more because the old person cannot pay what the law demands. Sin is its nature and of itself it cannot not sin. Therefore, the law is death and suffering to it. The law is not bad in itself. The old evil nature cannot do what is good and the law demands good. Just as a sick person cannot stand it when he or she is required to run and jump and do the works of a healthy person.

St. Paul, therefore, concludes that the law, correctly understood and thoroughly grasped, can only remind us of our sin, put us to death, and make us liable to eternal wrath. All this is fully learned and experienced by our conscience, when it is truly struck by the law. Because of this, we need something other than the law, something more than the law, to make us righteous and to save us. But they who do not correctly understand the law are blind. They go ahead in their presumption, thinking to satisfy the law by means of their deeds, not knowing how much the law demands, namely, a willing and happy heart. Because they do not see Moses clearly; a veil is placed between them and him, and hides him (Exodus 34:29–35; 2 Corinthians 3:12–16).

Then he shows how spirit and flesh struggle with one another within us. He uses himself as an example, so that we may learn how properly to understand the work of slaying sin within us. He calls both the spirit and the flesh "laws." It is the nature of the divine law to drive humans and make demands of them. Similarly, the flesh drives humans and makes demands—raging against the spirit and insisting on its own way. The spirit, in turn, drives humans and makes demands contrary to the flesh, and will have its own way. This tension lasts in us as long as we live; though in one person it is greater, in another less, depending on whether the spirit or the flesh is stronger. Human beings are both spirit and flesh; they struggle within themselves until they become wholly spiritual.

In chapter 8, he comforts such strugglers, telling them that this flesh does not condemn them. He shows further what the nature of flesh and spirit is, and how the Spirit comes from Christ. Christ has given us his Holy Spirit, makes us spiritual and subdues the flesh. Christ assures us that we are still God's children, however intensely sin may rage within us. In this way, then, we follow the spirit, as we resist and put sin to death. Because nothing crushes the flesh like the cross and suffering, he comforts us in our suffering with the support of the Spirit of love and all creation. Indeed, the Spirit sighs within us and the creation longs within us that we may be rid of the flesh and sin. These three chapters (6–8) clearly drive home the one task of faith: to slay the old Adam and crush the flesh.

In chapters 9, 10, and 11, Paul teaches about God's eternal predestination, from which originally proceeds who shall believe or not believe, who can or cannot get rid of sin—in order that our salvation may be taken entirely out of our hands and put in the hands of God alone. This is also necessary, because we are so weak and undependable that if it depended on us, none of us would be saved. The devil would surely overpower us all. But because God is dependable, predestination is certain. Because no one can resist God, we still have hope in the face of sin.

Here, now, for once we must put a stop to those wicked and high-flying spirits who first apply their own reason to this matter. They begin at the top to search the abyss of divine predestination, and worry in vain about whether they are predestinated. They are bound to plunge to their own destruction, either through despair, or through throwing caution to the winds.

But you had better follow the order of this epistle. Worry first about Christ and the gospel, that you may recognize your sin and his grace. Then fight your sin, as the first eight chapters here have taught. Then, when you have reached the eighth chapter, and are under the cross and suffering, this will teach you correctly about predestination in chapters 9, 10, and 11, and how comforting it is. For in the absence of suffering and the cross and the perils of death, one cannot deal with predestination without harm and without secret anger against God. The old Adam must first die before he can tolerate this thing and drink the strong wine. On account of this, beware that you do not drink wine while you are still a suckling. There is a limit, a time, and an age for every doctrine.

In chapter 12 he teaches what true worship is, and makes all Christians priests. They are to offer not money or cattle, as under the law, but their own bodies, with slaying of the lusts. Then he describes the outward conduct of Christians, under the spiritual government, telling how they are to teach, preach, rule, serve, give, suffer, love, live, and act toward friend, foe, and all people. These are the works that a Christian does; for, as has been said, faith takes no holidays.

In chapter 13 he teaches honor and obedience to worldly government. Although worldly government does not make people righteous before God, nevertheless it is instituted in order to accomplish at least this much—that the good may have outward peace and protection and the bad may not be free to do evil in peace and quietness, and without fear. Therefore the good too are to honor it even though they themselves do not need it. Finally, he comprehends it all in love, and sums it up in the example of Christ: as he has done for us, we are also to do, following in his footsteps.

In chapter 14 he teaches that consciences weak in faith are to be led gently, spared, so that we do not use our Christian freedom to harm, but to help the weak. Wherever that is not done, the result is discord and contempt for the gospel; and the gospel is the all-important thing. It is better, therefore, to yield a little to the weak in faith, until they grow stronger, than to have the teaching of the gospel come to nothing. This is a specific work of love, for which there is great need especially now—when some folks are so rudely and roughly—and needlessly—shaking tender consciences (who do not yet know the truth) by their eating of meat and other liberties.

In chapter 15 he sets up Christ as an example: we are to tolerate also those other weak ones who fail in other ways, in open sins or in unpleasing habits. We are not to cast them off, but to bear with them until they, too, grow better. For so Christ has done with us, and still does every day; he bears with our many faults and bad habits, and with all our imperfections, and helps us constantly.

Then, at the end, he prays for them, praises them, and commends them to God. He speaks of his own office and of his preaching, and asks them kindly for a contribution to the poor at Jerusalem. All that he speaks of or deals with is pure love.

The last chapter is a chapter of greetings. But he mingles with them a noble warning against human doctrines, which break in alongside the teaching of the gospel and cause offense. It is as if he had certainly foreseen that out of Rome and through the Romans would come the seductive and offensive canons and decretals and the whole squirming mass of human laws and commandments that have now drowned the whole world and wiped out this epistle and all human scriptures, along with the spirit and faith itself, so that nothing remains anymore except the idol, the valley, whose servants St. Paul here rebukes. God save us from them. Amen.

This letter shows us, with utmost clarity, what Christians need to know: what is law, gospel, sin, punishment, grace, faith, righteousness, Christ, God, good works, love, hope, and the cross. At the same time, this letter shows us how to act toward our neighbor: righteous or sinner, strong or weak, friend or foe, and even toward our own selves. And St. Paul so compellingly supports this with Scripture and proves by his own example (and that of the prophets) that no one could wish for anything more. On account of this, it appears that he wanted in this one letter to sum up briefly all Christian and evangelical doctrine, and to prepare an introduction to the entire Old Testament. Without a doubt, those who have this document in their hearts also have the light and power of the Old Testament. May all Christians, therefore, know it well. And may they exercise themselves in it continually. To this end, may God give us grace.[9] Amen.

Confession Concerning Christ's Supper: Part III (1528)[1]

In 1527, pressure on Luther mounts: He's physically ill. Katie's late-term pregnancy turns problematic and their baby will die soon after birth. Bubonic plague hits Wittenberg and the university moves classes to Jena (about a hundred miles away) for safety, but Luther remains and assumes pastoral duties during the epidemic. His reform proposal and its disposition have emboldened disparate protest movements across Europe, but attempts to unify them are failing. He's racked with self-doubt.

In November, he gathers himself to write a three-part "confession." In this concluding section, published in February 1528, Luther affirms classic, creedal teachings on the Trinity and the Person of Jesus Christ. He confesses a distinctively Lutheran view of the sacraments and the church. He connects the vocations of all believers to serve their neighbors with the divinely established "orders of creation."

As I see it, the fractures in the church's unity, along with the errors that go with them, continue to multiply as time goes on. And I can see that Satan's wrath and rage have no end. I, therefore, want to confess my faith before God and all the world, point by point. That way, no one during my lifetime or after my death should be able to misuse me or my writings in support of their false ideas—as the "communion-baptism-fanatics"[2] are already doing. I commit myself to remain in this faith until I die. And, with God's help, I will trust this faith as I leave this world and present myself before our Lord Jesus Christ's seat of judgment. That way, if a person claims, once I've died, that Luther would teach and maintain such and such a thing differently, if he were still living, because he did not think through, then allow me to say finally: by the grace of God, I have carefully considered each of these doctrines. I have looked at their biblical bases carefully. And I am now prepared to preserve them once and for all—just as I have safeguarded the sacrament of the altar.

I am not drunk[3] or unaware of what this means. I have considered the issues carefully and I know what I'm talking about. I have a clear sense of what might be at stake here for me when the Lord Jesus Christ returns in final Judgment. This is no joke and it is nothing to be taken lightly. This is indeed serious stuff. Because of God's grace, I have come to recognize Satan when I see him. If the devil can twist and pervert God's Word and the Bible, then how much more could the evil one do to the words of others, as well as to mine?

First, I believe from my heart in the supreme article of the majesty of God, that the Father, Son, and Holy Spirit, three distinct persons, are by nature one true and genuine God, the Maker of heaven, earth and all things; in opposition to the Arians, Macedonians, Sabellians, and similar heretics (Genesis 1:1).[4] This is how it has been held until now, in the Church of Rome and in other Christian churches throughout the whole world.

Second, I believe in and I hold to this Scriptural truth: only the second person of the Godhead—that is, the Son—became a true human being. The Holy Spirit conceived him, apart from any cooperation of a male. And the pure, holy Virgin Mary brought him into the world as a natural mother. St. Luke clearly speaks of this and the prophets proclaim that neither the Father nor the Holy Spirit became human, as certain heretics have taught.

Also, I believe that God the Son did not take on only a body without a soul, as some heretics have taught, but rather his humanity was full and complete, soul and all. As a true descendant of Abraham and David as promised, he was the natural-born son of Mary. The Son was a complete and true human being in every way. He was like every other person (as I am myself)—outside of the fact that he came without sin, from the Virgin by means of the Holy Spirit.

Also, I believe that this particular person is true God—one, eternal, indivisible being from God who became human. Therefore, the holy Virgin Mary is unquestionably a true mother—not only of the human Christ, as the Nestorians teach, but she is also mother of the Son of God, as Luke 1:35 says, "the holy Child shall be called the Son of God." In other words, he is my Lord and the Lord of all creation. Jesus Christ, the only begotten Son, by nature of both God and Mary, true God and true human.

I believe also that this Son of God and son of Mary, our Lord Jesus Christ, suffered for us poor sinners, was crucified, dead, and buried, in order that he might redeem us from sin, death, and the eternal wrath of God by his innocent blood. I also believe that on the third day he rose from the dead, ascended into heaven, and sits at the right hand of God the Father almighty. Christ is Lord over all lords and King over all kings. Christ is above creation, in heaven and on earth and under the earth; above death and life, and above sin and righteousness.

This I confess and this I can prove from the Bible: every human being is a descendant from a single person, Adam. And everyone, by birth, has received and inherited the fall, guilt, and sin of this particular individual. Adam started it in the garden (even though the evil deceit of the devil brought it on). Therefore, we all enter the world, we live, and we die in sin. We are just like Adam. If Jesus Christ had not come to our aid—taking to himself our guilt and sin, and suffering like an innocent lamb, a ransom for us—then we would deserve death. And even more, Christ continues to intercede and advocate for us, as the faithful, merciful Mediator, Savior. Indeed, Christ is the only Priest and Bishop of our souls.

Along with this, then, I do not accept and must condemn as unqualified errors any doctrines that overly stress the role of our free will. They are completely contrary to the assistance and grace of Jesus Christ our Savior. Without Christ, death and sin enslave us and the devil is our lord and god. We have neither the ability nor the power, neither the intellect nor the capacity, to prepare ourselves to receive life and righteousness—or to pursue it. Indeed, the reverse is true. Our weakness and captivity to sin continue. The devil owns us, so we do and think whatever he wishes and whatever contradicts the commandments of God.

In addition, I condemn the Pelagians, old and new.[5] They will not acknowledge that original sin is sin. Rather, they conceive of it as a sort of illness or defect. I condemn them because death confronts us all. And that means original sin must be more than simply some sort of sickness. Indeed, it is massive sin—as St. Paul says, "The wages of sin is death."[6] "The sting of death is sin."[7] David puts it this way in Psalm 51: "Indeed, I was born guilty, a sinner when my mother conceived me." He does not say, "My mother conceived me with sin," but, "I was a sinner when my mother conceived me" and "I was born guilty." The Hebrew text, put another way, says that I have grown from sinful seed.

Furthermore, I do not accept and must condemn all monastic orders, rules, cloisters, and religious foundations as absolute lies. They are mere devilish errors, concocted by humans and instituted apart from and above Scripture. With these errors, they would hold the Word captive by their vows and obligations. In spite of the numerous celebrated saints who had lived monastic lives as God's elect, monasticism led them astray. But now, because faith in Jesus Christ redeemed them, they have gotten out.

Because monastic rules, foundations, and cults continued to grow with the notion that their disciplines and acts contribute to and obtain salvation (and thereby escape sin and death), they are shameful, disgusting blasphemies. They reject the irreplaceable help and grace of Jesus Christ, our only Savior and Mediator. Because "there is no other name given by which we must be saved"[8] than Jesus Christ, there cannot be other saviors (or other paths) to salvation than through our Savior Jesus Christ and the specific kind of righteousness he gives to us—the righteousness Christ, our one "mercy seat," offers to God for us.[9]

It would be acceptable if monasteries and religious foundations were kept for the purpose of teaching young people the Word of God, the Scriptures, and Christian ethics. That way, we could educate and train upstanding, skilled men to serve as bishops, pastors, and other workers in the church. We could not only nurture competent, learned men for civil government, we could also raise good, respectable, educated women who can keep house and train children in a Christian manner. As ways of seeking salvation, however, these institutions are the devil's dogma and creed.[10]

But the holy orders and true religious institutions established by God are these three: the office of priest, the estate of marriage, the civil government.[11] All who are engaged in the clerical office or ministry of the Word are in a holy, proper, good, and God-pleasing order and estate, such as those who preach, administer sacraments, supervise the common chest, sextons and messengers or servants who serve such persons. These are engaged in works that are altogether holy in God's sight.

Again, all fathers and mothers who regulate their household wisely and bring up their children to the service of God are engaged in pure holiness, in a holy work and a holy order. Similarly, when children and servants show obedience to their elders and masters, here too is pure holiness, and whoever is thus engaged is a living saint on earth.

What is more, princes and lords, judges, civil officers, state officials, notaries, male and female servants and all who serve such persons, and all their obedient subjects—all are engaged in true holiness and the pursuit of a holy life before God. These three religious institutions or orders are found in God's Word and commandment. And whatever is contained in God's Word must be holy because God's Word is holy and makes everything holy that is connected with it and involved in it.

Higher than these three institutions and orders is the secular order of Christian love, in which one serves not only the three orders, but also every needy person in general with all kinds of benevolent deeds—feeding the hungry, providing drink to the thirsty, forgiving one's enemies, praying for all people on earth, enduring all kinds of evil on earth, etc. You see, each of these are good and holy acts. None of these orders, however, is a means of salvation. There remains only one way above them all: faith in Jesus Christ.

So we distinguish between "being saved" and "being holy." We are saved through Christ alone; but we become holy both through this faith and through these divine foundations and orders. The godless may have much about them that is holy, but that does not save them, because God desires that we do such works to the praise and glory of the Almighty. And everyone whom Christ saves through faith certainly does these works and maintains these orders.

What we said about the estate of marriage, however, applies also to widows and unmarried women, because they, too, belong to the domestic sphere. Now if these orders and divine institutions do not save, what can we say about the effects of the devil's institutions and monasteries that have arisen apart from the Word of God; and now they rage and fight against the one and only way of faith?

Third, I believe in the Holy Spirit, who with the Father and the Son is one true God and proceeds eternally from the Father and the Son, yet is a distinct person in the one divine essence and nature. The same Holy Spirit, as a living, eternal, divine gift and trust, provides all believers with faith, along with various spiritual gifts, raises them from death, frees them from sin, and fills them with joy and confidence—making them free and certain in their conscience. This witness of the Spirit in our hearts assures us that God would be our Father, forgive our sin, and provide eternal life to us.

These are the three persons and one God, who has entirely and fully given himself to everyone, along with everything God is and has. The Father gives himself to us, in addition to earth and sky and all creatures—and by them, we are helped and blessed. The giftedness of creation, however, has become hidden and virtually unusable through Adam's fall. On account of that, the Son of God offered himself and provided all his work, passion, wisdom, and righteousness—reconciling us to the Father. And all of that to bring us new life and put us right with God. That way, we can know and have the good gifts of the Father.

But because this grace would benefit no one if it remained so profoundly hidden and could not come to us, the Holy Spirit comes to us also, wholly and completely. And the Spirit gives for us and teaches us to understand this deed of Christ which has been manifested to us, helps us receive and preserve it, use it to our advantage and impart it to others, increase and extend it. He does this both inwardly and outwardly—inwardly by means of faith and other spiritual gifts, outwardly through the gospel, baptism, and the sacrament of the altar, through which as through three means or methods he comes to us and inculcates the sufferings of Christ for the benefit of our salvation.

Therefore, I maintain and know that just as there is no more than one gospel and one Christ, so also there is no more than one baptism. And that baptism in itself is a divine ordinance, as is his gospel also. And just as the gospel is not false or incorrect for the reason that some use it or teach it falsely, or disbelieve it, so also baptism is not false or incorrect even if some have received or administered it without faith, or otherwise misused it. Accordingly, I altogether reject and condemn the teaching of the Anabaptists and Donatists, and all who rebaptize.

Similarly, I assert and confess that in the Sacrament of the Altar the true body and blood of Christ are eaten and drunk in the bread and wine, even if the priests who distribute them or those who receive them do not believe or otherwise misuse the sacrament. It does not rest on one's belief or unbelief but on the Word and ordinance of God—unless they first change God's Word and ordinance and misinterpret them, as the enemies of the sacrament do at the present time. They, indeed, have only bread and wine, for they do not also have the words and instituted ordinance of God but have perverted and changed it according to their own imagination.

In addition, I believe that there is one holy Christian Church on earth, i.e., the community or number or assembly of all Christians in all the world, the one bride of Christ, and his spiritual body of which he is the only head. The bishops or priests are not her heads or lords or bridegrooms, but servants, friends, and—as the word "bishop" implies—superintendents, guardians, or stewards.

This Christian Church exists not only under the rule of the Church of Rome or pope, but in all the world, as the prophets foretold that the gospel of Christ would spread throughout the world (Psalms 2 and 19). The Church of Christ is physically dispersed among the pope, Turks, Persians, Tartars, etc., but it is spiritually gathered in one gospel and faith, under one head, who is Jesus Christ. The papacy, therefore, is assuredly the real realm of the Antichrist, the true anti-Christian tyrant, who sits in God's temple and rules with human laws (as Christ in Matthew 24 and Paul in 2 Thessalonians 2 declare). The Turk and all other heresies, no matter where they are, are also included in this abomination that the prophets say will stand in the holy place—but they are not comparable to the papacy.

Wherever the Christian church exists, we find the forgiveness of sins. It is a realm of grace and true absolution. So in the church we find the gospel, baptism, and the sacrament of the altar. The church offers the forgiveness of sins, and in the church, we hold and receive it. More than that, Christ and his Spirit and God are there. Outside this Christian Church there is no salvation or forgiveness of sins—only everlasting death and condemnation. Even though holiness and lots of good works may seem splendid, they amount to nothing. That is why we do not expect the forgiveness of sins only one time (as the Novatians teach about baptism), but over and over again, as many times as we need it, until we die.

This is why I value private confession so much: God's word and forgiveness are declared personally and privately to each believer—and each individual's sins are forgiven. Plus, as many times as one feels a need for it, he or she may return to its absolution, consolation, wisdom, and direction. For believers, it remains a valuable and blessed practice—as long as the church does not force them to do it, by law and decrees. Sinners have the freedom to use it, based on their circumstances, wherever and whenever they desire. Similarly, we have the freedom to obtain counsel and comfort, guidance and instruction when and where our need or our inclination moves us. And we do not need to list all our sins, but only those that bother us most intensely or those that someone would probably mention anyway (I have discussed this in my Little Book on Prayer).[12]

However, the absolutions or indulgences that the pope's church has and metes out are blasphemous lies. It not only makes them up, but it has invented a specific kind of forgiveness over and above the general forgiveness that the gospel and the sacrament provide to the entire Christian Church. Because it establishes and founds satisfaction for sins on human works and the merits of saints, it blasphemes and nullifies the general forgiveness—when, on the contrary, only Christ makes proper satisfaction on our behalf.[13]

Regarding prayers for the dead, Scripture gives us no information on the subject, so I think that it is not a sin to pray openly like this or in a similar manner: "Dear God, if your mercy would touch my loved ones, please be gracious to them." Then, after you've prayed such a prayer a time or two, then let it rest. Vigils and annual celebrations of requiem masses are useless. They are little more than yearly rites of the devil.[14]

Furthermore, Scripture does not mention purgatory. It was certainly invented by mischievous imps. Therefore, I maintain it is not necessary to believe in it; although all things are possible to God, and he could very well allow souls to be punished after their departure from the body. The Lord, however, did not say anything about this. Thus, God does not want us to believe in it as an article of faith. I do know of another kind of purgatory, but it would not be right to teach anything about it in the church or to address it with endowments or vigils.[15]

I am not the first person to call into question the practice of praying to the saints—and for that, I'm glad. I believe that we should only call on Christ as our Mediator, a Truth that is as certain as it is scriptural. Scripture does not mention prayer to the saints and, therefore, we do not need to believe in such an unreliable practice.[16]

If anointing the sick and dying were practiced in accordance with the gospel (i.e., Mark 6:13 and James 5:14), then I would allow for it. However, to make it into a sacrament is ridiculous. Similarly, we would be better listening to sermons on death and eternal life, rather than holding vigils and masses for the dead. Survivors could also pray during the funeral ceremony and meditate upon their own mortality. Apparently the early church did it this way, so it would be good to visit the sick, to pray, and to encourage the faithful. Finally, anointing with oil they should be left free to be done in the name of God or not done at all.

Further, we do not need to make marriage and ordination into sacraments. They are already holy orders. Also, penance is simply the practice and the power of baptism. Two sacraments remain: Baptism and the Lord's Supper, along with the gospel, in which the Holy Spirit richly offers, gives, and accomplishes the forgiveness of sins.

I contend that the mass, when it is preached as a sacrifice or sold as a good work, is an abomination of the highest degree and the basis of the system of religious foundations and monasteries.

Yet, if it be God's will it will soon be undone. Even though I am excessively, gravely, and shockingly sinful—and I wasted my youth in insensitive and condemnable ways—my greatest sins were that I was such a holy monk. I so terribly vexed, tormented, and inundated my dear Lord with so many masses for some fifteen years. Oh praise be to God for such inexpressible, eternal grace! And thanks to the Spirit, who led me out of this abomination and continues to uphold and strengthen me every day in true faith, despite how ungrateful I have been.[17]

Along the same lines, I continue to tell people to abandon religious foundations and monasteries and their vows. Let them come out into authentic Christian orders. That way, they can escape these abhorrent masses and the sacrilegious "holiness" of poverty, chastity, and obedience (by which so many imagine they are saved).[18] As good as it might have been in the early Church to maintain the state of virginity, it is now an abomination, because it is used to deny the help and the grace of Christ. It is entirely possible to maintain virginity, widowhood, and chastity without this blasphemous heresy.

I maintain that religious art, bells, eucharistic vestments, liturgical decorations, altar candles, and such are nonessential items. Those who would not use them may do so (or not). I consider art derived from Scripture and from solid stories quite helpful. They are, however, nonessential and optional. Ergo, I have nothing in common with the iconoclasts.[19]

Finally, I believe in the resurrection of the dead, both the godly and the ungodly, when Christ returns. Everyone will then receive in their bodies what they deserve, based on their merits. The godly will live eternally with Christ and the wicked will perish eternally with the devil and his demons. I do not agree with those who teach that the devil also will finally be restored to salvation.[20]

This is my faith, as genuine Christians believe and the Holy Scriptures instruct. On those topics that I have not confessed thoroughly enough here, my other writings will bear witness—in particular, those I have penned in the last few years. I would humbly ask that everyone of pious hearts testify to this and pray for me, that I may continue firmly in this faith to the end of my life. Because if, God forbid, I would say something different in the assault of temptation or the pangs of death, then disregard it! I am publicly declaring here that statements other than this would be wrong and uttered under the influence of the devil.

May my Lord and Savior Jesus Christ help me. Blessed be Christ forever. Amen.

Small Catechism:
For Regular Pastors and Preachers
(1529)[1]

[A Handbook][2]

1529: Luther publishes this work first as a series of posters or "broadsheets" for use in churches and in homes. The previous fall, his site visits to Saxon parishes had shocked him. These visits, and the visits of others, uncovered a deep need for quality parish education. So, like Augustine, bishop of Hippo (AD 354–430) before him, he writes a handbook of Christian teaching to educate the faithful in the basics of Christian doctrine.

Luther's work on reforming catechesis had begun years earlier, when John Staupitz added to Luther's academic duties the assignment to preach in Wittenberg's city church. Thus would Luther deliver sermons on the various parts of the catechism, beginning as early as the fall of 1516.

"Catechism," to Luther, means more than a specific document. The Catechism was the core message of the Christian faith—something each informed believer could and should know. The truths presented here were, from the Reformer's perspective, a sort of "Bible for the laity" and a summary of basic Christian doctrine.

PREFACE TO THE CATECHISM

From Martin Luther to all honest and upright pastors and preachers: Grace, mercy, and peace in Jesus Christ our Lord.[3]

I am publishing this catechism, this Christian teaching, in this

small, common, and straightforward format, because of the pa-
thetic, wretched deficiencies I saw firsthand not long ago—when
I served as an observer in area parishes. Help, dear God, the
misery I saw. The misinformed folks, particularly in the rural
areas, know practically nothing about Christian teaching and,
sadly, many of the clergy are simply inept and incompetent
teachers. They all bear the name Christian, are baptized, and
partake in the Holy Sacrament. And yet, they do not know the
Lord's Prayer, the Creed, or the Ten Commandments.[4] So they
live like ignorant farm animals and stupid pigs. And, where the
gospel has arrived, they have learned all too well how to misuse
their freedom.

Oh, you bishops! How could you, in any way imaginable, respond to Christ? You have so shamefully ignored your people
and you have not exercised the duties of your ministry, not
one bit. You might yet avoid the punishment you deserve for
this! You forbid the wine of the Lord's Supper and enforce
your human laws. And all the while you do not even ask
whether folks know the Lord's Prayer, the Creed, the Ten
Commandments—or a single section of God's Word. May
shame be on your heads forever!

Therefore, I request that you all, my dear gentlemen and
brothers (both pastors and preachers), for the sake of God, in-
vest in your ministries wholeheartedly. Care enough about the
folks who are entrusted to you, and help us bring the catechism
to the people, especially to the youth. And I ask those who cannot do any better to follow these structures and formulas—
reading them out loud, word for word, in the following manner:

First, more than anything, preachers are to make sure to avoid
variations or deviations in the words and forms of the Ten Commandments, the Lord's Prayer, the Creed, the Sacraments, etc.
Rather than that, make a particular form your own. Stay with it.
Consistently use the same form year after year, because youth
and regular people need to be taught with a definite text and
form. If not, it is too easy for folks to misunderstand when someone teaches one way today and another way in a year—even for
the sake of making improvements. Then all that time and effort
will amount to nothing.

Our beloved forebears in the early church understood this well. They made use of a particular form for the Lord's Prayer, the Creed, and the Ten Commandments. So let us, then, teach youth and regular people like that—neither changing a single syllable nor reciting it differently from one year to the next. Pick whatever version you want and stay with it for the long haul.

If you are preaching to educated and scholarly people, then you might want to place your learning and skill before them—discussing these various aspects of the catechism in their complexities and turning them over as masterfully as you can.

With the young people, however, stay with a set, consistent version and process: start with teaching them these parts: the Ten Commandments, the Creed, the Lord's Prayer, etc., word for word. That way, they are able to repeat it out loud and learn it by heart.

Those persons who will not learn these things need to be told they are denying Christ and they are not Christians. We should not permit them to receive the Sacrament of the Altar or serve as baptismal sponsors for children. They should not be allowed to participate in any of the liberties permitted to Christians.[5] Just let them go back home to the pope and his functionaries (and, along with them, to the devil). Also, parents and the heads of houses should deny such folks food and drink—warning them that the prince is inclined to expel uncivilized people like them from his territory.

No one can or should force someone else to believe.[6] Yet one should require and hold folks to this standard: that they know what the people around them consider right and wrong. And they should be held accountable for such knowledge if they want to dwell, eat, and live among these people.[7] Because if a person would want to enjoy the benefits of a particular city's local laws, then that person should know and keep them—no matter if he or she believes in them (or not), if they are, at bottom, rascals or rogues.

Second, after folks have memorized the words, then teach them to understand what they have memorized. That way, they can know the meaning of the words. Return once again to the form given here or another short form that you choose. And stay with it—altering not even a single syllable (as noted above).

Further, provide plenty of time for this instruction. It is not necessary to deal with each of the sections all at once. Rather, take up each of them one at a time. After people grasp the meaning of the First Commandment well, then move on to the Second, etc. That way, you will not overwhelm them with so much that they can scarcely recall anything.

Third, once you have taught folks a short catechism like this, then move to a large catechism—enriching and broadening their knowledge. With that catechism, clarify every commandment, prayer, and section. Point out their respective works, benefits, and blessings; along with the dangers, and potentially negative consequences. Numerous booklets discuss such things.

Be sure to emphasize the commandment or section that addresses the greatest need of your people. For example, focus on the Seventh Commandment (the prohibition of stealing) with skilled workers and merchants (as well as farmers and domestic workers), because there is so much corruption and thievery among these folks.

Similarly, teach the Fourth Commandment with care to children and common folk. That way, they can be well ordered, faithful, quiet, loyal, dutiful, and peaceful. Refer always to the many examples from the Scriptures, specifically where they show how God either punished or blessed such people.

And especially encourage the magistrates and parents to exercise their authority well—specifically in sending their children to school. Show them that they have an obligation to do this and how they commit a horrible, awful sin if they do not do it. Because, by such actions, they act like they are the worst enemies of both God and humanity. Their actions would undermine the rule of law in this world and destroy the rule of God in the next. Make it clear as crystal, so they understand the kind of despicable damage they do when they do not help the formation of young people into pastors, preachers, civil servants, etc. Tell them that, because of this, they face a horrible punishment from God. In our time and place, we must preach about such matters. I do not have enough words to describe how badly parents and magistrates are sinning at this point. In these matters, the devil has something horrible in mind.

A final example of how to apply the catechism: folks no longer desire the Sacrament of the Altar, because the pope's cruel domination has been dethroned. They disrespect it. Emphasize this, knowing that we should not try to force others to believe or to receive the Sacrament. And we should not pass any laws or set mandatory times or places for it. Now, we should preach so that people desire the Sacrament without any legal compulsion; so that folks compel themselves to come and they would compel us to give them communion. Try preaching like this:

We have got to be concerned about anyone who will not or does not receive the Sacrament four times (or so) per year—that such a person rejects the Sacrament and is not a Christian. It's equivalent to this: those who will not listen to or believe in the gospel cannot be Christian. Because Christ did not say, "Leave this out if you want." Nor did he say, "Reject this." Rather, he said, "Do this as often as you drink it." He truly desires that we do it and not leave it out or reject it. "Do this," says Christ.[8]

Whoever does not value the Sacrament as treasure signals that they must have no sin, no lust, no devil, no world, no death, no threats, no damnation. In other words, they believe that they do not possess any of these things—even though they are up to their ears in them. They are doubly the devil's, because at the same time they are demonstrating they have no need of grace, life, paradise, heaven, Christ, God, or any other blessings. If they believed that they possessed such evils and needed such blessings, then they would not neglect the Sacrament. It offers so much help in the face of so much evil—delivering so much good to us.

We would no longer need to demand, by threat of law, that folks receive the sacrament. They would come to it of their own accord, hurrying and hustling all the way. They would demand the sacrament for themselves and they would demand the sacrament from you.

On these grounds, then, one does not need to pass laws (as the pope has done) about the Sacrament of the Altar. Simply focus intensely on the help and the harm, the bane and the blessing, the risk and the redemption in this sacrament. Folks will undoubtedly come of their own volition, without being forced. If they do not come, then let them go. Tell them, however, that it comes from the devil that they neither recognize nor feel their great need and God's gracious help.

If you do not intentionally encourage folks to receive it, then it is your fault if they reject the sacrament as if it were poisonous—now that you are no longer making a law out of it. What else are they supposed to do but spurn the sacrament, if you are asleep and say nothing? So, pastors and preachers, take a look around! Our ministry is now something different from what it was under the pope. It has become both more profound and more important. It also now has many more duties and much more work; and many more traps and devilish attacks. And with all of that, we receive precious little compensation and gratitude in this world. Christ, however, more than makes up for it. That way, we can do this work with integrity.

Father of all grace, help us! You are the one whom we praise and thank forever. Through Christ our Lord, Amen.

THE TEN COMMANDMENTS, AS A HEAD OF THE HOUSEHOLD SHOULD REGULARLY TEACH THEM TO A HOUSEHOLD

The First Commandment: You shall have no other gods.[9]

What is this?
Answer: We are to fear, love, and trust God above all things.

The Second Commandment: You shall not misuse your God's name.

What is this?
Answer: We are to fear and love God, so that we do not use God's name as a curse-word, to swear, to do magic, to lie, and to cheat. Rather, whenever we are in need, we

are to call on God's name—praying, praising, and giving thanks.

The Third Commandment: You shall keep the Sabbath holy.

What is this?
　　Answer: We are to fear and love God, so that we do not disrespect preaching and God's word. Rather, we are to regard them as holy—eagerly hearing and learning.

The Fourth Commandment: Honor your father and your mother.

What is this?
　　Answer: We are to fear and love God, so that we do not hate or anger our parents and others in authority. Rather, we are to hold them in high esteem, to serve them, to obey them, to love them, and to value them.

The Fifth Commandment: You shall not kill.

What is this?
　　Answer: We are to fear and love God, so that we do not put our neighbors' lives at risk or hurt them. Rather, we are to assist them and support them in all their physical needs.

The Sixth Commandment: You shall not commit adultery.

What is this?
　　Answer: We are to fear and love God, so that we live virtuously and decently, in word and deed, so all people love and respect their spouse.

The Seventh Commandment: You shall not steal.

What is this?
　　Answer: We are to fear and love God, so that we do not pilfer our neighbors' money or material possessions; nor

do we obtain them under false pretenses or fraud. Rather, we are to help our neighbors enhance and protect their properties and incomes.

The Eighth Commandment: You shall not bear false witness against your neighbor.

What is this?

Answer: We are to fear and love God, so that we do not lie about our neighbors—betraying or libeling them; nor do we ruin their good name. Rather, we are to defend them, speak well of them, and interpret everything in the best possible way.

The Ninth Commandment: You shall not covet your neighbor's house.

What is this?

Answer: We are to fear and love God, so that we do not try to manipulate our neighbors from their land or house. We do not attempt to obtain either one for ourselves by falsely claiming to have a legal right to it, etc. Rather, we are to assist and serve them as they maintain what is theirs.

The Tenth Commandment: You shall not covet your neighbor's wife, servant, livestock, or anything that is your neighbor's.

What is this?

Answer: We are to fear and love God, so that we do not lure, coerce, or take our neighbor's spouse, workers, livestock, etc. Rather, we are to encourage them to remain where they are, so that they fulfill their responsibilities to our neighbors.

What does God say about all of these commandments?

Answer: God says: "I, the Lord your God, am a jealous God. And I punish those who hate me to have the sins of their fathers pass along to their children, to the third and the fourth generation. I will, however, do well by those who love me and keep my commandments—to the thousandth generation."[10]

What is this?

Answer: God threatens to punish those who disobey these commandments, and thus we are to fear the wrath of God and obey these commandments. Still, God promises grace and every good thing to everyone who keeps these commandments. On account of this, then, we are to love and trust God—and happily obey God's commandments.

THE CREED, AS A HEAD OF A HOUSEHOLD SHOULD MOST REGULARLY TEACH IT TO THE HOUSEHOLD

The First Article: About Creation

I believe in God, the Father Almighty, creator of heaven and earth.

What is this?

Answer: I believe that God has created me together with every created thing. God has given me, and continues to sustain: my body and soul, eyes, ears, and every body part, reason and all my senses. Also, God richly and daily provides clothes and shoes, food and drink, house and yard, spouse and children, fields, livestock, and all good things— along with everything we need, including food, for this body and this life. God also guards me against all danger— protecting and preserving me from all evil. All of this flows from pure, fatherly, and divine goodness and mercy, without any merit or worthiness on my part at all. Because of all this, I owe God a debt of gratitude and praise, service and obedience. This is certainly true.[11]

The Second Article: About Redemption

And [I believe] in Jesus Christ, God's only Son, our Lord, who was conceived by the Holy Spirit; who was born of Mary the virgin; who suffered under Pontius Pilate, who was crucified, died, and was buried; who descended to hell; who, on the third day, rose again from the dead; who ascended into heaven; who is sitting at the right hand of God, the almighty Father, from whom he will come to judge the living and the dead. This is certainly true.

What is this?

Answer: I believe that Jesus Christ, true God, begotten of the Father in eternity, and truly human, born of the virgin Mary, is my Lord—who has redeemed me, a lost and condemned person. Christ has bought and freed me from all sins, from death, and from the power of the devil, not with gold or silver but with his holy, priceless blood and with his guiltless suffering and death. Christ has done all this in order that I may belong to him, live under him in his kingdom, and serve him in eternal righteousness, guiltlessness, and blessedness, just as he rose from the dead, lives and rules eternally. This is certainly true.

The Third Article: About Sanctification[12]

I believe in the Holy Spirit, the holy Christian church,[13] the communion of saints, the forgiveness of sins, the resurrection of the body, and the life everlasting.

What is this?

Answer: I believe that I am not able to believe in Jesus Christ my Lord or come to him—not from my own reason or power. But I do believe that the Holy Spirit has called me through the gospel, enlightened me with his gifts, sanctified me, and kept me in the true faith. Likewise, the Spirit calls, gathers, enlightens, and sanctifies the whole Christian church on earth and keeps it with Jesus Christ in the one, true faith. Every day in the Church, the Holy Spirit generously forgives sins—all of my sins and the sins of all believers. On the last day, the Holy Spirit will raise me and all the dead and will give to me and all believers in Christ eternal life. This is certainly true.

THE LORD'S PRAYER: AS A HEAD OF A HOUSEHOLD SHOULD MOST REGULARLY TEACH THE HOUSEHOLD

Our Father, you who are in heaven.

What is this?
Answer: Here God wants to encourage us to believe that he is our true Father and we are God's true children. Because of that, we may pray boldly and with utter confidence, just as dear children approach their loving father.

The First Request: May your name be holy.

What is this?
Answer: The name of God is certainly holy in itself, but we ask in this prayer that it would also be holy among us.
How does this happen?
When we teach the clear and pure Word of God, and when we also live holy lives as God's children according to that Word. Help us to do that, dear Heavenly Father. However, whoever teaches and lives otherwise than the Word of God teaches, dishonors the name of God among us. Protect us from that, Father in Heaven.

The Second Request: May your kingdom come.

What is this?
Answer: Certainly, the kingdom of God comes by itself, without our prayer. However, we request in this prayer that it would also come to us.
How does this happen?
Answer: Whenever our Father in Heaven gives us the

Holy Spirit in order that, by the grace of the Spirit, we believe God's holy word and live in ways that please God, here in time and in eternity.

The Third Request: Your will be done on earth as in heaven.

What is this?
Answer: In fact, God's good and gracious will is done without our prayer, but we ask in this prayer that it may also be done in and among us.
How does this happen?
Answer: Whenever God thwarts and disrupts the evil plots and evil intentions that would not allow us to keep God's name holy and would prevent the coming of the kingdom (like the will of the devil, the world, and our flesh). And whenever God empowers us and keeps us securely in the Word and in the faith until the end of our lives. That is God's gracious and good will.

The Fourth Request: Give us today our daily bread.

What is this?
Answer: God gives daily bread, without our requesting it, including all evil people. But we request in this prayer that God would allow us to see what our daily bread is, and gratefully receive it.
Then what qualifies as "daily bread"?
Answer: Everything that belongs to the nourishment and needs of our bodies: items like food, drink, clothes, shoes, a home, garden, fields, livestock, money, property, a good spouse, respectful children, honest workers, moral and dedicated rulers, good government, decent weather, peace, health, discipline, honor, good friends, real neighbors, and so on . . .

The Fifth Request: Forgive us our debts, as we forgive our debtors.

What is this?
Answer: We request in this prayer that our Father in

Heaven would not look at our sins or deny these requests because of them. We are not worthy and we do not deserve the things we are requesting. Yet, God would give us everything from grace, on account of how much we sin every day and we really do deserve nothing but punishment. Therefore, we truly want to forgive from our hearts and gladly do good to those who sin against us.

The Sixth Request: Lead us not into temptation.

What is this?

Answer: Truly, God does not tempt anyone. We request, however, in this prayer, that God would preserve and keep us so that the devil, the world, and our flesh would not betray us or mislead us into false belief, despair, and other kinds of massive shame and vice. And, although we may be assaulted by them, we request that we would endure to the end and remain victorious.

The Seventh Request: And deliver us from evil.

What is this?

Answer: We request in this prayer, which is a sort of summary of all the other requests, that the Heavenly Father would protect us in the midst of every evil—those that afflict the body or soul, possessions or character. And finally, when our own time is finished, we would pray for God to bestow on us a blessed ending and, with grace, take us from this vale of tears to be with him in heaven.

Amen.[14]

What is this?

Answer: I ought to be sure that these requests (and others like them) are received and listened to by the Heavenly Father. God commands us to pray like this and promises to listen to us. "Amen, amen," means "Yes, yes, it is going to happen."

THE SACRAMENT OF HOLY BAPTISM: AS A HEAD OF A HOUSEHOLD SHOULD REGULARLY TEACH IT TO THE HOUSEHOLD

What is baptism?

Answer: Baptism is not just water by itself. Rather, it takes water, as commanded by God, and connects it with God's word.

What is this word of God?

Answer: Our Lord Christ says in Matthew 28, "Go therefore and make disciples of all nations, baptizing them in the name of the Father and of the Son and of the Holy Spirit."[15]

What gifts or benefits does baptism give?

Answer: It accomplishes the forgiveness of sins, delivers from death and the devil, and grants eternal salvation to everyone who believes it, as the words and promise of God declare.

What are these words and God's promise?

Answer: Our Lord Christ says it in the final chapter of the Gospel of Mark, "The one who believes and is baptized will be saved; but the one who does not believe will be condemned."[16]

How can water accomplish such profound things?

Answer: The water, obviously, does not do it. Rather, the word of God does it—with, and in conjunction with the water, along with the faith that trusts this word of God in the water. Because apart from God's word, water is simply water and is no baptism. However, with God's word, it is a baptism, a grace-rich water of life and a "bath of the new birth in the Holy Spirit," as St. Paul says to Titus, "through the water of rebirth and renewal by the Holy Spirit. This Spirit he poured out on us richly through Jesus Christ our Savior, so that, having been justified by his grace, we might become heirs according to the hope of eternal life. The saying is sure."[17]

What does this baptism with water mean?

Answer: It means that every day, the old person in us, together with every sin and evil desire, is to be drowned and die through remorse and repentance—and again, each day, a new person emerges, arising to live a life of righteousness and purity in God's presence, forever.

Where is this written?

Answer: St. Paul says in Romans, chapter 6, "We were buried with Christ through baptism into death, so that, just as Christ was raised from the dead through the glory of the Father, so we too might walk in newness of life."[18]

THE SACRAMENT OF THE ALTAR:[19] HOW THE HEAD OF A HOUSEHOLD SHOULD REGULARLY INSTRUCT THE HOUSEHOLD

What is the Sacrament of the Altar?

Answer: It is the true body and blood of our Lord Jesus Christ, under the bread and the wine, instituted by Christ himself for us Christians to eat and to drink.

Where is this written?

Answer: The holy evangelists Matthew, Mark, Luke, and St. Paul put it like this:

In the night in which he was betrayed, our Lord Jesus took bread, and gave thanks, broke it, and gave it to his disciples, saying: Take and eat; this is my body, given for you. Do this for the remembrance of me. Again, after supper, he took the cup, gave thanks, and gave it for all to drink, saying: This cup is the new covenant in my blood, shed for you and for all people for the forgiveness of sin. Do this for the remembrance of me.[20]

What good does such eating and drinking do?

Answer: That goodness is shown in the words "given

and shed for you for the forgiveness of sin." Specifically, the forgiveness of sin, life, and salvation are given to us in the sacrament through these words. Because where there is forgiveness of sin, there is also life and salvation.

How can bodily eating and drinking do such a great thing?

Answer: Eating and drinking certainly do not do it, but rather the words that are recorded: "given for you" and "shed for you for the forgiveness of sin." These words, when accompanied by the physical eating and drinking, are the essential thing in the sacrament, and whoever believes these very words has what they declare and state, namely, "forgiveness of sin."

Who, then, receives this sacrament worthily?

Answer: Fasting and bodily preparation are in fact a fine external discipline, but a person who has faith in these words, "given for you" and "shed for you for the forgiveness of sin," is really worthy and well prepared. However, a person who does not believe these words or doubts them is unworthy and unprepared, because the words "for you" require truly believing hearts.

THE MORNING BLESSING

In the morning, as soon as you get out of bed, you are to make the sign of the holy cross and say:

"God the Father, Son, and Holy Spirit watch over me. Amen."

Then, kneeling or standing, say the Apostles' Creed and the Lord's Prayer. If you wish, you may in addition recite this little prayer as well:

"I give thanks to you, heavenly Father, through Jesus Christ your dear Son, that you have protected me through the night from all harm and danger. I ask that you would also protect me today from sin and all evil, so that my life and actions may please you. Into your hands I commend myself: my body, my soul, and all that is mine. Let your holy angel be with me, so that the wicked foe may have no power over me. Amen."

After singing a hymn perhaps (for example, one on the Ten Commandments) or whatever else may serve your devotion, you are to go to your work joyfully.

THE EVENING PRAYER

In the evening, when you go to bed, you are to make the sign of the holy cross and say: "God the Father, Son, and Holy Spirit watch over me. Amen."

Then, kneeling or standing, say the Apostles' Creed and the Lord's Prayer. If you wish, you may in addition recite this little prayer as well:

"I give thanks to you, heavenly Father, through Jesus Christ your dear Son, that you have graciously protected me today. I ask you to forgive me all my sins, where I have done wrong, and graciously to protect me tonight. Into your hands, I entrust myself: my body, my soul, and all that is mine. Let your holy angel be with me, so that the evil enemy might not exert power over me. Amen."

After that, go to sleep quickly and cheerfully.

TABLE BLESSINGS

The children and the members of the household are to come devoutly to the table, fold their hands, and recite:

"The eyes of all wait upon you, O Lord, and you give them their food in due season. You open your hand and satisfy the desire of every living creature."

Then they are to recite the Lord's Prayer and the following prayer:

"Lord God, heavenly Father, bless us and these your gifts, which we receive from your bountiful goodness, through Jesus Christ our Lord. Amen."

Similarly, after eating they should in the same manner fold their hands and recite devoutly:

"Give thanks to the Lord, for the Lord is good, for God's mercy endures forever. God provides food for the cattle and for the young ravens when they cry. God is not impressed by the might of a horse, and has no pleasure in the speed of a runner, but finds pleasure in those who fear the Lord, in those who await God's steadfast love."

Then recite the Lord's Prayer and the following prayer:

"We give thanks to you, Lord God our Father, through Jesus Christ our Lord for all your benefits, you who live and reign forever. Amen."

On Translating:
An Open Letter (1530)

Summer 1530: Luther goes into hiding once again. It had been nearly a decade since the emperor had declared him a traitor and the pope declared him a heretic. This time, he holes up in the Coburg Castle, the farthest south and west fortress of the Saxon Prince (now John "the Steadfast," Frederick's brother). Emperor Charles V had convoked another legislative assembly, the Diet of Augsburg—this time to hear firsthand what Lutherans, not just Luther, believe, teach, and confess. Coburg is as close to Augsburg as Luther can safely stay (175 miles away). And, while couriers deliver regular updates on the proceedings to Luther and return to Augsburg with his responses, he continues to write and publish on related themes.

As the proceedings continue, Luther pens this piece on September 12 as an open letter to an acquaintance in Nuremberg. The recipient delivers it to a Nuremberg printer on the 15th and it appears in public shortly thereafter. Luther seeks to clarify two basic issues: first, the biblical, textual basis for his understanding of justification by faith alone; and second, the practice of praying to the saints.

. . . . .

To the Honorable and Upright Mr. X, my Esteemed Gentleman and Friend:

Grace and peace in Christ,

I have received your request for my response to your questions. First, you wonder why I translated Paul's words of Romans 3:28, *Arbitramur hominem justificari ex fide absque operibus*, like this: "We hold that a person is justified without the works of the law, by faith alone." You mention also that the papists are making a tremendous fuss, because the word *sola* (alone) is not in Paul's text, and that this addition of mine to the words of God is not to be tolerated. Second you ask whether the departed saints too intercede for us, because we read that angels indeed do intercede for us?

Regarding the first question, you may give your papist acquaintances the following answer from me, if you like:

First if I, Dr. Luther, thought that all the papists taken together would be able to translate a single chapter of the Scriptures correctly and well, I would certainly have mustered up enough humility to invite their aid and assistance in putting the New Testament into German. But because I knew—and still see with my own eyes—that none of them knows how to translate, or to speak German, I spared them and myself that trouble. It is evident, indeed, that they are using my German translation to learn how to speak and to write German. In short, they are stealing from me my language, of which they had little knowledge before. They do not thank me for it, however, but prefer to use it against me. However, I readily grant them this, for it tickles me that I have taught my ungrateful pupils, even my enemies, how to speak.

Second you may say that I translated the New Testament conscientiously and to the best of my ability. I have compelled no one to read it, but have left that open, doing the work only as a service to those who could not do it better. No one is forbidden to do a better piece of work. Those who do not want to read it, can drop it. I neither ask anybody to read it nor praise anyone who does so. It is my Testament and my translation, and it shall continue to be mine. If I have made some mistakes in it—though I am not conscious of any and would certainly be most unwilling to give a single letter a wrong translation intentionally—I will not allow the papists to judge. Their ears are still too long, and their hee-haws are too weak,[1] for them to criticize my translating. I know very well—and they know it even less than a miller's donkey—how much skill, energy, sense, and brains are required in a good translator. For they have never tried it.

There is a saying, "Whoever builds along the road has many bosses." That is the way it is with me too. Those who have never

spoken properly (to say nothing of actually translating) have suddenly become my teachers, and I must be their pupil. If I were to
have asked them to translate into German the first two words of
Matthew's Gospel, Liber Generationis, not one of them would
have even clucked as well as a chicken.[2] And now these fine fel-
lows sit in judgment on my whole work!

Similarly, St. Jerome endured this kind of thing when he translated the Bible into Latin. Everyone was his teacher; he alone was
incompetent. Those who were not worthy to clean his shoes criticized the good man's work. It takes a great deal of patience to do a
good thing publicly, for the world always thinks it can do better. It
is always putting the bit in the horse's rear,[3] criticizing everything
and doing nothing. It is its nature; it cannot help itself.

I should like to see a papist who would come forward and
translate even a single epistle of St. Paul or one of the prophets
without making use of Luther's German translation. Then we
should see a fine, beautiful, praiseworthy German translation!
We have seen the Dresden scribbler who played the master to my
New Testament. I shall not mention his name again in my books
as he has his Judge now,[4] and is already well known anyway. He
admits that my German is sweet and good.[5] He saw that he could
not improve on it. But eager to discredit it, he went to work and
took my New Testament almost word for word as I had written
it. He removed my introductions and explanations, inserted his
own, and thus sold my New Testament under his name. Oh my,
dear children, how it hurt me when his prince, in a nasty preface,
condemned Luther's New Testament and forbade the reading of
it; yet commanded simultaneously that that scribbler's New Testament be read, even though it was the very same one that Luther
had produced!

I'm not making this up. Simply take the two Testaments, Luther's and the scribbler's, and compare them; you will see who is
the translator of them both. He has cut and pasted in a few spots
and, even though some of that irks me, I can let it go. It really
doesn't matter, as far as the text itself is concerned. For this reason, I never intended to write against it. But I could not help but
chuckle that the same kind of good judgment that would so terribly mock, dismiss, and ban my New Testament, when it was

published under my name, would make it required reading, when published under someone else's name.

Where is the integrity in slandering and vilifying another's book, if you pirate it and publish it under your own name? And then to gain higher praise and status through the work of someone else (the very work you've just slandered)—well, I leave that for your Judge to decide. In the meantime, I am satisfied, even happy, that my work (as St. Paul also boasts [Philippians 1:18]) is being promoted, even by my foes, and that Luther's book, without Luther's name but under the name of his enemies, must now be read. What better revenge is there?

But that is not my main point. If your papist wants to whine about the word *sola* (alone) tell him this, "Dr. Martin Luther will have it so, and he says that papists and donkeys are the same." As Juvenal puts it, "I will it; I command it; my will is reason enough."[6]. We are not going to be the pupils and disciples of the papists, but their masters and judges. For once, we too are going to be proud and brag with these blockheads; and as St. Paul boasts over against his mad raving saints [2 Corinthians 11:21ff.], so I shall boast over against these donkeys of mine. Are they doctors? So am I. Are they learned? So am I. Are they preachers? So am I. Are they theologians? So am I. Are they debaters? So am I. Are they philosophers? So am I. Are they dialecticians? So am I. Are they lecturers? So am I. Do they write books? So do I.

And the list goes on: I can expound psalms and prophets; they cannot. I can translate; they cannot. I can read the Holy Scriptures; they cannot. I can pray; they cannot. And, to come down to their level, I can use their own dialectics and philosophy better than all of them put together; and besides I know for sure that none of them understands their Aristotle. They cannot understand a single passage from Aristotle any more than I can fly.

This is no idle boast. As a child, I was trained and drilled in all their "scholarship." And I understand how deep and broad it is—just as they know that I can do everything they can. Still, these sickos treat me like I were a newcomer to their field; as if I had just showed up this morning and had never seen or heard what they teach and know. They are so brilliant—parading around with all their academic achievements, teaching me what has already become old hat to me. Let them scream and shout. I'll sing with the working girls, "I have known for seven years that horseshoe-nails are iron."[7]

Let this be the answer to your first question. And please give these donkeys no other and no further answer to their useless braying about the word *sola* than simply this, "Luther will have it so, and says that he is a doctor above all the doctors of the whole papacy." It shall stay at that! From now on, I will just hold them in contempt, and have them held in contempt, so long as they are the kind of people—I should say, asses—that they are. There are shameless nincompoops among them who have never learned their own art of sophistry—like Dr. "Smithy"[8] and Dr. "Snot-nose,"[9] and their likes—and who set themselves against me in this matter, which transcends not only sophistry, but (as St. Paul says [1 Corinthians 1:19–25]), all the world's wisdom and understanding as well. Clearly, donkeys do not need to bray if we can see them. Their ears give them away.

To you and to our people, however, I shall show why I chose to use the word *sola*—though in Romans 3[:28] it was not *sola*, but *solum* or *tantum* that I used, so clearly do these donkeys stare at my work! That said, I admit that I have indeed used *sola fide* elsewhere, and I want both: *solum* and *sola*. I have constantly worked, as a translator, to produce true and clear German. In fact, it happened with some frequency that for weeks on end, we hunted and sought for a single word and, sometimes, we just couldn't find it. In translating the Book of Job, Master Philipp, Aurogallus, and I worked so hard, that there were times we scarcely handled three lines in four days.

Now that it is translated and finished, everyone can read it and criticize it. Now they can glide their eyes over three or four pages and not stumble once. And they don't even know what boulders and clods had once been where they now move along, as over finely polished wood. We had to sweat and toil there before we got those boulders and clods out of the way, so that others could go along so nicely. The plowing goes well when the field is cleared.[10] But rooting out the woods and stumps, and getting the field ready—this is a job nobody wants. There is no such thing as earning the world's thanks. Even God himself cannot earn it, not even by the sun and the whole of heaven and earth or even by his own Son's death. The world simply remains "the world," because the devil will not let it be anything else.

Here, in Romans 3:28, of course I knew that the word *solum* is not in the Greek or Latin text; the papists did not have to teach me that. True enough, the four letters *s o l a* are not there. And these blockheads stare at them like cows at a new gate.[11] At the same time they do not see that it conveys the sense of the text; it belongs there if the translation is to be clear and vigorous. I wanted to speak German, not Latin or Greek. It was German I had undertaken to speak in the translation. But it is the nature of our German language that in speaking of two things, one of which is affirmed and the other denied, we use the word *allein* [only] along with the word *nicht* [not] or *kein* [no]. For example, we say, "The farmer brings *allein* grain and *kein* money"; "No, really I do not have money, but only (*allein*) grain"; "I have only *allein* eaten and *nicht* yet had anything to drink"; "Did you *allein* write it, and *nicht* read it over?" There are innumerable cases of this kind in daily use.

In all these phrases, this is German usage, not Latin or Greek. The German language adds the word *allein* in order that the word *nicht* or *kein* may be clearer and more complete. Certainly, I can also say, "The farmer brings grain and *kein* money," but the words "*kein* money" do not sound as full and clear as if I were to say, "The farmer brings *allein* grain and *kein* money." Here the word *allein* helps the word *kein* so much that it becomes a complete, clear German expression.

These donkeys look only at the literal Latin text for clues as to how Germans speak. We, however, ask the mother in the home, the child down the lane, the worker in the marketplace. Their language and the way they speak guide us as we translate. That way they will understand what the text means and hear that we are speaking German to them.

Take the words of Christ in Matthew 12:34 and Luke 6:45, for example. If I follow these donkeys, who want me to follow the original word-for-word, then I would translate *Ex abundantia cordis os loquitur* as, "Out of the abundance of the heart, the mouth speaks." Tell me, what kind of German is that? No German could understand what that means. What is "the abundance of the heart"? Germans don't talk like that. That is, unless they are trying to say that some person was too nice or had too much courage (and even that would not be right). "Abundance of the heart" is not German, any more than "abundance of the house," "abundance of the stove," or "abundance of the bench" is German. Peasant women and men would more likely say, "The mouth expresses what wells up from the depth of the heart." Now that is the kind of good German I strive for, even though I do not always reach that goal or hit that target. The literal meaning of the Latin words stands in the way of good German.

So, for example, Judas the betrayer says, in Matthew 26:8, "Why this waste?" and in Mark 14:4, "Why was the ointment wasted in this way?" If I had followed these literalistic dopes, then I would have translated it: "Why has this loss of ointment happened?" But what kind of German is that? Who in Germany uses a phrase like, "Loss of the ointment has happened"? If they understand that at all, then they think the ointment is lost and must be looked for and found again (and even that is still obscure and ambiguous).

Now if that is such good German, why do they not come out and make us a fine, pretty, new German Testament like that, and leave Luther's Testament alone? I think that would really bring their talents to light! But a German would say *Ut quid*, etc.: "Why this waste?" Or, "Why this extravagance [*schade*]?" Indeed, "It's a shame about the ointment." That is good German, from which one understands that Magdalene[12] had wasted the ointment that she poured out and that Mary had been extravagant. That was what Judas meant, because he thought he could have used it to better advantage.

Again, when the angel greets Mary, he says, "Hail Mary, full of grace, the Lord is with you!" (Luke 1:28). In the past, that has simply been translated word-for-word from the Latin. Tell me whether that is also good German! When does a German speak like that, "You are full of grace"? What German understands what that is, to be "full of grace"? He would have to think of a keg "full of" beer or a purse "full of" money. So, I have translated it, "You gracious one,"[13] so that a German can at least think his way through to what the angel meant by this greeting. Here, however, the papists are going wild about me, because I have corrupted the Angelic Salutation; though I have still not hit upon the best German rendering for it. Suppose I had taken the best German, and translated the salutation thus: "Hello there, Mary"[14]—for that is what the angel wanted to say, and what he would have said, if he had wanted to greet her in German. Suppose I had done that! I believe that they would have hanged themselves out of tremendous fanaticism for the Virgin Mary, because I had thus destroyed the salutation.

Indeed, why should I listen to what they say? I cannot keep them from translating however they want. I will translate as I see fit and not to please them. If they do not like it, then they don't have to read it and they can keep their opinion to themselves. I won't look at it and I won't listen to it. They irresponsibly offer nothing better than my translation.

Maybe they will listen to this: I say "gracious Mary," and "dear Mary." They say, "Mary full of grace." Well, whoever understands German knows right away that "dear" (liebe) is a precious, heartfelt word: dear Mary, dear God, dear emperor, the dear prince, the dear one, the dear child. It is hard to imagine that "dear" can carry a set of associations more lovely and more sweet in Latin (or any other language) than it does in German—strumming our heartstrings and pulsing through all the senses.

I imagine that St. Luke, a true master of Greek and Hebrew, wanted to translate the Angel's Hebrew into Greek (Luke 1:28). I also imagine that Angel Gabriel would have addressed Mary as he had addressed Daniel, as "dear Daniel" (Daniel 9:23; 10:11, 19). That is simply how Gabriel talked in the book of Daniel. If I were to translate the angel's words literally, with the skill of these donkeys, I would have to say, "Daniel, man of desires." Now, that is terrible German. Germans would certainly hear the words "Man," "pleasure," and "desire" as "German-ish," but not true German. Pleasure and desire would be better by themselves. If Germans read the phrase "man of desires," they would assume that it meant: Daniel was lustful. Wouldn't that be in poor taste? I must sometimes let the literal words go and try to learn how Germans communicate what the Hebrew expresses. I have discovered that Germans actually use phrases like this: "dear Daniel" or "dear Mary," and "gracious lady," "lovely maiden," "gentle girl," etc. Translators need a large warehouse full of words. That way, they can employ them when literal renderings don't work.

And why should I talk so much about translating? If I were to point out the reasons and considerations back of all my words, I should need a year to write on it. I have learned by experience what an art and what a task translating is. That is why I will not tolerate these papal donkeys or mules to judge or criticize my work. They have never done it themselves. If they don't like my translating, then they can ignore it. Let them go to the devil, if they dislike my work or criticize it without my knowledge and consent! If it is to be criticized, I'll do it myself. If I don't do it, then let them leave my translations in peace. Let them translate for themselves in a way that suits them—what do I care?

I can say this without reservation: I poured my best into this work. I didn't ask for a penny to do it and I haven't received one, either. My Lord knows I have not done this for glory. I have tried to serve my dear Christians and to honor the One enthroned on high. God has so abundantly blessed me throughout my life that if I had worked 1,000 times harder and produced 1,000 times more text, I would not deserve even one hour's wage. All that I am and have is from God's grace and mercy; from Christ's precious blood and bitter sweat. It is for God's sake; I honestly hope only to bring honor to God.

The papacy's stumbling donkeys might condemn me, but true believers and Christ their Lord will bless me. If a single Christian acknowledges me as an honest worker, that would be more than enough payment. I could not care less about those papal donkeys. They do not have the skills required to evaluate my work. In fact, if they approved of it, then I would know something was wrong. Their condemnation has become my highest praise and honor. I am still a doctor of the church (perhaps even a bit distinguished at it) and that's a title they can never take from me. Of that I'm certain.

That doesn't mean I disregard the precise wording of the text. My team and I focus intensely on the specific words of the original. Everything depends on the specific wording of the original and I do not depart from it without good reason. For example, in John 6:27, Christ says, "It is on him that God the Father has set his seal." It would have been better German to say, "God the Father has signified him" or "God the Father means him." But I preferred to do violence to the German language rather than to depart from the word. Ah, this work is not for everyone, as these deluded saints imagine. Translating demands a heart that is: fair, faithful, honest, sincere, God-fearing, Christian, trained, informed, and experienced.

Ergo, I contend that no false Christian or fanatic can be a skilled translator. Look at the translation of the Prophets published at Worms.[15] It has been carefully done and approaches my German very closely. Some Jews, apparently, have their hands in it, and they do not show much reverence for Christ. Apart from that, there is plenty of competence and craftsmanship there.

So much for translating and the nature of the languages!

I did not depend only on the literal meaning of either language, when I translated the word *solum* (alone) in Romans 3:28. The text itself and St. Paul's intent require and demand it. To be specific, he deals in that passage with the chief article of Christian teaching: we are justified by faith in Christ without any works of the law. Paul cuts away all works so completely, as even to say that the works of the law—though it is God's law and word—do not help us toward justification (Romans 3:20). He cites Abraham as an example and says that he was justified so entirely without works that even the highest work—which, moreover, had been newly commanded by God, over and above all other works and ordinances, namely circumcision—did not help him for justification; rather he was justified without circumcision and without any works, by faith, as he says in chapter 4, verse 2: "For if Abraham was justified by works, he has something to boast about, but not before God." But when all works are so completely cut away—and that must mean that faith alone justifies—whoever would speak plainly and clearly about this cutting away of works must say, "Faith alone justifies us, and not works." The matter itself, as well as the nature of the language, demands it.

Still, they say, "It sounds offensive and people will think that good works are not necessary." So, what can we say? Is it not much more offensive that St. Paul does not use the phrase "faith alone" himself? Rather, he says it even more plainly and lays all his cards on the table: "without the works of the law." In Galatians 2:16 (as well as in many other places) he says, "Not by the works of the law," because "faith alone" can be misunderstood. The phrase "without the works of the law," however, is so bold, so

offensive, and so scandalous that no amount of interpretation can
help it. How much more might people learn from this "that they
need not do any good works," when they hear this preaching
about the works themselves put in such plain, powerful language?
"No works!" "Without works!" "Not by works!" If it is not "offensive" to preach, "without works," "no works," "not by works,"
then why is it "offensive" to preach, "by faith alone"?

And the "offense" even increases: St. Paul rejects, not only
commonplace works, but "works of the law." Now someone could
easily take offense at that even more and say that the law is condemned and accursed before God, and we ought to be doing nothing but evil—as they did in Romans 3:8, "Why not do evil that
good may come?" This is the very thing that one fanatic[16] started
to do in our time. St. Paul and I want to give such offense; we
preach so strongly against works and insist on faith alone, for no
other reason than that the people may be offended, stumble, and
fall, in order that they may learn to know that they are not saved
by their good works but only by Christ's death and resurrection.
Now if they cannot be saved by the good works of the law, how
much less shall they be saved by bad works, and without the law?
Ergo, it does not follow that, if good works do not help, then bad
works do help—no more than it follows that if the sun cannot help
blind persons see, then night and darkness must help them see.

It amazes me that someone would disagree over a case as
evident as this. Please tell me, yes or no: is Christ's death and
resurrection a work that we accomplish? Certainly not—and nor
is it the work of any law. Christ's death and resurrection alone
saves us and frees us from sin, as Paul says in Romans 4:25, He
"who was handed over to death for our trespasses and was raised
for our justification."

Furthermore, can you tell me: What is the work by which we
receive Christ's death and resurrection? It cannot be any external
accomplishment, but simply the internal faith of the heart. Faith
alone, indeed, all alone and without any works, lays hold of this
death and resurrection when the gospel is preached. Why then this
raging and raving, this making of heretics and burning them
at the stake? The case itself, at its core, clearly proves that faith
alone grasps Christ's death and resurrection, without any works.
His death and resurrection [alone] are our life and our righteous-

ness. If, then, the fact itself is so obvious that faith alone delivers, grasps, and imparts this life and righteousness, then why not say so? It is no heresy that faith alone lays hold of Christ and gives life. Yet it must be heresy, if someone says it out loud. Isn't that crazy, stupid, and irrational? They admit that this conclusion is correct, but label the saying of it wrong. But nothing can be both right and wrong at the same time.

Indeed, am I the only one, or even the first, to say that faith alone justifies? Ambrose and Augustine said it before me, as well as many others. If they are going to read St. Paul and understand him, they should say the same thing. They can say nothing else. Paul's words are too strong; they allow no works. None.

Now if it is not any work, then it must be faith alone. What a nice, constructive, and inoffensive doctrine that would be, if people were taught that they could be saved by works, as well as faith! That would be as much as to say that it is not Christ's death alone that takes away our sins, but that our works too have something to do with it. That would be a fine honoring of Christ's death, to say that it is helped by our works, and that whatever it does our works can do too—so that we are his equal in strength and goodness! This is the very devil; he can never quit abusing the blood of Christ.

The heart of the matter requires us to say, "Faith alone justifies." And the character of our German language leads us to say it like that. Also, I have the precedent of the holy fathers. Further, the risks to the faithful compel it, so they do not keep holding on to their works and wander away from faith and lose Christ. Particularly in these days, because they have gotten so used to works for so long, they must be ripped away from them by force.

Based on these reasons, it is more than the right thing to do, it is necessary. We proclaim it as openly and completely as possible, "Faith alone saves, without works!" I only regret that I did not also add the word "*any*," and say, "without *any* works of *any* laws," so that it would have been expressed with absolute clarity. Therefore, it will stay in the New Testament and all the papal donkeys can go crazy over it. They shall not take it from me.

That's enough for now. If God gives me grace, then I'll have more to say in my pamphlet On Justification.

Now, to your second question, whether the departed saints intercede for us, I shall give you only a brief answer now, for I am thinking of publishing a sermon on the angels in which, God willing, I shall treat this point more fully.

First, you know that the papacy not only teaches that the saints in heaven intercede for us, but the saints have also been made gods (even though we cannot know this, because the Scriptures tell us nothing about it). They must be our patrons, on whom we are to call—some of whom never even existed. To each saint, they have attributed a specific power and strength. One controls fire, another water, another pestilence, fever, and all kinds of diseases.

Indeed, now God has pretty much nothing to do—letting the saints work, acting in God's place. The papists themselves are now aware of this heretical practice; they are quietly putting up their pipes, and presently preening and primping themselves with this teaching about the intercession of the saints. I shall defer this subject for the present, but you can bet I shall not forget it and allow their preening and primping to go unpaid for.

Second, you know that there is not a single word of God commanding us to call on either angels or saints to intercede for us, and we have no example of it in the Scriptures. For we find that angels spoke with the fathers and the prophets, but none was ever asked to intercede for them. Even the patriarch Jacob did not ask the angel with whom he wrestled for any intercession, but merely took from him the blessing [Genesis 32:24–29]. We find the exact opposite in the book of Revelation: the angel would not allow himself to be worshipped by John (Revelation 22:9). Thus, the worship of saints shows itself to be nothing but human twaddle, man's own invention apart from the word of God and the Scriptures.

Because in the matter of worship, however, it is not right to undertake anything without God's command—whoever does so is tempting God—it is therefore neither to be advised nor tolerated that folks should call upon the departed saints to intercede for them (or teach others to invoke them). This is to be condemned, and believers should be taught to avoid it. Ergo, I will also not advise it and shackle my conscience with other people's sin. It was not easy for me to escape from the saints, because I was so steeped in it and it nearly drowned me. The light of the gospel now glows so brightly that there is no reason to remain in darkness. We all know what we should do.

In addition, this practice is not only dangerous, it is offensive—to worship without turning to Christ. Because people so easily get used to turning from Christ; they quickly learn to put more confidence in the saints than in Christ himself. Our nature is, in any case, all too prone to flee from God and Christ and to trust in others. Indeed, it is hard enough for us to learn to trust in God and Christ, though we have vowed [in baptism] and are duty bound to do so.

Therefore, we ought not to tolerate this offense, because by it, those of us who are weak and worldly commit idolatry—violating both the first commandment and our baptism. It will be hard enough to redirect our teaching and practice from the saints to Christ—coming to Christ and embracing him properly. There is no need to paint a welcome sign for the devil on the door; he will be there anyway.

In the end, we can be sure that God is not angry with us. And that we remain secure, even if we do not invoke the saints to pray on our behalf, because God never commanded us to do so. God is a jealous God, visiting their iniquities on those who do not keep the commandments [Exodus 20:5–6]. There is no commandment about this and no wrath to terrify us. If we can be certain on our side and their side takes the huge risk of insulting God's word, then why should we move from security to danger, where no word of God sustains, comforts, and saves us in time of need? As it is written, "Whoever loves danger will perish by it" (Ecclesiasticus 3:26), and, as God commands, "You shall not tempt the Lord your God" (Matthew 4:7).

"But," they say, "that way you condemn the whole of Christendom, which has always and everywhere taught thus and so." My response: I understand quite well that the priests and monks try to hide their atrocities in this cloak. They want Christendom to take responsibility for the damage their neglect has wrought. Then, when we say, "Christendom does not err," we are also saying that they, too, do not make mistakes. Then, they are not responsible for any falsehoods or errors, because Christendom teaches thus.

No pilgrimage can be wrong, regardless of how much the devil works in it. No indulgence can be wrong, regardless of how huge the lies are. In a word, there is nothing but holiness there! Therefore, when they say, "It is not a question of who is and who is not condemned," you should reply, "This is a different topic. They are inserting it into the discussion to lead us away from the subject at hand. We are now discussing God's word. What Christendom is or does is another issue. The question here is: What is or is not God's word? What is not God's word does not make Christendom."

We read that in the days of Elijah the Prophet there was apparently no word of God and no worship of God in all Israel. As Elijah says, "Lord, they have slain your prophets and thrown down your altars, and I am left completely alone" (1 Kings 19:10, 14). At that point, King Ahab and others might have said, "Elijah, with talk like that, you condemn the whole people of God." God, however, kept 7,000 to himself (1 Kings 19:18). How was that possible?

Don't you think God could preserve a remnant of believers within the papacy in the present—even though so many priests and monks in Christendom have really only been teachers of the devil and have now gone to hell? Countless children and young people have died in Christ, because even under the Antichrist, Christ powerfully works in baptism, the plain meaning of the gospel in the chancel, the Lord's Prayer, and the Creed. Christ uses these to rescue so many subjects and save his kingdom—without even telling the devil's teachers about it.

And even though Christians have contributed to this papal abomination, the pope's lackeys have not proved they did it on purpose; much less does it prove that they did the right thing. All Christians can err and sin, but God has taught them all to pray in the Lord's Prayer for forgiveness of sins. And God could very well forgive the sins they had to commit unwillingly, unknowingly, and under the compulsion of Antichrist—without saying anything about it to the priests and monks! This, however, can easily be proved, that in all the world there has always been a lot of secret murmuring and complaining against the clergy, that they were not treating Christendom properly. And the papal donkeys have valiantly withstood such murmuring with fire and sword,

down to the present day. This murmuring proves how happy
Christians have been over these abominations, and how right
they have been in doing them!

So, come right out with it you papal lapdogs and say that this
is the teaching of Christendom: those stinking lies you scoundrels and traitors have imposed upon Christendom by force—
murdering so many Christians for such untruths. Each letter of
every papal law points to the truth: the wisdom and consent of
Christendom have never taught these things. They give us nothing except, "We strictly command and teach."[17]

With this as their claim to the Holy Spirit, an oppressive form of
Christendom arose and now continues—robbing the church of the
sacrament and keeping it captive, through no fault of its own.[18] And
the donkeys would palm off on us this intolerable tyranny of their
own sinfulness, as a willing act and example of Christendom—and
so clear themselves.

This is getting too long. This response must suffice for now.
More another time. Forgive this long letter. Christ our Lord be
with us all. Amen.

Martin Luther

Your good friend.

The Wilderness,
September 8, 1530.

Sermon on Luke 2:1–14, Christmas Day (1530)

December 25: Luther preaches one of the five sermons he preached on the Christmas gospel that year in the City Church of Wittenberg. The Reformer loved the Festival of Christmas (preaching sixty sermons on the Christmas gospel in his career). The evocative story, with its poor couple, stable, shepherds, etc., allowed him to tell of God's love in ways that German peasants, living in a preindustrial, agriculturally based world, could readily grasp.

He emphasizes traditional views of the person of Christ here—that Mary's baby was simultaneously truly God and truly human, the savior of the world. However important doctrinal formulations might be, Luther indicates here that intellectual assent to a set of abstractions about Jesus is not all there is to faith. Belief addresses a sinner's deepest needs in a way that general religious propositions cannot.

The Reformer, therefore, speaks about "the second faith"—not simply to accept as information the idea that the child born in Bethlehem is the Lord of the universe, but to trust that this baby is my Lord and Savior. Such faith, such trust of the heart, is an active, dynamic reliance on Christ, engendered by the grace of God revealed at Bethlehem.

This morning we heard about how our Lord Christ was born from the Gospel of St. Luke. We heard how the angel proclaimed who the baby boy was.[1] Now we move on to the content of the angel's message. So far today, you have heard only that the child was born and that he is Lord and Savior. We spoke of the story, how it unfolded, and who the persons in it were. This article of faith is so overwhelming that only a few in our day believe it.

Still, God has preserved it even through those who have not believed it. Look at the monasteries and universities. They consistently conduct disputations and lectures that explore the reality that Christ the Lord, born of Mary, is true human and God. But it went no further than saying and hearing it. But this belief is held by the devil too and the Turks and all the godless among the Christians, and is the kind of belief which everybody believes that it is true but would not die for it, as Eck and many others show today. If they had as much from Christ and the teaching of the gospel[2] as from the devil, they would also think as much of Christ. The Turk too admits that Christ was born of the Virgin Mary, that Mary was an immaculate virgin, and that Christ was more than a man; but the Word of God, as it is given in the gospel, he denies, and yet I fear that the Turk believes more of this article than does the pope. Therefore, it is a high article to believe that this infant, born of Mary, is true God; for nobody's reason can ever accept the fact that he who created heaven and earth and is adored by the angels was born of a virgin. That is the article. Nobody believes it except he who also knows this faith, namely, that this child is the Lord and Savior.

But for whom was Jesus born and for whom is he Lord and Savior? The angels declare that he was born Lord and Savior. The Turks, the pope, and the scholars say the same thing, but only to the extent that it brings in money and honor. But that anyone could say, "to *you* is born," as the angel says, this is the faith which we must preach about. But we cannot preach about it the way we would like. Indeed, who could ever grasp [the full meaning of] these words of the evangelist: "a Savior, who is the Lord," and, "to you!" I know well enough how to talk about it and what to believe about it, just like everyone else. Many folks believe this. They do not doubt this first belief: Christ is the Lord, the Savior, and the virgin's Son. This I too have never doubted.

But if these words are planted no deeper than in my thoughts, then their roots are not strong enough. We might be sure that the angel proclaimed this, but firm faith does not follow. Reason does not understand both sides of this faith: Christ is a human being and Christ is Savior and Lord. This needs to be revealed from heaven. If someone truly has the first faith, then that same person also has the second.

And to whom is this joyful news proclaimed? The fainthearted and those who know the burden of their sins—like the shepherds. The angels proclaim the message to them and let the lords and ladies in Jerusalem sleep. The rich and the powerful don't accept this proclamation. Beyond the first faith, there is also the second faith: Christ is not just the virgin's Son; Christ is also the Lord of the heavenly host and the world's Savior.

For example, anyone—the sacramentarians, the fanatics, the sectarians, and the Turks—can learn empty words. Words that do not come from the heart come only from hearing with the head and go no farther than such hearing. Accurate recall of what they have heard, the memory that they have heard a certain amount of information, is not faith. They do not risk anything. They do not wager their possessions, venture their lives, and bet their honor on what they've heard. We preach Christ, however, for the benefit of all those who belong with those who heard the angels' first proclamation.

Our theology is this: we preach so we might understand the angel's message. Mary bore the child and took him to her breast and nursed him—and the Heavenly Father has a Son who lies in the manger and on his mother's lap. Why did God do all this? Why does Mary guard the child as mothers do? Our reason says: "So that we might idolize and venerate the mother." Mary receives such attention without her knowledge and consent—all the hymns and the reverence and the honor addressed to her as the mother.

The passage, however, does not emphasize the mother's honor. The angel says, "Do not be afraid; for see—I am bringing you good news of great joy for all the people: to you is born this day in the city of David a Savior" (Luke 2:10–11). Therefore, look at the child and his coming into the world. The mother's role cannot be ignored (a birth, obviously, requires a mother), but we try not to focus on her. We do not believe in the mother, but only in the fact that the child was born. The angel wants us to see the baby only. The other angels, as if they wore blinders, saw nothing but the child who was birthed by the virgin. They intended that we see all creation as nothing compared with this child. Therefore, let us not allow anything (like harps, gold, goods, honor, power, etc.) to take precedence over their message.

Even if I acquire the costliest and most precious treasure the world can provide, it will never measure up to the Savior's name. And if the Turkish Empire were ten times stronger than it is now, it could not for one second fix my weakness, to say nothing of the death that threatens me. And even less can such power save me from the smallest sin or from death itself. In my sin, my death, I must let go of all created things. No created thing can help me: sun, moon, stars, all the animals, physicians, emperors, kings, magi, rulers, and whatever else.

When I die, I will see only black and darkness, except for this light that remains for me and fills all heaven and earth: "To you is born this day a Savior" (Luke 2:11). The Savior will help me when everyone else has let me down. When the skies and the stars and all creatures stare at me with horrible hatred, I will stare only at this child and nothing else in heaven and earth.

The light that proclaims my Savior is so brilliant to me that I could even say:

"Mary, you did not bring this child into the world for yourself alone. This baby does not belong to you and you didn't deliver him for yourself, but for me. You are his mother and you rocked him in your arms and you swaddled him warmly and you carried him from one place to another. Yet, I still have an honor that exceeds your honor as his mother. Your honor relates to being the mother of this newborn's physical body. My honor, however, lies here: that you have my treasure. I know no other, neither human nor angelic, who can help me except this child whom you, Oh Mary, hold in your arms."

If one could put out of mind all that is and has; that is, except this child. And if for him everything—money, goods, power, or honor—fades into darkness and he despises everything on earth compared with this child, so that heaven with its stars and earth with all its power and all its treasures become nothing compared to him. When that happens, one would have the true gain and fruit of this message of the angel. And for us the time must come when suddenly all will be darkness and we shall know nothing but this message of the angel: "I am bringing you good news of great joy for all the people: to you is born this day in the city of David a Savior" (Luke 2:10–11).

This, then, is the faith we preach. The Turks and the pope and all the sectarians know nothing about it. Without a doubt, the fanatics have latched on to the angels' words, but we can clearly see they are not serious about it. They receive the Word merely as letters on a page, as the communion vessels receive the body and blood of Christ. The paper does no more than hold something and pass it on to others, yet it remains paper. We copy something from one paper to another paper; from my tongue the Word sounds in your ear, but it does not go to the heart. In the same way, they receive this greatest of treasures to their great harm and still think they are Christians. It's as if the paper were to say: "I certainly have in me the written words, 'to you is born this day the Savior'; therefore, I shall be saved." But then the fire comes and burns up the paper.

Therefore, this is the chief article, which separates us from all the heathen: that you, my friend, may not only learn that Christ, born of the virgin, is the Lord and Savior, but also learn that he is your Lord and Savior, that you may be able to say in your heart: I hear the Word that comes from heaven and says: This child who is born of the virgin is not only his mother's son. I have more than the mother's estate; he is more mine than Mary's, for he was born for me, for the angel said, "To you" is born the Savior. Then ought you to say, Amen, I thank you, dear Lord.

But then reason speaks: Who knows? I believe that Christ, born of the virgin, is the Lord and Savior and he may perhaps help Peter and Paul, but for me, a sinner, he was not born. But even if you believed as much as they did, it would still not be enough, unless there were added to it the faith that he was born for you.

Christ was not born merely in order that I should honor the mother, that she should be praised because he was born of the virgin mother. This honor belongs to none except her and it is not to be despised, for the angel said, "Blessed are you among women!" (Luke 1:28). However, we must not hold her in too high esteem, so we don't deny what is written here: "To you is born this day a Savior." He was not only concerned to be born of a virgin; it was infinitely more than that. As Mary sings in the Magnificat: "He has helped his servant Israel" (Luke 1:54), not "he was born of me and my virginity." She would say that he was born for you and for your benefit, not only for her honor.

Get a hold of yourself! Examine yourself and see whether you are a Christian! If you can sing: The Son, who is proclaimed to be a Lord and Savior, is my Savior; and if you can confirm the message of the angel and say yes to it and believe it in your heart, then your heart will be filled with assurance and joy and confidence, and you will not worry much about even the costliest and best that this world offers. For when I can speak to the virgin from the bottom of my heart and say: O Mary, noble, tender virgin, you have borne a child; this I want more than robes and money, more than my body and life; then you are closer to the treasure than everything else in heaven and earth, as Psalm 73[:25][3] says, "There is nothing upon earth that I desire besides you."

You see how folks rejoice when they receive new robes or ten gold coins. But how many shout and jump for joy when they hear the message of the angel? "To you is born this day a Savior." Indeed, the majority look upon it as a sermon that must be preached, and when they have heard it, consider it a trifling thing, and go away just as they were before. This shows that we have neither the first nor the second faith. We do not believe that the virgin mother bore a son and that he is the Lord and Savior unless, added to this, we believe the second thing, namely, that he is *our* Savior and Lord. When I can say: This I accept as my own, because the angel meant it for me, then, if I believe it in my heart, I shall not fail to love the mother Mary, and even more the child, and especially the Heavenly Father.

If it is true that the child, the one born of the virgin, is mine, then I have no angry God and I must know and feel that there is nothing but laughter and joy in the heart of the Father and no sadness in my heart. For, if what the angel says is true, that Christ is our Lord and Savior, what can sin do to us? "If God is for us, then who is against us?" [Romans 8:31].[4] Greater words than these I cannot speak, nor all the angels and even the Holy Spirit, as is sufficiently testified by the beautiful and devout songs that have been made about it. I do not trust myself to express it. I most gladly hear you sing and speak of it, but as long as no joy is there, so long is faith still weak or even nonexistent, and you still do not believe the angel.

You can see what our papists and Junkers, who have chosen innumerable saviors, have felt about this faith. Indeed, the papists still want to retain the mass, the invocation of saints, and their invented works by which we are to be saved. This is as much as to say, I do not believe in the Savior and Lord whom Mary bore; and yet they sing the words of the angel, hold their triple masses [at Christmas] and play their organs. They speak the words with their tongues but their heart has another savior. And the same is true in the monasteries: if you want to be saved, remember to keep the rule and regulations of Francis and you will have a gracious God! And at the Diet of Augsburg they decided to stick to this. In the name of all the devils, let them stick there! It has been said sufficiently that this Savior lies in the manger. But if there is any other thing that saves me, then I rightly call it my savior. If the sun, moon, and stars save, I can call them saviors. If St. Bartholomew or St. Anthony or a pilgrimage to St. James or good works can save me, then they surely are my savior. If St. Francis, then he is my savior. But then what is left of the honor of the child who was born this day, whom the angel calls Lord and Savior, and who wants to keep his name, which is Savior and Christ the Lord? If I set up any savior except this child, no matter who or what it is or is called, then he is not the Savior. But the text says that he is the Savior. And if this is true—and it is the truth—then let everything else go.

One who hears the message of the angel—and believes it—will be filled with fear, as were the shepherds. Admittedly, it is too much for me to believe that I should come into this treasure without any merit[5] on my part. And yet, that is how it is. Under the papacy, we did not proclaim this message from our pulpits. Indeed, I am afraid it will disappear again. The devil instituted that other message and has continued it through the papacy. All their hymns point to it.

Among the Turks, the devil has eradicated it completely. Therefore, remember it, sing it, and learn it, while there is still time! I am afraid that the time will come when we won't be allowed to hear, believe, and sing this message in public. At present, few if any understand it. Satan allows it to be spoken with the mouth (per the papists), but he would not allow us to proclaim or sing that Christ is born *for you*:

> In our sweet rejoicing, our gladness we are voicing
> In the stable lies the boy, the one who is our hearts' true joy
> From his mother's lap, He shines like a blast
> You are the first, you are the last![6]

What we have said, then, concerns that second faith: we believe that the One who lies on the virgin's lap is *our* Savior (not only that He is Mary's son). Lay hold of this and then give thanks to God, who so loved you that he gave you a Savior. He is yours! As a sign, God sent the angel from heaven to announce this birth. That way, nothing else should be preached except that this child is our Savior and far more precious than heaven and earth. Because of all this, we acknowledge him and receive Him. We confess that Christ is our Savior. In every need, we can call upon him, and believe that he will save us from all misfortune. Amen.

A Regular Way to Pray
(Written for a Good Friend) (1535)

Fall 1534: Luther walks into the barbershop of Peter Beskendorf for a trim, as is his habit for the last twenty years. This time, however, Peter asks the most famous theologian in Europe how he prays. This document is the Reformer's response. Written as an open letter, it shows Luther's long-standing attention to the practical concerns of the Christian life. In many ways, Luther wanted to reform how the church prays, how Christians relate to God, and how believers interpret God's presence in their lives. His response here shows how he viewed this kind of practical Reformation—believers living at the nexus of the Word of God, the catechism, and prayer. Luther recommends that believers regularly "pray" the chief articles of the church's confession as found in the catechism, adapting the ancient practice of *lectio divina* as a lifestyle—even for barbers.

Dear Master Peter: I will try my best to tell how I pray. May our dear Lord give you and everyone the means to do it better. Amen.

First, when I feel cold and miserable praying, because of my duties or thoughts (with the flesh and the devil continually holding us back and hindering us from prayer), I take my Book of Psalms, hurry to my room, or, if the day and time are right, I go to a church—where a community of believers has assembled. As time allows, then, I say quietly to myself and word-for-word the Ten Commandments, the Creed, and, if I have time, some words of Christ or of Paul, or some Psalms, just as a child might do.

It is especially good for prayer to be the first business of the morning and the last at night. Guard yourself carefully against those false, misleading notions that say, "I can wait a little while. I'll pray in an hour; right after I've done this or that thing." Such thoughts distract you from prayer and get you focused on other activities which so capture your attention and involve you that nothing comes of prayer for that day. Of course, it might be that you do have some tasks that are as good as or better than formal prayer, especially in an emergency. St. Jerome supposedly said, "The one who works faithfully prays twice"—and that everything a believer does is prayer.

He can say such things because believers fear and honor God in their work and remember the commandment not to wrong anyone or steal, defraud, or cheat. Such thoughts and such beliefs undoubtedly transform their work into prayer and a sacrifice of praise.

The flipside is also true: a work done without faith is downright cursing. Indeed, whoever works without faith curses twice. Nonbelievers work with no thought of God, but only how to avoid Divine law and exploit their neighbors—thieving, cheating. Can this attitude be anything other than a curse against God and one's neighbor? This is what makes unbelievers' labors and endeavors a double curse—they end up also cursing themselves as scroungers and bunglers. Christ spoke about this continual prayer in Luke 11:9–13, "Pray without ceasing,"[1] because one must unceasingly guard against sin and wrongdoing, something one cannot do unless one fears God and keeps his commandment in mind, as Psalm 1:1 says, "Blessed is the one who meditates upon God's law, day and night."

Let us take care that we do not break the habit of authentic prayer and consider other habits as necessary, when they are not. We could end up lackadaisical and lazy, cool and casual toward prayer. The devil that oppresses us, however, is never lazy or casual. In the meantime, our flesh remains ready and willing to sin and neglect prayer.

If you have warmed up your heart with the Ten Commandments, the Creed, and the words of Christ and you are ready, then kneel or stand with your hands folded and your eyes toward heaven and speak or consider as briefly as you can: "Our Father in Heaven, dear God, I am a poor unworthy sinner. I do not deserve to raise my eyes or hands toward you or to pray. But because you have commanded us all to pray and have promised to hear us and through your dear Son Jesus Christ have taught us both how and what to pray, I come to you in obedience to your word, trusting in your gracious promise. I pray in the name of my Lord Jesus Christ together with all your saints and Christians on earth as he has taught us: 'Our Father in Heaven.'" Then continue through the whole prayer, word-for-word. Then repeat one section or more, as you wish, probably the first request of the Lord's Prayer:

The First Request: "Hallowed be your name," paraphrase, "Yes, Lord God, dear Father, may your name be holy—both in us and in the whole world. Destroy and uproot all the immorality, false worship, and false teaching of the Turk, the papacy; likewise, all the heretics and fanatics who use your name falsely and shamefully; all who use it in vain and horribly blaspheme it. They constantly brag that they teach your word and the laws of the church. However, they use the deceptions and tricks of the devil, in your name. They dreadfully seduce so many poor souls on earth. They even murder and shed innocent blood along the way. They even contend that their persecutions serve you.

"My dear Lord and God, bring them to repentance and restrain them. Convert those whom you can convert, so that they with us and we with them may keep your name holy and praise it—with both true and pure doctrine, as well as with good and holy lives. Restrain those who refuse to be converted so that they can no longer misuse, defile, and dishonor your holy name. Keep them from misleading the poor people. Amen."

The Second Request: "Your kingdom come," paraphrase, "Oh dear Lord, God and Father, you see how worldly wisdom and reason not only profane your name and ascribe the honor due to you to lies and to the devil, but how they also misuse the power, might, wealth, and glory which you have given them on earth for ruling the world and thus serving you. And now they misuse it to oppose your kingdom with their own ambition. They are many and mighty; they plague and hinder the tiny flock of your kingdom who are weak, despised, and few. They will not tolerate your flock on earth and think that by plaguing them they render a great and godly service to you. Dear Lord, God and Father, convert them and defend us. Convert those who are still to become children and members of your kingdom so that they with us and we with them may serve you in your kingdom in true faith and unfeigned love and that from your kingdom which has begun, we may enter your eternal kingdom. Defend us against those who will not direct their might and power away from the destruction of your Reign. When they are dethroned and humbled, they will stop. Amen."

The Third Request: "Your Will be done on earth as it is in heaven." Paraphrase, "Oh dear Lord, God and Father, you know that the world, if it cannot destroy your name or root out your kingdom, is busy day and night. It seeks to destroy your name, word, kingdom, and children with wicked tricks and schemes, strange conspiracies and intrigue. The world huddles together in secret counsel, giving mutual encouragement and support, raging and threatening and going about with every evil intention to destroy your name. Therefore, dear Lord, God and Father, convert them and defend us. Convert those who have yet to acknowledge your goodwill that they with us and we with them may obey your will and for your sake gladly, patiently, and joyously bear every evil, cross, and adversity, and thereby acknowledge, test, and experience your benign, gracious, and perfect will. But defend us against those who in their rage, fury, hate, threats, and evil desires do not cease to do us harm. Make their wicked schemes, tricks, and devices come to nothing so that these may be turned against them, as we sing in Psalm 7[:16]."

The Fourth Request: "Give us this day our daily bread." Paraphrase, "Dear Lord, God and Father, bless us also in this temporal and physical life. Graciously grant us blessed peace. Protect us against war and disorder. Grant to our Sovereign Leader fortune and success against all enemies. Grant wisdom and insight to govern earthly domains peacefully and prosperously. Grant to all kings, princes, and rulers good counsel and the will to preserve their domains and their subjects in tranquility and justice. Especially aid and guide our dear prince N., under whose protection and shelter you preserve us and our lives, so that he may be protected from every danger, and may his rule be blessed. Keep him from evil influences and treacherous people. Grant to

all his subjects grace to serve him loyally and obediently. Grant
to every estate—urban and rural—to be diligent and to display
charity and loyalty toward each other. Give us favorable weather
and good harvest. I commend to you my house and property,
spouse, and child. Grant that I may lead well, supporting and
educating them as a Christian should. Defend us against the De-
stroyer and all the wicked angels who would harm and injure us
in this life. Amen."

The Fifth Request: "Forgive us our trespasses as we forgive
those who trespass against us." Say: "Oh dear Lord, God and
Father, do not judge us, because no one living is justified before
you. Do not count it against us as a sin that we are so unthank-
ful for your ineffable goodness, spiritual and physical, or that
we stray into sin many times every day, more often than we can
know or recognize, Psalm 19[:12]. Do not look upon how good
or how wicked we have been but only upon the infinite compassion which you have bestowed upon us in Christ, your dear Son.
Grant forgiveness also to those who have harmed or wronged
us, as we forgive them from our hearts. They inflict the greatest
injury upon themselves by arousing your anger in their actions
toward us. We are not helped by their ruin; we would much
rather that they be saved with us. Amen." (Anyone who feels unable to forgive, let him ask for grace so that he can forgive; but
that belongs in a sermon.)

The Sixth Request: "And lead us not into temptation." Say:
"Oh dear Lord, Father and God, keep us fit and alert, eager and
diligent in your word and service, so that we do not become
complacent, lazy, and slothful as though we had already achieved
everything. Do this, Lord, and the dreadful devil cannot swoop
down on us, surprise us, and deprive us of your precious word or
stir up strife and factions among us and lead us into other sin
and disgrace, both spiritually and physically. Rather grant us
wisdom and strength through your spirit that we may valiantly
resist him and gain the victory. Amen."

The Seventh Request: "But deliver us from evil." Say: "Oh
dear Lord, God and Father, this wretched life is so full of misery
and calamity, of danger and uncertainty, so full of malice and
faithlessness (as St. Paul says, "The days are evil" [Ephesians
5:16]) that we might rightfully grow weary of life and long for

death. But you, dear Father, know our weaknesses; therefore, help us to pass in safety through so much wickedness and villainy; and, when our last hour comes, in your mercy grant us a blessed departure from this vale of sorrows so that in the face of death we do not become fearful or despondent but in firm faith commit our souls into your hands. Amen."

Finally, mark this, that you must always speak the Amen firmly. Never doubt that God in his mercy will surely hear you and say "Yes" to your prayers. Never think that you are kneeling or standing alone, rather think that the whole of Christendom, all devout Christians, are standing there beside you and you are standing among them in a common, united request which God cannot reject. Do not leave your prayer without having said or thought, "Very well, God has heard my prayer; this I know as a certainty and a truth." That is what Amen means.

You should also know that I do not want you to repeat all these words in your prayer. That would make it nothing but idle chatter and babble, recited word-for-word out of a book (as were the rosaries by the laity and the prayers of the priests and monks). I want your heart to be stirred and guided concerning the thoughts that ought to be comprehended in the Lord's Prayer. These thoughts may be expressed, if your heart is rightly warmed and inclined toward prayer, in various ways and with more words or fewer. I do not bind myself to such words or syllables, but say my prayers in one way today, in another tomorrow, depending upon my mood and feeling. I stay however, as nearly as I can, with the same general thoughts and ideas. It may happen occasionally that I may get lost among so many ideas in one request that I pass on the other six. If such an abundance of good thoughts comes to us we ought to disregard the other petitions, make room for such thoughts, listen in silence, and under no circumstances obstruct them. The Holy Spirit preaches here, and one word of the Spirit's sermon is far better than a thousand of our prayers. Often, I have learned more from one prayer than I might have learned from all kinds of reading and study.

It is vital to prepare the heart for prayer, so you can pray eagerly. As the Preacher says, "prepare yourself; do not be like one who puts the Lord to the test" (Ecclesiasticus 18:23). What else is it but tempting God when your tongue keeps wagging, while your mind has wandered on to other thoughts? Like the priest who prayed: *"Deus in adjutorium meum intende* (Psalm 70:1a ['Be pleased, Oh God, to deliver me!'])—Farmhand, did you unhitch the horses?" and *"Domine ad adjuvandum me festina* (Psalm 70:1b ['Oh LORD, make haste to help me!'])—Maid, get out there and milk the cow." And *"Gloria patti et filio et spiritui sancto* ('Glory to the Father and to the Son and to the Holy Ghost.')—Get going, kid! Stop playing like you're sick!"

I have heard many such prayers in my experience under the papacy; most of their prayers are of this sort. This abomination would be better if they only played at it, as if they cannot or do not care to do better. In my day, I have prayed many such canonical hours myself, regrettably, and so quickly that the psalm or the allotted time came to an end before I even realized whether I was at the beginning or in the middle.

Though not all of them blurt out the words like the above-mentioned cleric did, and mix business and prayer. They do it by the thoughts in their hearts. They jump from one topic to another internally and when it is all over they do not know what they have done or what they talked about. They start with praise and immediately they wander into a fool's paradise. It seems to me that if someone could see what arises as prayer from a cold and inattentive heart he would conclude that he had never seen a more ridiculous kind of buffoonery. But, praise God, it is now clear to me that a person who forgets what he has said has not prayed well. In a good prayer one fully remembers every word and thought from the beginning to the end of the prayer.

A good, attentive barber concentrates his thoughts, attention, and eyes on the razor and hair and does not forget how far he has gotten with his shaving or cutting. If he wants to chat too much or let his mind wander or look somewhere else he might cut his customer's mouth, nose, or even his throat. Thus, if anything is to be done well, it requires the full attention of all one's senses and members, as the proverb says, "Whoever thinks of many things, thinks of nothing and does nothing right." How much more does prayer need focus and singleness of heart, if it is to be a good prayer?

To review: this is the way I pray the Lord's Prayer. To this day, I am drawn to it like a baby to the breast and now, even though

I am old, I am fed by it and can never get enough. This prayer is superb—better even than the Psalms (which I so dearly love). Clearly, a true master wrote and taught it.

That is why it is so sad that all over the world folks babble and chatter this masterful prayer with such irreverence! How many people recite the Lord's Prayer several thousand times during a year, and if they were to keep on "praying" like that for a thousand years, then they would not have tasted nor prayed one "jot and tittle"[2] of it? In a word, the Lord's Prayer is the greatest martyr on earth (as are God's name and God's word). Everybody tortures and abuses it; few take comfort and joy in its proper use.

If I have had time and opportunity to go through the Lord's Prayer, I do the same with the Ten Commandments. I take one part after another and free myself as much as possible from distractions, so I can pray. I divide each commandment into four parts, as I form a garland of four strands. That is, I think of each commandment as, first, instruction, which is what it is intended to be, and consider what the Lord God demands of me so earnestly. Second, I turn it into a thanksgiving; third, a confession; and fourth, a prayer. I do so in thoughts or words such as these:

"I am the Lord your God," etc. "You shall have no other gods before me," etc. Here I earnestly consider that God expects and teaches me to trust him sincerely in all things and that it is his most earnest purpose to be my God. I must think of him in this way at the risk of losing eternal salvation. My heart must not build upon anything else or trust in any other thing, be it wealth, prestige, wisdom, might, piety, or anything else. Second, I give thanks for his infinite compassion by which he has come to me in such a fatherly way and, unasked, unbidden, and unmerited, has offered to be my God, to care for me, and to be my comfort, guardian, help, and strength in every time of need. We poor mortals have sought so many gods and would have to seek them still if he did not enable us to hear him openly tell us in our own language that he intends to be our God. How could we ever—in all eternity—thank him enough! Third, I confess and acknowledge my great sin and ingratitude for having so shamefully despised such sublime teachings and such a precious gift throughout my whole life, and for having fearfully provoked his wrath by

countless acts of idolatry. I repent of these and ask for his grace.
Fourth, I pray and say: "Oh my God and Lord, help me by your
grace to learn and understand your commandments more fully
every day and to live by them in sincere confidence. Preserve my
heart so that I shall never again become forgetful and ungrateful, that I may never seek after other gods or other consolation
on earth or in any creature, but cling truly and solely to you, my
only God. Amen, dear Lord God and Father. Amen."

Next, if I am motivated and time permits, then I also pray the
Second Commandment in four strands: "You shall not take the
name of the Lord your God in vain," etc. I learn first that I need
to honor God's name as holy and beautiful. I ought not use it to
swear, curse, boast, or make myself look good. I must not use
God's name to gain honor or status for myself. Rather, I humbly
invoke God's name as I offer my prayers, praise, and reverence—
letting it be my sole honor and glory that this is my God and that
I am simply a lowly creature and unworthy servant. Second, I
thank God for costly gifts like these: that the Almighty has revealed the Divine name to me and given it to me, that I can celebrate this name and be known as a servant and a creature of
God, that the name of God protects the righteous like a mighty
fortress to which the righteous can flee and find protection, as
Solomon says [Proverbs 18:10]. Third, I confess and acknowledge
that I have grievously and shamefully sinned against this commandment all my life. I have not only failed to invoke, extol, and
honor his holy name, but have also been ungrateful for such gifts
and have, by swearing, lying, and betraying, misused them in the
pursuit of shame and sin. This I bitterly regret and ask grace and
forgiveness, etc. Fourth, I ask for help and strength henceforth to
learn [to obey] this commandment and to be preserved from such
evil ingratitude, abuse, and sin against his name, and that I may
be found grateful in revering and honoring his name.

I repeat here what I previously said about the Lord's Prayer:
during such thoughts, if the Holy Spirit begins to preach in your
heart with rich, enlightening thoughts, honor him by letting go
of this written scheme. Be still and listen to the one who can do
better than you can. Remember what the Spirit says and note it
well and you will behold wondrous things in the law of God, as
David says [Psalm 119:18].

"Remember the Sabbath day, to keep it holy." I learn from this, first, that the Sabbath day has not been instituted for the sake of being idle or indulging in worldly pleasures, but in order that we may keep it holy. However, it is not sanctified by our works and actions, but by the word of God. Our works are not holy. The word of God alone is totally pure and sacred. It sanctifies everything that it encounters—time, place, person, labor, rest, etc. St. Paul says that every creature is consecrated by word and prayer (1 Timothy 4:5) and our works are consecrated through the word. I realize therefore that on the Sabbath I must, above all, hear and contemplate God's word. Thereafter I should give thanks in my own words, praise God for all his benefits, and pray for myself and for the whole world. The one who does this on the Sabbath keeps it holy. The one who fails to do so is worse than the person who works on the Sabbath.

Second, I thank God in this commandment for the great and beautiful divine goodness and grace which has been given to us in the preaching of God's word. And God has instructed us to make use of it, especially on the Sabbath day, for the meditation of the human heart can never exhaust such a treasure. The word of God is the only light in the darkness of this life, a word of life, consolation, and supreme blessedness. Where this precious and saving word is absent, nothing remains but a fearsome and terrifying darkness, error and faction, death and every calamity—the tyranny of the devil himself, as we see each day with our own eyes.

Third, I confess and acknowledge great sin and wicked ingratitude on my part because all my life I have made disgraceful use of the Sabbath and have thereby despised God's precious and dear word in a wretched way. I have been too lazy, listless, and uninterested to listen to it, let alone to have desired it sincerely or to have been grateful for it. I have let my dear God proclaim the word to me in vain, have dismissed the noble treasure, and have trampled it underfoot. God has tolerated this with great and divine mercy and has not ceased in his fatherly, divine love and faithfulness to keep on preaching to me and calling me to the salvation of my soul. For this I repent and ask for grace and forgiveness.

Fourth, I pray for myself and for the whole world that our

gracious Father may preserve us in his holy word and not withdraw it from us because of our sin, ingratitude, and laziness. May God preserve us from factious spirits and false teachers. May God send faithful and honest laborers into the harvest (Matthew 9:38), that is, devout pastors and preachers. May God grant us grace humbly to hear, accept, and honor their words as the word of God and to offer our sincere thanks and praise.

"Honor your father and your mother." First, I learn to acknowledge God, my Creator, and how wonderfully I have been created, body and soul; and how God has given me life through my parents and has given them the desire to care for me, the fruit of their bodies, with all their power. He has brought me into this world, has sustained and cared for me, nurtured and educated me with great diligence, carefulness, and concern, through danger, trouble, and hard work. At this very moment, God, who created me, also protects me, and helps me in countless dangers and troubles. It is as though I am continually being created anew by God—even though the devil does not willingly concede us one single moment of life.

Second, I thank our gracious Creator, who has so richly established and assured us all, in this commandment, to multiply and preserve humanity, at both the household and governmental levels. Without these two institutions or governments the world could not exist a single year. Without government, there can be no peace, and where there is no peace there can be no family; without family, children cannot be begotten or raised, and fatherhood and motherhood would cease to be. It is the purpose of this commandment to guard and preserve both family and state, to admonish children and subjects to be obedient, and to enforce it, too, and to let no violation go unpunished—otherwise children would have disrupted the family long ago by their disobedience, and subjects would have disorganized the state and laid it to waste, for they outnumber parents and rulers. There are no words to fully describe the benefit of this commandment.

Third, I confess and lament my wicked disobedience and sin; in defiance of God's commandment I have not honored or obeyed my parents; I have often provoked and offended them, have been impatient with their parental discipline, have been resentful and scornful of their loving admonition and have rather gone along

with loose company and evil companions. God himself condemns such disobedient children and withholds from them a
long life; many of them succumb and perish in disgrace before
they reach adulthood. Whoever does not obey father and mother
must obey the executioner or otherwise come, through God's
wrath, to an evil end, etc. Of all this I repent and ask for grace
and forgiveness.

Fourth, I pray for myself and for all the world that God would
bestow his grace and pour his blessing richly upon the family
and the state. Grant that from this time on we may be devout,
honor our parents, obey our superiors, and resist the devil when
he entices us to be disobedient and rebellious, and so may we
help improve home and nation by our actions and thus preserve
the peace, all to the praise and glory of God for our own benefit
and for the prosperity of all. Grant that we may acknowledge
these his gifts and be thankful for them.

At this point we should add a prayer for our parents and superiors, that God may grant them understanding and wisdom to
govern and rule us in peace and happiness. May he preserve
them from tyranny, from riot and fury, and turn them to honor
God's word and not oppress it, nor persecute anyone or do injustice. Such excellent gifts must be sought by prayer, as St. Paul
teaches; otherwise the devil will reign in the palace and everything fall into chaos and confusion.

If you are a father or mother, you should at this point remember your children and the workers in your household. Pray
earnestly to the dear Father, who has set you in an office of
honor in his name and intends that you be honored by the name
"father." Ask that he grant you grace and blessing to look after
and support your wife, children, and servants in a godly and
Christian manner. May he give you wisdom and strength to
train them well in heart and will to follow your instruction with
obedience. Both are God's gifts, your children and the way they
flourish, that they turn out well and that they remain so. Otherwise the home is nothing but a pigsty and school for rascals, as
one can see among the uncouth and godless.

The Fifth Commandment: "You shall not kill." Here I learn,
first, that God desires me to love my neighbor, so that I do him
no bodily harm, either by word or action, neither injure nor take

revenge upon him in anger, vexation, envy, hatred, or for any evil reason, but realize that I am obliged to assist and counsel him in every bodily need. In this commandment, God commands me to protect my neighbor's body and in turn commands my neighbor to protect my body. As Sirach says, "He has committed to each of us his neighbor" (Ecclesiasticus 9:14).

Second, I give thanks for such indescribable love, providence, and faithfulness toward me by which God has placed this mighty shield and wall to protect my physical safety. Everyone is bound to care for me and protect me, and I, in turn, must behave likewise toward others. He upholds this command and, where it is not observed, he has established the sword as punishment for those who do not live up to it. Were it not for this excellent commandment and ordinance, the devil would instigate such a massacre among men that no one could live in safety for a single hour—as happens when God becomes angry and inflicts punishment upon a disobedient and ungrateful world.

Third, I confess and lament my own wickedness and that of the world, not only that we are so terribly ungrateful for such fatherly love and solicitude toward us—but what is especially scandalous, that we do not acknowledge this commandment and teaching, are unwilling to learn it, and neglect it as though it did not concern us or we had no part in it. We amble along complacently, feel no remorse that in defiance of this commandment we neglect our neighbor, and, yes, we desert him, persecute, injure, or even kill him in our thoughts. We indulge in anger, rage, and villainy as though we were doing a fine and noble thing. Really, it is high time that we started to deplore and bewail how much we have acted like rogues and like unseeing, unruly, and unfeeling persons who kick, scratch, tear, and devour one another like furious beasts and pay no heed to this serious and divine command, etc.

Fourth, I pray the dear Father to lead us to an understanding of this sacred commandment and to help us keep it and live in accordance with it. May he preserve us from the murderer who is the master of every form of murder and violence. May God grant us grace so that we and all others may treat each other in kindly, gentle, charitable ways, forgiving one another from the heart, bearing each other's faults and shortcomings in a Christian and brotherly manner, and thus living together in true peace and concord, as the commandment teaches and requires us to do.

The Sixth Commandment: "You shall not commit adultery." Here I learn once more what God intends and expects me to do, namely, to live virtuously, decently, and temperately, in thoughts, words, and deeds. I do not violate the honor of my neighbor's spouse or child or servant. More than this, I ought to assist, save, protect, and guard marriage and decency to the best of my ability; I should silence the idle thoughts of those who want to destroy and slander their reputation. All this I am obliged to do, and God expects me not only to leave my neighbor's spouse and family unmolested, but I owe it to my neighbor to preserve and protect his good character and honor, just as I would want my neighbor to do for me and mine in keeping with this commandment.

Second, I thank my faithful and dear Father for his grace and benevolence by which he accepts my husband, son, servant, wife, daughter, maidservant into his care and protection and forbids so sternly and firmly anything that would bring them into disrepute. He protects and upholds this commandment and does not leave violations unpunished, even though he himself should act when someone disregards and violates the commandment and precept. No one escapes him; he must either pay the penalty or eventually atone for such lust in the fires of hell. God desires chastity and will not tolerate adultery. That can be seen every day when the impenitent and profligate are overtaken by the wrath of God and perish miserably. Otherwise it would be impossible to guard one's wife, child, and servants against the devil's filth for a single hour or preserve them in honor and decency. What would happen would be unbridled immorality and beastliness, as happens when God in his wrath withdraws his hand and permits everything to go to wrack and ruin.

Third, I confess and acknowledge my sin, my own and that of all the world, how I have sinned against this commandment my whole life in thought, word, and action. Not only have I been ungrateful for these excellent teachings and gifts, but I have complained about and rebelled against the divine requirement of such decency and chastity, that God has not permitted all sorts of fornication and rascality to go unchecked and unpunished.

He will not allow marriage to be despised, ridiculed, or condemned, etc. Sins against this commandment are, above all others, the grossest and most conspicuous and cannot be covered up or whitewashed. For this I am sorry, etc.

Fourth, I pray for myself and all the world that God may grant us grace to keep this commandment gladly and cheerfully in order that we might live honorably—helping and supporting others in their relationships.

Then I continue with the other commandments as I have time or opportunity or am in the mood for it. As I have said before, I do not want anyone to feel bound by my words or thoughts. I only want to offer an example for those who may wish to follow it; let anyone improve it who is able to do so and let him meditate either upon all commandments at one time or on as many as he may desire. For the mind, once it is seriously occupied with a matter, be it good or evil, can ponder more in one moment than the tongue can recite in ten hours or the pen write in ten days. There is something quick, subtle, and mighty about the mind and soul. It is able to review the Ten Commandments in their fourfold aspect very rapidly if it wants to do so and is in earnest.

The Seventh Commandment: "You shall not steal." First, I can learn here that I must not take my neighbors' possessions or obtain them against their will, either in secret or openly. I must not be misleading or dishonest in business, service, or deed. I ought not to profit by fraud, but must support myself by the sweat of my brow and enjoy my bread in honor. Furthermore, I need to ensure that my neighbor is not defrauded in any way, just as I desire for myself. I also learn in this commandment that God's fatherly oversight protects me with a sort of hedge around my possessions and specifically prohibits others from stealing them. Where that is ignored, God imposes a penalty and has put up gallows and the rope in the hands of the executioner. Where that cannot be done, God Almighty metes out punishment and they become beggars in the end. As the proverbs say, "Unjust gain does not remain," or, "To win by cheating is self-defeating."[3]

Second, I give thanks for his steadfast goodness in that he has given such excellent teachings, assurance, and protection to me and to all the world. If it were not for his protection, not a penny or a crumb of bread would be left in the house.

Third, I confess my sins and ingratitude in such instances where I have wronged, deprived, or cheated anyone in my life.

Fourth, I ask that he grant to me and all the world grace to learn from this commandment, to ponder it, and to become better people, so that there may be less theft, robbery, usury, cheating, and injustice and that the Judgment Day, for which all saints and the whole creation pray, Romans 8[:20–23], shall soon bring this to an end. Amen.

The Eighth Commandment: "You shall not bear false witness." This teaches us, first of all, to be truthful to each other, to shun lies and calumnies, to be glad to speak well of each other, and to delight in hearing what is good about others. Thus a wall has been built around our good reputation and integrity to protect it against malicious gossip and deceitful tongues; God will not let that go unpunished, as he has said in the other commandments.

We owe him thanks both for the teachings and the protection that he has graciously provided for us.

Third, we confess and ask forgiveness that we have spent our lives in ingratitude and sin and have maligned our neighbor with false and wicked talk, though we owe him the same preservation of honor and integrity that we desire for ourselves.

Fourth, we ask for help from now on to keep the commandment and for a healing tongue, etc.

The Ninth and Tenth Commandments: "You shall not covet your neighbor's house." Similarly, "his wife," etc.

First, we learn here that we ought not manipulate our neighbors out of their goods under false pretense of legal claims, or lure away, alienate, or extort what belongs to them. Rather, we should help them keep what is theirs, just as we would want ourselves to be treated. This commandment also protects us against the intricacies and deceptions of devious exploiters. They will be punished in due time. Second, we should thank God. Third, we should contritely and sorrowfully confess to God our sins. Fourth, we should ask for help and strength faithfully to follow divine commandments like these.

These are the Ten Commandments in their fourfold meaning. Each is a school book, a song book, a penitential book, and a prayer book. These four dimensions of meaning help the heart come to itself and grow increasingly fervent in prayer. Take care, however, not to undertake all of this or so much that one becomes weary in spirit. Likewise, a good prayer should not be lengthy or drawn out, but frequent and ardent. It is enough to consider one section or half a section that kindles a fire in the heart.[4] This the Spirit will grant us and continually instruct us in when, by God's word, our hearts have been cleared and freed of outside thoughts and concerns.

Nothing can be said here about the part of faith and Holy Scriptures [in prayer] because there would be no end to what could be said. With practice one can take the Ten Commandments on one day, a psalm or chapter of Holy Scripture the next day, and use them as flint and steel to kindle a flame in the heart.

A SIMPLE EXERCISE FOR CONTEMPLATING THE CREED

If you have more time, or the inclination, you may treat the Creed in the same manner and make it into a garland of four strands. The Creed, however, consists of three main parts or articles, corresponding to the three Persons of the Divine Majesty, as it has been so divided in the Catechism and elsewhere.

The First Article of Creation

"I believe in God the Father Almighty, maker of heaven and earth."

Right here, at the beginning, a great light shines into your heart, if you would allow it. In just a few words, it teaches you who you are, where you came from, and how heaven and earth came to be. All the languages of the world and all of their books cannot describe or put this into words: You are God's creation, God's handiwork, God's good work. In other words, of yourself and in yourself you are nothing. You cannot accomplish anything, you know nothing, you are capable of nothing. What were you a thousand years ago? What were heaven and earth six thousand years ago? Nothing. Like that which will never be created is nothing.

What you are, know, can do, and can achieve is God's creation, as you confess [in the Creed] by word of mouth. Therefore, you have nothing to boast of before God except that you are nothing and he is your Creator who can annihilate you at any moment. Reason is not able to see this light. Many great people have sought to know what heaven and earth, humans and creatures are and have found no answer. But here we declare and faith affirms that God has created everything out of nothing. Creation becomes the soul's garden of pleasure, along whose paths we enjoy the works of God—but it would take too long to describe all that.

In addition, we ought to thank God who, out of Divine kindness, has created us out of nothing and still, out of nothing, provides for our daily needs. God has made us to be such excellent beings with body and soul, intelligence, five senses. God has even ordained us to be masters of earth, of fish, bird, and beast, etc. Here consider Genesis, chapters 1 to 3.

Third, we should confess and lament our lack of faith and gratitude in failing to take this to heart, or to believe it, contemplate it, and acknowledge it. We are more stupid than irrational brutes.

Fourth, we pray for a true and confident faith that sincerely esteems and trusts God to be our Creator, as this article declares.

The Second Article of Redemption

"And in Jesus Christ, his only Son, our Lord," etc.

Again, a great light shines forth and teaches us how Christ, God's Son, has redeemed us from death which, after the creation, had become our lot through Adam's fall and in which we would have perished eternally. Now think: just as in the first article you were to consider yourself one of God's creatures and not doubt it, now you must think of yourself as one of the redeemed and never doubt that. Emphasize one word above all others, for instance, Jesus Christ, *our* Lord. Likewise, suffered for *us*, died for *us*, arose for *us*. All this is ours and pertains to us; that us includes yourself, as the word of God declares.

Second, you must be sincerely grateful for such grace and rejoice in your salvation.

Third, you must sorrowfully lament and confess your wicked unbelief and mistrust of such a gift. Oh, what thoughts will come to mind—the idolatry you have practiced repeatedly, how much you have made of praying to the saints and of innumerable good works of yours which have opposed such salvation.

Fourth, pray now that God will preserve you from this time forward to the end in true and pure faith in Christ our Lord.

The Third Article of Sanctification

"I believe in the Holy Spirit," etc.

This is the third great light which teaches us where such a Creator and Redeemer may be found and plainly encountered in this world, and what this will all come to in the end. Much could be said about this, but here is a summary: Where the holy Christian church exists, there we can find God the Creator, God the Redeemer, God the Holy Spirit, that is, him who daily sanctifies us through the forgiveness of sins, etc. The church exists where the word of God concerning such faith is rightly preached and confessed.

Again you have occasion here to ponder long about everything that the Holy Spirit accomplishes in the church every day, etc.

Therefore, be thankful that you have been called and have come into such a church.

Confess and lament your lack of faith and gratitude, that you have neglected all this, and pray for a true and steadfast faith that will remain and endure until you come to that place where all endures forever, that is, beyond the resurrection from the dead, in life eternal. Amen.

St. Paul's Main Point in His Letter to the Galatians (1535)[1]

Midwinter semester break, 1531–32, Luther sits at his famous table and talks with friends: "The Letter to the Galatians is my dear letter. I trust it completely. It is my Katie von Bora."[2] He spoke these words after a term of delivering lectures on the first four chapters of Galatians. Chapters 5 and 6 were slated for the spring.

As a professor of the Bible, he would lecture on Galatians some six times. And those 1531–32 lectures, transcribed and prepared for publication by colleagues, would become his most substantial commentary on this letter of Paul. He loved Galatians' honesty, clarity, beauty—the kinds of things that attracted him to his wife. Ergo, the Reformer counted St. Paul's letter to the Galatians as one of the most important documents in the Bible, a key to interpreting all of Scripture.

Luther's short preface and orientation to Paul's main point opened the 1535 publication of the lectures Luther had presented during the 1531–32 academic year at Wittenberg. An experienced teacher, Luther makes a classic pedagogical move: at the outset, he shares a summary of his approach and overall understanding of the subject at hand. For the Reformer, interpreting the Bible is an art that starts with the clear meaning of the text and then interprets the unclear parts of the Bible in light of the Scriptures' central message.

PREFACE

In the Lord's name, we return to lecture on Paul's Letter to the Galatians—not because we intend to teach anything new or something you do not know. Indeed, by the grace of God, you are now well acquainted with Paul. However, as I would often warn you, the devil presents a clear and present threat to take the pure doctrine of faith from us and put in its place doctrines of works and human traditions. That is why we must study and listen to this doctrine of faith constantly, and in public. How well we know it or how prudently we have learned it is not the point. Our enemy is not dead. The devil creeps around, wanting to consume us.[3] Plus, our flesh continues to live, with all kinds of temptations that afflict us and dominate us from every side. We can never talk about and teach this doctrine enough. If we lose it and it dies, then, at the same time, all knowledge of truth, life, and salvation disappears and dies. If grace thrives, then every kind of good thrives: faith, praise, and worship of God. Then follows wise insight into all things and true knowledge of our society.

So, let us continue from where we stopped. As Ecclesiasticus 18:7 says, "When human beings have finished, they are just beginning."

THE ARGUMENT OF ST. PAUL'S EPISTLE TO THE GALATIANS

First, we must speak of Paul's line of reasoning, that is, of the issue with which Paul deals in this epistle. It runs like this: Paul wants to establish the doctrine of faith, grace, the forgiveness of sins or Christian righteousness. That way, we may have a perfect knowledge and know the difference between Christian righteousness and all other kinds of righteousness. For righteousness is of different kinds. First, the political righteousness of worldly affairs that concern emperors, princes, philosophers, and lawyers. This includes also the ceremonial righteousness of human traditions that concerns the pope and others who observe various ritual traditions. Parents and teachers may teach this righteousness without danger, because they do not attribute to it any power to make satisfaction for sin, to placate God, and to earn grace; but they teach that these ceremonies are necessary only for moral discipline and for certain observances. There is, in addition to these, yet another righteousness, the righteousness of the Law or of the Ten Commandments, which Moses teaches. We, too, teach this, but after the doctrine of faith.

Over and above all these stands the righteousness of faith or the righteousness of Christians—a righteousness that we distinguish carefully from all the others. We do this because they are all contrary to this righteousness, both because they proceed from the laws of emperors, the traditions of the pope, and the commandments of God, and because they consist in our works and can be achieved by us with "purely natural endowments," [4] as the Scholastics teach, or from a gift of God. For these kinds of the righteousness of works, too, are gifts of God, as are all the things we have.

But this most excellent righteousness, the righteousness of faith, which God imputes to us through Christ without works, is neither political nor ceremonial nor legal nor work righteousness but is quite the opposite; it is a merely passive righteousness, while all the others listed above are active. For here we work nothing, render nothing to God; we only receive and permit someone else to work in us, namely, God. Therefore, it is appropriate to call the righteousness of faith or Christian righteousness "passive." This is a righteousness hidden in a mystery, which the world does not understand. In fact, Christians themselves do not adequately understand it or grasp it when they find themselves tempted. Therefore, we must continually teach and practice it. Anyone who does not cling to it or lay hold of it in afflictions and terrors of conscience[5] cannot stand. For there is no comfort of conscience so solid and certain as is this passive righteousness.

But such is human weakness and misery that in the terrors of conscience and in the danger of death we look at nothing except our own works, our worthiness, and the Law. When the Law shows us our sin, our past life immediately comes to our mind. Then the sinner, in his great anguish of mind, groans and says to himself: "Oh, how damnably I have lived![6] If only I could live longer! Then I would amend my life." Ergo, human reason cannot stop looking at active righteousness, that is, its own righteousness;

nor can it shift its gaze to passive, that is, Christian righteousness, but it simply rests in the active righteousness. So deeply is this evil rooted in us, and so completely have we acquired this unhappy habit! Taking advantage of the weakness of our nature, Satan increases and aggravates these thoughts in us. Then it is impossible for the conscience to avoid being more seriously troubled, confounded, and frightened. For it is impossible for the human mind to conceive any comfort of itself, or to look only at grace amid its consciousness and terror of sin, or consistently to reject all discussion of works. To do this is beyond human power and thought. Indeed, it is even beyond the Law of God. For although the Law is the best of all things in the world, it still cannot bring peace to a terrified conscience but makes it even sadder and drives it to despair. For by the Law sin becomes exceedingly sinful (Romans 7:13).

Therefore, the afflicted conscience has no remedy against despair and eternal death except to take hold of the promise of grace offered in Christ, that is, this righteousness of faith, this passive or Christian righteousness, which says with confidence: "I do not seek active righteousness. I ought to have and perform it; but I declare that even if I did have it and perform it, I cannot trust in it or stand up before the judgment of God on the basis of it. Thus I put myself beyond all active righteousness, all righteousness of my own or of the divine Law, and I embrace only that passive righteousness which is the righteousness of grace, mercy, and the forgiveness of sins." In other words, this is the righteousness of Christ and of the Holy Spirit, which we do not perform but receive, which we do not have but accept, when God the Father grants it to us through Jesus Christ.

As the earth itself does not produce rain and is unable to acquire it by its own strength, worship, and power but receives it only by a heavenly gift from above, so this heavenly righteousness is given to us by God without our work or merit. As much as the dry earth of itself is able to accomplish in obtaining the right and blessed rain, that much can we men accomplish by our own strength and works to obtain that divine, heavenly, and eternal righteousness. Thus we can obtain it only through the free imputation and indescribable gift of God. Therefore, the highest art and wisdom of Christians is not to know the Law, to ignore works and all active righteousness, just as outside the people of God the highest wisdom is to know and study the Law, works, and active righteousness.

It is a marvelous thing and unknown to the world to teach Christians to ignore the Law and to live before God as though there were no Law whatever. For if you do not ignore the Law and thus direct your thoughts to grace as though there were no Law but as though there were nothing but grace, you cannot be saved. "For through the Law comes knowledge of sin" (Romans 3:20). On the other hand, works and the performance of the Law must be demanded in the world as though there were no promise or grace. This is because of the stubborn, proud, and hardhearted, before whose eyes nothing must be set except the Law, in order that they may be terrified and humbled. For the Law was given to terrify and kill the stubborn and to exercise the old being within us. Therefore, the Apostle says law and grace need to be properly distinguished (2 Timothy 2:25ff.).

A faithful and wise pastor is called to apply the Law within its limits. If I teach Law so believers imagine that they justify themselves with it before God, then I exceed the limit of the Law, confusing these two kinds of righteousness, the active and the passive. Muddled thinkers do not properly distinguish between the two.

Furthermore, if I try to reach beyond the old Adam or Eve, then I likewise go beyond the Law—because the flesh (or the old person) is connected to the Law and works. Similarly, the spirit (or the new person) is connected to the promise and to grace. When I see, therefore, that someone is deeply contrite, condemned by the Law, terrified by sin, and longing for comfort, then I take away the Law and active righteousness. The time has come to direct them, through the Gospel, to passive righteousness. Passive righteousness excludes Moses and the Law and welcomes the promise of Christ, who came for anguished and sinful folk.

At this point, one is raised up again and receives hope—no longer under the Law, but under grace. As the apostle says (Romans 6:14): "You are not under law but under grace." How can one not be under the law? The Law does not apply to the new person. The Law had its limits until Christ, as Paul says (Galatians 3:24): "The Law, until Christ . . ." When Christ came, Moses and the Law stopped—no more circumcision, sacrifices, and Sabbath. Even all the prophets stopped.

This is our theology: we teach a precise distinction between these two kinds of righteousness, the active and the passive. That way, morality and faith, works and grace, secular society and community of faith may not be confused. Both are necessary and both need to be kept within their limits. Christian righteousness applies to the new Adam or Eve and the righteousness of the Law applies to the old person (who is born of flesh and blood). Upon this old person, like a beast of burden, a load must be put that will oppress it. The old person cannot enjoy the freedom of the spirit or the freedom of grace unless the new has been put on, which happens through faith in Christ. This, however, does not happen fully until the next life. Then the new Adam or Eve may enjoy the kingdom and the wonderful gift of grace.

Let nobody, then, suppose that we reject or prohibit good works. The papists falsely accuse us of this, because they do not understand what they are saying and what we are teaching. They know nothing except the righteousness of the Law and yet they claim the right to judge a doctrine that is far above and beyond the Law. The old person cannot judge this doctrine. Inevitably, then, they take offense. They are unable to see above the Law and what is higher than the Law offends them greatly.

We set forth two worlds, as it were, one of them heavenly and the other earthly. Into these we place these two kinds of righteousness, which are distinct and separated from each other. The righteousness of the Law is earthly and deals with earthly things; by it we perform good works. But as the earth does not bring forth fruit unless it has first been watered and made fruitful from above—for the earth cannot judge, renew, and rule the heavens, but the heavens judge, renew, rule, and fructify the earth, so that it may do what the Lord has commanded—so also by the righteousness of the Law we do nothing even when we do much; we do not fulfill the Law even when we fulfill it. Without any merit or work of our own, we must first be justified by

Christian righteousness, which has nothing to do with the righteousness of the Law or with earthly and active righteousness. But this righteousness is heavenly and passive. We do not have it of ourselves; we receive it from heaven. We do not perform it; we accept it by faith, through which we ascend beyond all laws and works. "As, therefore, we have borne the image of the earthly Adam," as Paul says, "let us bear the image of the heavenly one" (1 Corinthians 15:49), who is a new person in a new world, where there is no Law, no sin, no conscience, no death, but perfect joy, righteousness, grace, peace, life, salvation, and glory.

Then do we do nothing and work nothing in order to obtain this righteousness? I reply: Nothing at all. For this righteousness means to do nothing, to hear nothing, and to know nothing about the Law or about works but to know and believe only this: that Christ has gone to the Father and is now invisible; that He sits in heaven at the right hand of the Father, not as a Judge but as one who has been made for us wisdom, righteousness, sanctification, and redemption from God (1 Corinthians 1:30); in short, that He is our High Priest, interceding for us and reigning over us and in us through grace. Here one notices no sin and feels no terror or remorse of conscience. Sin cannot happen in this Christian righteousness; for where there is no Law, there cannot be any transgression (Romans 4:15). If, therefore, sin does not have a place here, there is no conscience, no terror, no sadness. Therefore, John says: "No one born of God commits sin" (1 John 3:9). But if there is any conscience or fear present, this is a sign that this righteousness has been withdrawn, that grace has been lost sight of, and that Christ is hidden and out of sight. Where we truly see Christ, however, we experience perfect joy in the Lord and peace in our heart. Then the heart declares: "Although I am a sinner according to the Law, judged by the righteousness of the Law, I still do not despair. I will not die, because Christ lives. Christ is my righteousness, my everlasting, heavenly life. In that righteousness and life I have no sin, conscience, and death. I am indeed a sinner according to the present life and its righteousness, as a son of Adam where the Law accuses me, death reigns and devours me. But above this life I have another righteousness, another life, which is Christ, the Son of

God, who does not know sin and death but is righteousness and eternal life. For His sake this body of mine will be raised from the dead and delivered from the slavery of the Law and sin, and will be sanctified together with the spirit."

Thus as long as we live here, both remain. The flesh is accused, exercised, saddened, and crushed by the active righteousness of the Law. But the spirit rules, rejoices, and is saved by passive righteousness, because it knows that it has a Lord sitting in heaven at the right hand of the Father, who has abolished the Law, sin, and death, and has trodden all evils underfoot, has led them captive and triumphed over them in Himself (Colossians 2:15). In this epistle, therefore, Paul is concerned to instruct, comfort, and sustain us diligently in a perfect knowledge of this most excellent and Christian righteousness. For if the doctrine of justification is lost, the whole of Christian doctrine is lost. And those in the world who do not teach it are either Jews or Turks or papists or sectarians. For between these two kinds of righteousness, the active righteousness of the Law and the passive righteousness of Christ, there is no middle ground. Therefore, he who has strayed away from this Christian righteousness will necessarily relapse into the active righteousness; that is, when he has lost Christ, he must fall into a trust in his own works.

We see this today in the fanatics and sectarians, who neither teach nor can teach anything correctly about this righteousness of grace. They have taken the words out of our mouth and out of our writings, and these only they speak and write. But the substance itself they cannot discuss, deal with, and urge, because they neither understand it nor can understand it. They cling only to the righteousness of the Law. Therefore, they are and remain disciplinarians of works. They cannot move beyond their active righteousness. Thus they remain exactly what they were under the pope. Clearly, they invent new names and new works; but the content remains the same: Turks do different works from the papists, and the papists perform different works from the Jews, and so forth. But although some do works that are more splendid, great, and difficult than others, the content remains the same, and only the quality is different. That is, the works vary only in appearance and in name. For they are still works. And those who do them are not Christians; they are hirelings, whether they are called Jews, Mohammedans, papists, or sectarians.

Therefore, we always repeat, urge, and inculcate this doctrine of faith or Christian righteousness, so that it may be observed by continuous use and may be precisely distinguished from the active righteousness of the Law. (For by this doctrine alone and through it alone is the church built, and in this it consists.) Otherwise we shall not be able to observe true theology but shall immediately become lawyers, ceremonialists, legalists, and papists. Christ will be so darkened that no one in the church will be correctly taught or comforted. Therefore if we want to be preachers and teachers of others, we must take great care in these issues and hold to this distinction between the righteousness of the Law and that of Christ. This distinction is easy to speak of; but in experience and practice it is the most difficult of all, even if you exercise and practice it diligently. For in the hour of death or in other conflicts of conscience these two kinds of righteousness come together more closely than you would wish or ask.

Therefore I admonish you, especially those of you who are to become instructors of consciences, as well as each of you individually, that you exercise yourselves by study, by reading, by meditation, and by prayer, so that in temptation you will be able to instruct consciences, both your own and others, console them, and take them from the Law to grace, from active righteousness to passive righteousness, in short, from Moses to Christ. In affliction and in the conflict of conscience it is the devil's habit to frighten us with the Law and to confront us with our sin and our wicked past, the wrath of God and Divine judgment, hell and eternal death. That way, he would drive us into despair, dominate us, and pluck us from Christ. It is also his habit to set against us those passages in the Gospel in which Christ himself requires works from us and with plain words threatens damnation to those who do not perform them. If here we cannot distinguish between these two kinds of righteousness; if here by faith we do not take hold of Christ, who is sitting at the right hand of God, who is our life and our righteousness, and who makes intercession for us miserable sinners before the Father (Hebrews 7:25), then we are under the Law and not under grace, and Christ is no longer a Savior. Then He is a lawgiver. Then there can be no salvation left, but sure despair and eternal death will follow.

Therefore let us learn diligently this art of distinguishing between these two kinds of righteousness, in order that we may know how far we should obey the Law. We have said above that in a Christian the Law must not exceed its limits but should have its dominion only over the flesh, which is subjected to it and remains under it. When this is the case, the Law remains within its limits. But if it wants to ascend into the conscience and exert its rule there, see to it that you are a good dialectician and that you make the correct distinction. Give no more to the Law than it has coming, and say to it: "Law, you want to ascend into the realm of conscience and rule there. You want to denounce its sin and take away the joy of my heart, which I have through faith in Christ. You want to plunge me into despair, in order that I may perish. You are exceeding your jurisdiction. Stay within your limits, and exercise your dominion over the flesh. You shall not touch my conscience. For I am baptized; and through the Gospel I have been called to a fellowship of righteousness and eternal life, to the kingdom of Christ, in which my conscience is at peace, where there is no Law but only the forgiveness of sins, peace, quiet, happiness, salvation, and eternal life. Do not disturb me in these matters. In my conscience not the Law will reign, that hard tyrant and cruel disciplinarian, but Christ, the Son of God, the King of peace and righteousness, the sweet Savior and Mediator. He will preserve my conscience happy and peaceful in the sound and pure doctrine of the Gospel and in the knowledge of this passive righteousness."

When I have this righteousness within me, I descend from heaven like the rain that makes the earth fertile. That is, I come forth into another kingdom, and I perform good works whenever the opportunity arises. If I am a minister of the Word, I preach, I comfort the saddened, I administer the sacraments. If I am a father, I rule my household and family, I train my children in piety and honesty. If I am a magistrate, I perform the office which I have received by divine command. If I am a servant, I faithfully tend to my master's affairs. In short, whoever knows for sure that Christ is his righteousness not only cheerfully and gladly works in his calling but also submits himself for the sake of love to magistrates, also to their wicked laws, and to everything else in this present life—even, if need be, to burden and danger. For he knows that God wants this and that this obedience pleases Him.

So far the argument of the epistle, which Paul sets forth because of the false teachers who had obscured this righteousness of faith among the Galatians. Against them he asserts his authority and office.

The Smalcald Articles (1538)

In June 1536, Pope Paul III called for a general council to meet the following year, in Mantua, Italy, in May 1537. The Lutherans needed to respond, and Saxon Elector John Frederick took the lead. He decided early not to attend, but he used the council as a pretext to get Luther to write a response that could be delivered to the council. The prince wanted a sort of doctrinal "last will and testament" from the Reformer (who had been aging and in ill health)—a clear summary of the critical issues at stake in his reform program. So in December 1536, Luther began to write this document.

The Lutheran princes (and their court theologians) gathered in Smalcald, Hesse, in February 1537 (whence comes the name, "Smalcald Articles," hereafter SA). However, critical illness kept Luther from the proceedings and the princes decided simply to reaffirm the Augsburg Confession and its Apology (and add a statement on the papacy) as summaries of their collective faith. Although the princes did not discuss or approve Luther's articles at Smalcald, the majority of the assembled theologians did.

The Articles have a Trinitarian structure. Part I confesses ancient ecumenical doctrine, on which both the papal party and the Lutherans had always publicly agreed. Luther uses the creeds of the early church to summarize this consensus. Part II confesses the heart of the biblical message: Christ's atoning work and the human response of faith (a response engendered by God's grace). Luther, then, based on this understanding of the gospel, critiques "the Mass," "Foundations and Monasteries," and "the Papacy." Part III applies the emphases of Part I (the creedal faith of the church) and the emphases of Part II (the evangelical, "Lutheran" reform proposal) to a series of practical issues of faith and practice.

Luther wrote a preface to the Articles in 1538 further outlining his program for reform, made further revisions, and published the Articles that summer. Eventually these articles were formally recognized as such a clear witness to Luther's faith that they gained official confessional status for Lutherans. They were adopted into *The Book of Concord* in 1580.

Before, during, and after the writing of this document, the aging Luther suffered a series of debilitating bouts with illness. He and those around him thought he was dying. Ergo, SA has a testamentary character—Luther's theological bequest to posterity. Although he was to live another eight years, the impetus of his supposed impending death contributed to Luther's interest in crafting SA as one of the clearest and personally most significant writings to flow from his pen.

Postscript: The council called for the spring of 1537, which prompted Luther to write these articles, did not meet until December 1545—as the famous Council of Trent. Trent officially rejected Luther and his followers and set Roman Catholic teaching until the early 1960s.

ARTICLES OF CHRISTIAN DOCTRINE, WHICH SHOULD HAVE BEEN PRESENTED

by our side at the council in Mantua, or wherever else it might happen, and which were to indicate what we could or could not accept or give up, etc. Written by Dr. Martin Luther in the year 1537[1]

THE PREFACE OF DR. MARTIN LUTHER

Pope Paul III called a council to meet at Mantua last year during Pentecost. Afterward, he moved it from Mantua, so that we still do not know where he intends to hold it, or whether he can hold it.[2] We on our side had to prepare for the possibility that, whether summoned to the council or not, we would be condemned. I was therefore instructed to compose and collect articles of our teaching in case there was discussion about what and how far we would and could compromise with the papists, and in which things we thought we had to persist and remain strong.

So, I collected these articles and presented them to our side. They were accepted and unanimously confessed by us, and it was resolved that we should publicly present the articles as our confession of faith—if the pope and his adherents should ever become so bold as seriously, genuinely, and without deception or treachery to convene a truly free council, as would be his duty.

But the Roman court is so dreadfully afraid of a free council and so shamefully flees from the light that it has deprived even those who are on the pope's side of their hope that he will ever tolerate a free council, much less actually convene one. They are understandably greatly offended and are troubled when they observe that the pope would as soon see all of Christendom lost and every soul damned as allow himself or his followers to be reformed even a little and permit limits on his tyranny.

Therefore, I wanted to make these articles available through the public press now, in case I die prior to the council actually happening (as I fully expect and hope). I wanted to do this, both because the scoundrels, who flee from the light and avoid the day, go to such great pains to postpone and hinder the council, and so that those who live and remain after me will have my testament and confession, in addition to the confession that I have already published. I have held fast to this confession until now and, by God's grace, I will continue to hold to it. What should I say? Why should I complain? I am still alive—every day I write, preach, and teach. Yet there are such poisonous people, not only among the adversaries, but false believers who want to be on our side and who dare to use my writings and doctrine directly against me. They let me look on and listen, even though they know that I teach otherwise. They want to conceal their poison with my work and mislead the poor people by my name. What will happen in the future after my death?

Should I indeed respond to everything while I am still living? Certainly. But then again, how can I alone stop all the mouths of the devil, especially those (they are, however, all poisoned) who do not want to hear or pay attention to what we write? Instead, they devote all their energy to one thing: how they, without any shame at all, might twist and corrupt our words and every letter. I will let the devil (or ultimately God's wrath) answer them as they merit it. I often think of the good Gerson, who doubted whether one should make good writings public. If one does not, then many souls that could have been saved are neglected. But if one does, then the devil is there with innumerable vile, evil mouths that poison and distort everything so that it bears no fruit. Yet, what they gain, we see in the light of day. Because, even though they so shamelessly slandered us and wanted to keep the people on their side with their lies, God has continually furthered his work. God has made their number decrease, while our number increases. God allows them to be ruined with their lies and continues to do so.

I have to tell a story: A doctor, sent here to Wittenberg from France, told us openly that his king was persuaded beyond the shadow of a doubt that there was no church, no government, no marriage among us, but rather everything went on in public as with cattle, and all did what they want. Now imagine, how will we be viewed on that day before the judgment seat of Christ, by those who have represented as pure truth such great lies to the king and to foreign lands through their writings? Christ the Lord and judge of us all knows quite well that they lie and have lied. They must hear that judgment. I am sure of that. May God bring to repentance those who can be converted. For the rest, there will be eternal suffering and woe.

I return to the subject: I would indeed very much like to see a true council, so that many matters and people might be helped. Not that we need it, for through God's grace our churches are now enlightened and supplied with the pure word and right use of the sacrament, an understanding of the various created orders, and true works. We do not ask, therefore, for a council for our sakes. In such matters, we know there is nothing good to hope for or expect from the council. Rather, we see in bishoprics everywhere so many parishes empty and deserted that our hearts are ready to break because of it. And yet, neither bishops nor cathedral canons ask how the poor people live or die—people for whom Christ died. And should not these people hear this same Christ speak to them as the true "shepherd with his sheep?"[3] It horrifies and frightens me that Christ might cause a council of angels to descend upon Germany and totally destroy us all like Sodom and Gomorrah, because we mock him so blasphemously with the council.[4]

In addition to such necessary concerns of the church, there are also innumerable, important things in the secular estate that need improvement: There is disunity among the princes and the estates. Greed and unfair lending have crashed over us like a great flood. And now they have even attained a semblance of legality. We've been inundated by recklessness; lewdness; extravagant dress; gluttony; gambling; pompousness; all kinds of vice and wickedness; disloyalty of servants, workers, subjects, and artisans of all kind; extortion by the peasants (Who can count all such offenses?). Now, no one could set things right again with ten councils and twenty imperial diets. If attendees at the council were to deal with the chief concerns in the spiritual and secular orders that are against God, then their hands would be so full that they would indeed forget the child's games and foolish play of long gowns, large shaved heads,[5] broad cinctures, bishop's and cardinal's hats, crosiers, and similar sleight of hand. If we already had fulfilled God's command and precept in the spiritual and secular orders, then we would have found enough time to reform food, clothes, shaved heads, and chasubles. But if we swallow such camels and strain out gnats, let logs stand and dispute about specks, then we might also be satisfied with such a council.

I, therefore, have provided only a few articles, because we already have received from God so many mandates to carry out in the church, in the government, and in the home that we can never fulfill them. What help is it to make many decretals and regulations in the council, especially if we neither honor nor observe these chief things commanded by God? It is as if we expect God to honor our magic tricks while we trample his real commands underfoot. But our sins burden us and do not permit God to be gracious to us, because we also do not repent and want to defend every abomination.

oh dear Lord Jesus Christ, hold a council and redeem your people through your glorious return! The pope and his people are lost. They do not want you. Help us who are poor and miserable, who sigh[6] to you and earnestly seek you, according to the grace you have given us through your Holy Spirit, who with you and the Father lives and reigns, forever praised. Amen.

PART I

The first part of the articles is about the lofty articles of the divine majesty, namely:

1. That Father, Son, and Holy Spirit, three distinct persons in one divine essence and nature, is one God, who created heaven and earth, etc.

2. That the Father was begotten by no one, the Son was begotten by the Father, the Holy Spirit proceeds from the Father and the Son.

3. That neither the Father nor the Holy Spirit, but the Son became a human being.

4. That the Son became a human being (i.e., "incarnate") in this way: he was conceived by the Holy Spirit without male participation and was born of the pure, holy Virgin Mary. After that, he suffered, died, was buried, descended to hell, rose from the dead, ascended to heaven, is seated at the right hand of God, in the future will come to judge the living and the dead, etc., as the Apostles' and the Athanasian Creeds and the common children's catechism teach.[7]

These articles are not matters of dispute or conflict, for both sides confess them. We do not need, therefore, to deal with them at greater length.

PART II

The Second Part is about the articles that pertain to the office and work of Jesus Christ, or to our redemption.

The First Article: Here is the first and chief article:

That Jesus Christ, our God and Lord, "was handed over to death for our trespasses and was raised for our justification" (Romans 4:25); and he alone is "the Lamb of God, who takes away the sin of the world" (John 1:29); and "the Lord has laid on him the iniquity of us all" (Isaiah 53:6); furthermore, "All have sinned," and "they are now justified without merit by his grace, through the redemption that is in Christ Jesus . . . by his blood" (Romans 3:-23–25). Now because this must be believed and may not be obtained or grasped otherwise with any work, law, or merit, it is clear and certain that this faith alone justifies us, as St. Paul says in Romans 3:28, 26: "For we hold that a person is justified by faith apart from works prescribed by the law"; and also, "that God alone is righteous and justifies the one who has faith in Jesus." Nothing in this article can be conceded or given up, even if heaven and earth or whatever is transitory passed away. As St. Peter says in Acts 4:12: "There is no other name . . . given among mortals by which we must be saved." "And by his bruises we are healed" (Isaiah 53:5). Upon this article stands all that we teach and practice against the pope, the devil, and the world. We must, therefore, be completely certain and have no doubt about it. Otherwise everything is lost, and the pope and the devil and whatever opposes us will gain victory and be proved right.

The Second Article:

That the mass under the papacy must be the greatest and most terrible abomination, as it directly and violently opposes this chief article. Despite this, it has been the supreme and most precious of all the various papal idolatries. For it is held that this sacrifice or work of the mass (even when performed by a rotten scoundrel) delivers people from sin both here in this life and beyond in purgatory, even though the Lamb of God alone should and must do this, as mentioned above. Nothing is to be conceded or compromised in this article either, because the first article does not allow it. And wherever there might be reasonable papists, a person would want to speak with them in a friendly way like this: "Why do you cling so tenaciously to the mass?"

1. After all, it is nothing but a mere human invention, not commanded by God. And we may discard all human inventions, as Christ says in Matthew 15:9: "In vain do they worship me with human precepts."

2. It is not necessary and you can easily omit it without sin or danger.

3. You can receive the sacrament in a much better and more blessed way (indeed, it is the only blessed way) when you receive it per Christ's institution. Why do you want to force the world into misery and destitution for the sake of unnecessary fabrications—especially when the sacrament can be had in another better and more blessed way? Let it be publicly preached to the people that the mass, as a human trifle, may be discontinued without sin and that no one will be damned who does not observe it but may in fact be saved in a better way without the mass. What do you want to bet that the mass falls of its own accord, not only among the mad mob but also among all upright, Christian, reasonable, and God-fearing hearts? How much more would this be the case were they to hear that the mass is a dangerous thing, fabricated and invented without God's Word and will?

4. Because such innumerable, unspeakable abuses have arisen throughout the whole world with the buying and selling of masses, they should properly be abandoned (if only to curb such abuses), even if in and of themselves masses did contain something useful and good. How much the more should they be abandoned in order to guard forever against such abuses, since the masses are completely unnecessary, useless, and dangerous, and everything can be had in a more necessary, useful, and certain manner without the mass.

5. As the canon of the mass and all the handbooks say, the mass is and can be nothing but a human work (even a work of rotten scoundrels), performed in order that

individuals might reconcile themselves and others to God, acquire the forgiveness of sins, and merit grace. (When the mass is observed in the very best possible way, it is observed with these intentions. What purpose would it otherwise have?) Thus the mass should and must be condemned and repudiated, because it is directly contrary to the chief article, which says that it is not an evil or devout servant of the mass with his work, but rather the Lamb of God and the Son of God, who takes away our sin (John 1:29).

If some want to justify their position by saying that they want to celebrate mass by themselves, for the sake of their own piety, they cannot be taken seriously. For if they seriously desire to commune, then they would do so with certainty and in the best way—by using the sacrament administered according to Christ's institution. On the contrary, to commune oneself is a human notion, uncertain, unnecessary, and even forbidden. Such people also do not know what they are doing, because they are following a false human notion and innovation without the sanction of God's Word. Thus it is not right (even if everything else were otherwise in order) to use the common sacrament of the church for one's own devotional life and to play with it according to one's own pleasure apart from God's Word and outside the church community.

This article on the mass will be the decisive issue in the council because, even if they were able to give in to us on every other article, they could not give in on this one. As Campeggio said at Augsburg, he would sooner allow himself to be torn to pieces before he would abandon the mass.[8] In the same way I, too, with God's help, would sooner allow myself to be burned to ashes before I would allow a servant of the mass (whether good or evil) and his work to be equal to or greater than my Lord and Savior Jesus Christ. Thus, we are and remain eternally divided and opposed to one another. They understand if the mass falls, the papacy falls. Before they would allow that to happen, they would kill us all—if they could do it.

Besides all this, the mass, like a dragon's tail, has produced the excrement of so many idolatries (along with its accompanying maggots).[9] For example:

First, purgatory. Here they "traded" in purgatory, with masses for the dead and vigils after seven days, thirty days, and a year, and, finally, with the "Common Week," All Souls' Day, and Soul Baths,[10] so that the mass is only used on behalf of the dead, although Christ instituted the sacrament only for the living. Purgatory, therefore, with all its pomp, requiem masses, and transactions, is to be regarded as an apparition of the devil. For it, too, is against the chief article that Christ alone (and not human works) is to help souls. Besides, concerning the dead we have received neither command nor instruction. For these reasons, it may be best to abandon it, even if it were neither error nor idolatry.

At this point, the papists cite Augustine and some of the Fathers, who have supposedly written about purgatory. They suppose that we do not see why and how they use such passages. St. Augustine does not write that there is a purgatory and cites no passage of Scripture that persuades him to adopt such a position. Instead, he leaves it undecided whether there is a purgatory or not and says simply that his mother asked to be remembered at the altar, or sacrament. Now all of this is nothing but the human opinions of a few individuals, who can establish no article of faith (something God alone can do). But our papists employ such human words in order to make people believe in their shameful, blasphemous, accursed fairs of masses offered up into purgatory for the souls of the dead, etc. They will never prove such a thing from Augustine. When they have given up their purgatorial "mass fairs" (something Augustine never dreamed of), then we will discuss with them whether St. Augustine's word, lacking support from Scripture, may be tolerated and whether the dead may be commemorated at the sacrament. It will not do to formulate articles of faith on the basis of the holy Fathers' works or words. Otherwise, their food, clothes, houses, etc., would also have to be articles of faith—as has been done with relics. This means that the Word of God—and no one else, not even an angel—should establish articles of faith.

Second, because of their teaching on the mass, evil spirits have caused so much mischief—appearing as souls of the departed and demanding masses, vigils, pilgrimages, and other alms with unspeakable lies and cunning. We all had to hold these matters as articles of faith and live by them. The pope confirms this along with the mass and all the other horrors. Here, too, there is no room for compromise or concession.

Third, pilgrimages. Masses, the forgiveness of sins, and God's grace were also sought here, for the mass ruled everything. Now, it is certain that, lacking God's Word, such pilgrimages are neither commanded nor necessary. For we can have forgiveness and grace in a much better way and can omit pilgrimages without any sin or danger. Why would one neglect one's own parish, God's Word, spouse and child, etc.—which are necessary and commanded—and run after unnecessary, uncertain, shameful, devilish will-o'-the-wisps? Only because the devil has driven the pope into praising and confirming such practices, so that the people routinely deserted Christ for their own works and (worst of all!) became idolatrous. Apart from this, they are not necessary, optional, silly, uncertain, and even harmful. Therefore here, too, there is nothing to concede or give up, etc. Let it be preached that it is unnecessary as well as dangerous, and then see where pilgrimages stand.

Fourth, fraternities. The monasteries, foundations, and lower clergy have assigned and conveyed to themselves (by lawful and open sale) all masses, good works, etc., for both the living and the dead. They are, however, nothing more than human trifles, lacking God's Word, completely unnecessary, and not commanded. And, they are contrary to the first article of redemption, and therefore they can in no way be tolerated.

Fifth, relics. Here so many open lies and foolishness are based on the bones of dogs and horses. Because of such shenanigans— at which even the devil laughs—they should have long ago been condemned, even if there were something good in them. In addition, they lack God's Word, being neither commanded nor advised, and are a completely unnecessary and useless thing. The worst part is that relics, like the mass, etc., were also to have produced an indulgence and the forgiveness of sin as a good work and act of worship.

Sixth, those precious indulgences belong here, which are given (for money, of course) to both the living and the dead. The accursed Judas, or pope, sells the merits of Christ together with the superabundant merits of all the saints and the entire church, etc. All of this is not to be tolerated, not only because it is without God's Word, not necessary, and not commanded, but because it is contrary to the first article. Christ's merit is not acquired through our work or pennies, but through faith by grace, without any money and merit—not by the authority of the pope, but rather by preaching a sermon, that is, God's Word.

The Invocation of the Saints

The invocation of saints is also one of the abuses of the Antichrist that is in conflict with the first, chief article and that destroys the knowledge of Christ. It is neither commanded nor recommended, has no precedent in the Scripture, and—even if it were a precious possession, which it is not—we have everything a thousand times better in Christ.

Although the angels in heaven pray for us (as Christ himself also does), and in the same way also the saints on earth and perhaps those in heaven pray for us, it does not follow from this that we ought to invoke angels and saints; pray to them; keep fasts and hold festivals for them; celebrate masses, make sacrifices, establish churches, altars, or worship services for them; serve them in still other ways; and consider them as helpers in time of need, assign all kinds of assistance to them, and attribute a specific function to particular saints, as the papists teach and do. This is idolatry. Such honor belongs to God alone. As a Christian and saint on earth, you can pray for me, not only in one kind of need but in all necessities. However, on account of that, I ought not pray to you, invoke you, hold a festival, keep a fast, make a sacrifice, perform a mass in your honor, and put my faith in you for salvation. There are other good ways I can honor, love, and thank you in Christ. Now if such idolatrous honor is taken away from the angels and dead saints, then the honor that remains will do no harm and will indeed soon be forgotten. When physical and spiritual benefit and help are no longer expected, then the saints will be left in peace, both in the grave and in heaven. For no one will long remember, esteem, or honor them simply out of love with no hope of return.

In summary, then, we cannot tolerate and must condemn what the mass is, what has resulted from it, and what is connected to it, so that we may retain the holy sacrament in purity and with certainty and may use and receive it with faith according to the institution of Christ.

The Third Article:

That foundations and monasteries, established in former times with good intentions for the education of learned people and decent women, should be returned to such use so that we may have pastors, preachers, and other servants of the church, as well as other people necessary for earthly government in cities and states, and also well-trained young women to head households and manage them. Where they are not willing to serve in this way, it is better if they were abandoned or torn down than that they—with their blasphemous worship, devised by human beings—should be regarded as something better than everyday Christian walks of life and the offices and orders established by God. For all of this, too, is contrary to the first and chief article concerning redemption in Jesus Christ. Furthermore, they (like all other human inventions) are also not commanded, not necessary, not useful—while causing dangerous and futile effort besides. The prophets call such worship *aven*, which means, in Hebrew, "wasted effort."

The Fourth Article:

The pope is not the head of all Christendom "by divine right" or on the basis of God's Word, because that belongs only to the one who is called Jesus Christ. Instead, the pope is only bishop, or pastor, of the church at Rome and of those who willingly or through a human institution (that is, through secular authority) have joined themselves to him in order to be Christians alongside him as a brother and companion but not under him as a lord—as the ancient councils and the time of St. Cyprian demonstrate. But now, however, no bishop dares to call the pope "brother," as at that time, but instead must address him as his "most gracious lord," as if he were a king or emperor. We will not, should not, and cannot impose this upon our consciences. But whoever wants to do so does it without our support.

It follows from this that everything the pope has undertaken and done on the basis of such false, offensive, blasphemous, arrogant power was and still is a purely diabolical affair and business, which corrupts the entire holy Christian church (however much it depends on him) and negates the first, chief article on redemption by Jesus Christ. (The only exception concerns the area of political government, where God sometimes allows much good to come to a people through a tyrant or scoundrel.)

All his bulls and books are available, in which he roars like a lion (the angel of Revelation 10:3 indicates this) that Christians cannot be saved unless they are obedient and submit to him in all things—what he wills, what he says, what he does. This is as much to say: "Even if you believe in Christ and have everything that is necessary for salvation in him, nevertheless it is nothing and all in vain unless you consider me your god and are subject and obedient to me." Yet, it is obvious that the holy church was without a pope for over five hundred years, at least, and even today the Greek church and many churches that use other languages have never been under the pope and still are not. Thus, as has often been said, it is a human fiction. It is not commanded. There is no need for it. And it is useless. The holy Christian church can survive quite well without such a head. It would have been much better off if such a head had not been raised up by the devil. The papacy is not necessary in the church, because it exercises no Christian office, and thus the church must continue to endure without the pope.

Suppose for the sake of argument that the pope wanted to renounce his claim; suppose that he was not the supreme head of the church "by divine right," that is, by God's command. Suppose instead, in order that the unity of Christendom might be better preserved against sects and heretics, that there must be a head to whom all others adhere. Now such a head would be elected by the people, and it would remain incumbent upon their power and choice whether to change or depose this head. This is virtually the way the council at Constance handled the popes, deposing three and electing the fourth. Now just suppose, I say, that the pope and the see of Rome relinquished their authority and accepted this view (which, of course, is impossible because he would have to suffer the overthrow and destruction of his entire government and position with all his laws and books; in short, he cannot do it).

Even if he could, Christianity would not be helped in any way, and there would be even more sects than before, because they would not have to submit to such a head on the basis of God's command but rather as a matter of human goodwill. He would rather easily and quickly be despised, until finally he would not have even one adherent. He would also no longer have to reside in Rome or at some other set place, but wherever and in whatever church God provided a man suitable for the position. Oh, that would be a complicated and disorganized state of affairs!

Therefore, the church cannot be better ruled and preserved than if we all live under one head, Christ, and all the bishops—equal according to the office (although they may be unequal in their gifts)—keep diligently together in unity of teaching, faith, sacraments, prayers, and works of love, etc. So St. Jerome writes that the priests at Alexandria ruled the churches together in common, as the apostles also did and afterward all bishops throughout Christendom, until the pope elevated himself over them all.

This business shows overwhelmingly that he is the true Antichrist who has raised himself over and set himself against Christ, because the pope will not let Christians be saved without his authority (which amounts to nothing, since it is not ordered or commanded by God). This is precisely what St. Paul calls "setting oneself over God and against God." Neither the Turks nor the Tartars, despite being great enemies of the Christians, do any such thing. They allow whoever desires it to have faith in Christ, and they receive physical tribute and obedience from the Christians.

The pope, however, will not allow faith in Christ to be enough, but asserts instead that anyone who is obedient to him will be saved. We are unwilling to do this, even if we have to die in God's name on account of it. All of this stems from his claim to be head of the Christian church "by divine right." Therefore he had to set himself up as equal to and even greater than Christ and let himself be praised first as the head of the church, then as its lord, and finally as lord of the entire world and nothing short of an earthly god—until he even dared to command the angels in heaven.

When the pope's teaching is distinguished from that of the Holy Scriptures or compared to them, it turns out that the pope's teaching—at its very best—is taken from the imperial, pagan law and teaches about secular dealings and judgments, as his decretals show. Beyond this, it gives instruction about ceremonies involving churches, vestments, foods, personnel, along with child's play, imaginary work, and fool's work without limit. But in all these things, there is absolutely nothing about Christ, faith, and God's commandments.

Finally, that the pope in contradiction to God promotes his lies about masses, purgatory, monastic life, one's own works, and worship (which are the essence of the papacy) is nothing but the devil through and through. He damns, slays, and plagues all Christians who do not exalt and honor his abominations above all things. Therefore, as little as we can worship the devil himself as our lord or god, so we cannot allow his apostle, the pope or Antichrist, to govern as our head or lord. His papal government is characterized by lying and murder and the eternal ruin of body and soul, as I have demonstrated in many books.

These four articles will furnish them with enough to condemn at the council. They neither can nor will concede to us the tiniest fraction of these articles. Of this we may be certain, and we must rely upon the hope that Christ our Lord has attacked his enemies and will carry the day, both by his Spirit and at his return. Amen.

At the council, we will not stand (as at Augsburg) before the emperor or the secular authority, who issued a most gracious summons and allowed the matters to be heard in a fair manner. We will stand before the pope and the devil himself, who does not intend to listen but only to damn us on the spot, to murder us, and to force us into idolatry. Therefore here we must not kiss his feet or say, "You are my gracious lord." Rather, we ought to speak as the angel spoke to the devil in Zechariah 3:2, "The Lord rebuke you, O Satan!"

PART III

We could discuss the following matters or articles with learned, reasonable people or among ourselves. The pope and his kingdom do not value these things very much, because the conscience means nothing to them; money, honor, and power mean everything.

Concerning Sin:

Here we must confess (as St. Paul says in Romans 5:12) that sin comes from that one human being, Adam, through whose disobedience all people became sinners and subject to death and the devil. This is called the original sin, or the chief sin.

The fruits of this sin are the subsequent evil works, which are forbidden in the Ten Commandments, such as unbelief, false belief, idolatry, being without the fear of God, presumption, despair, blindness, and, in short, not knowing or honoring God. Beyond that, there is lying, swearing [falsely] by God's name, not praying or calling on God's name, neglect of God's Word, being disobedient to parents, murdering, behaving promiscuously, stealing, deceiving, etc.

This inherited sin has caused such a deep, evil corruption of nature that reason does not comprehend it; rather, it must be believed on the basis of the revelation in the Scriptures (Psalm 51:5 and Romans 5:12; Exodus 33:20; Genesis 3:6ff.). Therefore, the Scholastic theologians have taught pure error and blindness against this article:

1. That after the fall of Adam the natural powers of the human being have remained whole and uncorrupted and that each human being possesses by nature sound reason and a good will, as the philosophers teach.

2. That the human being has a free will, either to do good and reject evil or to reject good and do evil.

3. That the human being is able, by using natural powers, to keep and carry out every command of God.

4. That human beings are able, using natural powers, to love God above all things and their neighbors as themselves.

5. That if human beings do as much as is in their power, then God will certainly give grace to them.

6. That if someone wants to go to the sacrament, it is not necessary to have a proper intention to do good, but it is enough for that person not to have an evil intention to commit sin, because human nature is so completely good and the sacrament is so powerful.

7. That there is no basis in Scripture that the Holy Spirit with his grace is necessary for performing a good work.

These and many similar things have arisen from a lack of understanding and ignorance about both sin and Christ our Savior. We cannot tolerate these purely pagan teachings, because, if these teachings were right, then Christ has died in vain. For there would be no defect or sin in humankind for which he had to die—or else he would have died only for the body and not for the soul, because the soul would be healthy and only the body would be subject to death.

Concerning the Law:

Here we maintain that the law was given by God, in the first place, to curb sin by means of the threat and terror of punishment and also by means of the promise and offer of grace and favor. All of this failed because of the evil that sin worked in humankind. Some, who are enemies of the law because it prohibits what they want to do and commands what they do not want to do, became worse because of it. On account of this, insofar as they are not restrained by punishment, they act against the law even more than before. These are the coarse, evil people who do evil whenever they have an opportunity. Others become blind and presumptuous, imagining that they can and do keep the law by their own powers (as has just been said above about the Scholastic theologians). This attitude produces hypocrites and false saints.

The foremost office or power of the law is that it reveals inherited sin and its fruits. It shows all creatures into what utter depth the human nature has fallen and how completely corrupt it is. The law must say to them that they neither have nor respect any god or that they worship foreign gods. This is something that they would not have believed before without the law. Thus they are terrified, humbled, despondent, and despairing. They anxiously desire help but do not know where to find it; they start to become enemies of God, to murmur, etc. This is what is meant by Romans 4:15: "The law brings wrath," and Romans 5:20, "Sin becomes greater through the law."

Concerning Repentance:

The New Testament retains this office of the law and teaches it, as Paul does and says, in Romans 1:18: "The wrath of God is revealed from heaven against all" people. Also Romans 3:19–20, "So that . . . the whole world may be held accountable to God" and "no human being will be justified in his sight"; and Christ says in John 16:8, the Holy Spirit "will convict the world of sin."

Now this is the thunderbolt of God, by means of which he destroys both the open sinner and the false saint and allows no one to be right but drives the whole lot of them into terror and despair. This is the hammer of which Jeremiah speaks: "My word is a hammer that breaks a rock in pieces" (Jeremiah 23:29). This is not "active contrition," a contrived remorse, but "passive contrition," true affliction of the heart, suffering, and the pain of death.

This is really what it means to begin true repentance. Here a person must listen to a judgment such as this: "You are all of no account—whether you appear publicly to be sinners or saints. You must all become something different from what you are now and act in a different way, no matter who you are now and what you do. You may be as great, wise, powerful, and holy as you could want, but here no one is righteous," etc.

To this office of the law, however, the New Testament immediately adds the consoling promise of grace through the gospel. This we should believe. As Christ says in Mark 1:15, "Repent, and believe in the good news." This is the same as, "Become and act otherwise, and believe my promise." Even before Jesus, John the Baptizer was called a preacher of repentance—but for the purpose of the forgiveness of sins. That is, John was to convict them all and turn them into sinners, so that they would know how they stood before God and would recognize themselves as lost people. In this way they were to be prepared for the Lord to receive grace, to await and accept from him forgiveness of sins. Jesus himself says in Luke 24:47: "You must preach repentance and forgiveness of sins in my name to the whole world."

But where the law exercises such an office alone, without the addition of the gospel, there is death and hell, and the human creature must despair, like Saul and Judas. As St. Paul says: "The law kills through sin." Moreover, the gospel does not give consolation and forgiveness in only one way—but rather through the Word, sacraments, and the like (as we shall hear), so that with God there is truly rich redemption from the great prison of sin (Psalm 130:7–8).

Now we must compare the false penance of the sophists with true repentance, in order that they both might be better understood.

Concerning the False Penance of the Papists:

It was impossible for them to teach correctly about penance, because they do not recognize what sin really is. As mentioned above, they do not hold the correct position about original sin at all. Instead they say that the natural powers of humankind have remained whole and uncorrupted; that reason can teach correctly and the will can rightly act according to it; that God surely gives his grace if human beings do as much as is in their power, according to human free will.

From this it necessarily follows that they only do penance for actual sins, such as evil thoughts to which they consent (because evil impulses, lusts, and inclinations were not sin), evil words, and evil works (which the free will could well have avoided).

They divide such penance into three parts—contrition, confession, and satisfaction—with this comfort and pledge: that the person who is truly contrite, goes to confession, and makes satisfaction by these actions merits forgiveness and pays for sins before God. In this way, they directed the people who come to penance to place confidence in their own works. From this came the phrase that was spoken from the pulpit when they recited the general confession on behalf of the people: "Spare my life, Lord God, until I do penance and improve my life." Here there was no Christ. Nothing was mentioned about faith, but instead people hoped to overcome and blot out sin before God with their own works. We also became priests and monks with this intention: we wanted to set ourselves against sin.

They handled contrition like this: Because no one could recall every sin (particularly those committed during an entire year), they resorted to the following loophole: if believers remembered some unknown sins later, then they should also be contrite for them and confess them, etc. Meanwhile, they were commended to God's grace.

Moreover, because no one knew how much contrition one needs for it to suffice before God, they offered this consolation: Whoever could not have *contritio* (contrition) should have *attritio*, what I might call a halfway or beginning contrition. However, they have not understood either word, and they still know as little about what is being said as I do. Such *attritio* was then counted as *contritio* when people went to confession.

And if it happened that some said they could not repent or be sorrowful for their sins (as might happen in fornication or revenge, etc.), they were asked whether they at least wished or really desired to have contrition. If they said "yes" (because who would say "no," except the devil himself?), it was considered to be contrition, and their sins were forgiven on the basis of such a good work. Here they pointed to the example of St. Bernard.

Here we see how blind reason gropes around in the things of God and seeks comfort in its own works, according to its own darkened opinions. It cannot consider Christ or faith. If we look at this now in the light, then such contrition is a contrived and imaginary idea. It comes from one's own powers, without faith, without knowledge of Christ. In this state, a poor sinner who reflected on this lust or revenge would at times have more likely laughed than cried—except for those truly struck down by the law or falsely plagued by the devil with a sorrowful spirit. Otherwise, such contrition was certainly pure hypocrisy and did not kill the desire to sin. They had to be contrite, but would rather have sinned more—had it been without consequences.

Confession worked like this: Each person had to enumerate all of his or her sins (which is impossible). This was a great torment. Whatever the person had forgotten was forgiven only on the condition that when it was remembered it still had to be confessed. Under these circumstances people could never know whether they had confessed perfectly enough or whether confession would ever end. At the same time, people were directed to their works and told that the more perfectly they confessed and the more ashamed they were and the more they degraded themselves before the priest, the sooner and better they would make satisfaction for their sin. For such humility would certainly earn the grace of God.

Here, too, there was neither faith nor Christ, and the power of the absolution was not explained to them. Rather, their comfort was based on the enumeration of sins and humiliation. It is not possible to recount here what torments, rascality, and idolatry such confession has produced.

Satisfaction is truly the most intricate of the three because no one could know how much should be done for each individual sin, to say nothing of all sins. Here they came up with the following solution: they imposed a few satisfactions that a person could easily fulfill, such as saying the Lord's Prayer five times, fasting for a day, etc. For the penance that remained people were directed to purgatory.

Here, as well, there was only pure misery and destitution. Some imagined that they would never get out of purgatory because, according to the ancient canons, each mortal sin carried with it seven years of penance. Still, confidence was placed in our work of satisfaction and, if the satisfaction could have been perfect, confidence would have been placed totally in it, and neither faith nor Christ would have been of any use. But such confidence was impossible. If they had done penance for a hundred years in this way, they would still not have known whether they had been penitent enough. This means always doing penance but never arriving at repentance.

At this point, the Holy See of Rome came to the rescue of the poor church and established indulgences. With these the papacy forgave and remitted the need for "satisfaction," first for seven years (depending on the particularities of the case) and then for a hundred years, and so forth. The popes also distributed indulgences among the cardinals and bishops, so that one could grant a hundred years and another a hundred days. However, the popes reserved for themselves the right to write off the entire satisfaction.

Once this practice began to bring in money and the market became increasingly lucrative, the popes devised the jubilee year—which offered the forgiveness for all penalties and guilt—and attached it to Rome. The people came running, because everyone wanted to be set free from the heavy, unbearable burden of satisfaction. This was called "finding and digging up the treasures of the earth." Succeeding popes quickly followed suit and began to establish increasing numbers of jubilee years, one after another. The more money the papacy swallowed, the wider its gullet became. Therefore, through papal legates jubilee years were established far and wide. Eventually, every church and every home was overflowing with them. Finally, the papacy stormed into purgatory among the dead—first with masses and the establishment of vigils; after that, with indulgences and the jubilee year. In the end, souls became so cheap that one could be sprung for a nickel.

And this was of no avail. For although the popes taught the people to rely on and trust in such indulgences, they once again made the process uncertain—claiming, "Whoever desires to partake of the indulgence or the jubilee year should have contrition, do penance, and give money." We have heard above that such contrition and confession are uncertain and hypocritical among them.

Furthermore, no one knew which soul was in purgatory, and, of those that were supposedly there, no one knew which had been truly contrite and had confessed. Thus, the pope took the money, offered comfort to the people with his authority and indulgence, and still directed them once again to their uncertain works.

Now, there were a few who did not consider themselves guilty of any actual sins of thought, word, and deeds—such as myself and others like me, who wanted to be monks and priests in monasteries and foundations. We resisted evil thoughts with fasting, keeping vigils, praying, holding masses, using rough clothing and beds, etc. With earnestness and intensity we desired to be holy. Still, while we slept, the hereditary, inborn evil was at work according to its nature (as St. Augustine and St. Jerome, along with others, confess). However, each one held that some of the others were so holy that we taught they were without sin and full of good works. On this basis, we transferred and sold our good works to others, as exceeding what we needed to get into heaven. This really is true, and there are seals, letters, and copies available to prove it.

Such people did not need repentance. For why did they need to be contrite since they had not consented to evil thoughts? What did they need to confess, since they had avoided evil words? For what did they need to make satisfaction, since their deeds were guiltless to the point that they could sell their excess righteousness to other poor sinners? In Christ's day, the Pharisees and scribes were such saints, too.

At this point, the fiery angel St. John, the preacher of true repentance, comes and destroys both sides with a single thunderclap, saying: "Repent!" The one side thinks: "But we have already done penance." The other thinks: "We do not need repentance." John says, "All of you together repent! You here are false penitents; those over there are false saints. You all need the forgiveness of sins because you all still do not know what true sin is, let alone that you ought to repent of it or avoid it. Not one of you is any good. You are full of unbelief, stupidity, and ignorance regarding God and his will. For God is present over there, in the One from whose fullness we all must receive grace upon grace and without whom no human being can be justified before God. Therefore, if you want to repent, then repent properly. Your penance does not do it. And you hypocrites, who think you do not need repentance, you brood of vipers, who assured you that you will escape the wrath to come, etc.?"

St. Paul also preaches this way in Romans 3:10–12 and says, "No one has understanding . . . no one is righteous . . . , no one seeks God . . . ; no one shows kindness, not even one . . . , all have turned aside and become worthless." And in Acts 17:30, God commands all people everywhere to repent. He says, "all people"—no single human being is excluded. This repentance teaches us to recognize sin: namely, that we are all lost, neither hide nor hair of us is good, and we must become new and different people.

This repentance is not fragmentary or paltry—like the kind that does penance for actual sins—nor is it uncertain like that kind. It does not debate over what a sin is or not. Instead, it simply lumps everything together and says, "Everything is pure sin with us. What would we want to spend so much time investigating, dissecting, or distinguishing?" Therefore, here as well, contrition is not uncertain, because there remains nothing that we might consider a "good" with which to pay for sin. Rather, there is plain, certain despair concerning all that we are, think, say, or do, etc.

Similarly, such confession also cannot be false, uncertain, or fragmentary. All who confess that everything is pure sin with them embrace all sins, allow no exceptions, and do not forget a single one. Thus, satisfaction can never be uncertain either. It consists not in our uncertain, sinful works, but rather in the suffering and blood of the innocent "Lamb of God, who takes away the sin of the world" (John 1:29).

John the Baptizer preached about this repentance and, after him, Christ in the Gospels, and we, too. With this repentance, we topple the pope and everything that is built upon our good works, because it is all built upon a rotten, flimsy foundation: good works or law. In fact, there are no good works but exclusively evil works, and no one keeps the law (as Christ says in John 7:19), but all transgress it. Therefore the whole edifice is nothing but deceitful lies and hypocrisy, especially where it is at its holiest and most beautiful.

This repentance endures among Christians until death because it struggles with the sin that remains in the flesh throughout life. As St. Paul bears witness in Romans 7:23, he wars with the law in his members, etc.—not by using his own powers but with the gift of the Holy Spirit which follows from the forgiveness of sins. This same gift daily cleanses and sweeps away the sins that remain and works to make people truly pure and holy.

The pope, theologians, lawyers, and all human beings know nothing about this. Rather, it is a teaching from heaven, revealed through the gospel, which must be called heresy among the godless saints.

Then again, some fanatical spirits might arise—perhaps some already are present, just as I saw for myself at the time of the disturbance—who maintain that all who once have received the Spirit or the forgiveness of sin or have become believers, should they sin after that, would still remain in the faith, and such sin would not harm them. They shout, "Do what you will! If you believe, then nothing else matters. Faith blots out all sin," etc. They say, in addition, that if someone sins after receiving faith and the Spirit, then that person never really had the Spirit and faith. I have encountered many such foolish people, and I am concerned that such a devil is still present in some.

Therefore, it is necessary to know and teach that when holy people—aside from the fact that they still have and feel original sin and also daily repent of it and struggle against it—somehow fall into a public sin (such as David, who fell into adultery, murder, and blasphemy against God), at that point faith and the Spirit have departed. The Holy Spirit does not allow sin to rule and gain the upper hand so that it is brought to completion, but the Spirit controls and resists so that sin is not able to do whatever it wants. However, when sin does whatever it wants, then the Holy Spirit and faith are not there. St. John says (1 John 3:9): "Those who have been born of God do not sin . . . and cannot sin." Nevertheless, this is also the truth (as the same St. John writes 1:8): "If we say we have no sin, we deceive ourselves, and the truth of God is not in us."

Concerning the Gospel:

We now want to return to the gospel, which gives guidance and help against sin in more than one way, because God is extravagantly rich in his grace: first, through the spoken word, in which the forgiveness of sins is preached to the whole world (which is the proper function of the gospel); second, through baptism; third, through the holy Sacrament of the Altar; fourth, through the power of the keys and also through the mutual conversation and consolation of brothers and sisters. Matthew 18:20: "Where two or three are gathered . . ."

Concerning Baptism:

Baptism is nothing other than God's Word in the water, commanded by God's institution, or, as Paul says, "washing by the Word." Moreover, Augustine says, "Let the Word be added to the element, and a sacrament results." Therefore we do not agree with Aquinas and the Dominicans who forget the Word (God's institution) and say that God has placed a spiritual power in the water which, through the water, washes away sin. We also disagree with Scotus and the Franciscans, who teach that baptism washes away sin through the assistance of the divine will, that is, that this washing takes place only through God's will and not at all through the Word and the water.

Concerning Infant Baptism:

We maintain that we should baptize children because they also belong to the promised redemption that was brought about by Christ. The church ought to extend it to them.

Concerning the Sacrament of the Altar:

We maintain that the bread and the wine in the Supper are the true body and blood of Christ and that they are not only offered to and received by upright Christians but also by evil ones.

And we maintain that no one should distribute only one kind in the sacrament. Nor do we need the lofty learning which teaches us that there is as much under one kind as under both. This is how the sophists and the Council of Constance teach. Even if it were true that there is as much under one kind as under both, one kind is still not the complete order and institution as established and commanded by Christ. Especially do we condemn and curse in God's name those who not only allow distribution of both kinds to be omitted but also dictatorially prohibit, condemn, and slander the distribution of both kinds as heresy. Thereby they set themselves against and above Christ, our Lord and God, etc.

Concerning transubstantiation, we have absolutely no regard for the subtle sophistry of those who teach that bread and wine surrender or lose their natural substances and that only the form and color of the bread remain, but it is no longer real bread. For it is in closest agreement with Scripture to say that bread is and remains there, as St. Paul himself indicates in 1 Corinthians 10:16; 11:28: "The bread that we break . . ." and "Eat of the bread."

Concerning the Keys:

The keys are an office and authority given to the church by Christ to bind and loose sins—not only the crude and notorious sins but also the subtle, secret ones that only God knows. As it is written (Psalm 19:12), "But who can detect their errors?" And Paul himself complains in Romans 7:23 that with his flesh he served the "law of sin." For it is not in our power but in God's alone to judge which, how great, and how many sins there are. It is written in Psalm 143:2, "Do not enter into judgment with your servant, for no one living is righteous before you." And Paul also says in 1 Corinthians 4:4, "I am not aware of anything against myself, but I am not thereby acquitted."

Concerning Confession:

Because absolution or the power of the keys is also a comfort and help against sin and a bad conscience and was instituted by Christ in the gospel, confession, or absolution, should by no means be allowed to fall into disuse in the church—especially for the sake of weak consciences and for the wild young people, so that they may be examined and instructed in Christian teaching.

However, the enumeration of sins ought to be a matter of choice for each individual: each person should be able to determine what and what not to enumerate. As long as we are in the flesh we will not lie if we say, "I am a poor person, full of sin." Romans 7:23 states: "I see in my members another law. . . ." Because private absolution is derived from the office of the keys, we should not neglect it but value it highly, just like all the other offices of the Christian church.

In these matters, which concern the spoken, external Word, it must be firmly maintained that God gives no one his Spirit or grace apart from the external Word which goes before. We say this to protect ourselves from the fanatics, that is, the "spirits," who boast that they have the Spirit apart from and before contact with the Word.[11] On this basis, they judge, interpret, and twist the Scripture or oral Word according to their pleasure. Thomas Müntzer did this, and there are still many doing this today, who set themselves up as shrewd judges between the spirit and the letter without knowing what they say or teach. The papacy is also purely religious raving in that the pope boasts that "all laws are in the shrine of his heart" and that what he decides and commands in his churches is supposed to be Spirit and law—even when it is above or contrary to the Scriptures or the spoken Word. This is all the old devil and old snake, who also turned Adam and Eve into enthusiasts and led them from the external Word of God to "spirituality" and their own presumption—although he even accomplished this by means of other, external words. In the same way, our enthusiasts also condemn the external Word, and yet they themselves do not keep silent. Instead, they fill the world with their chattering and scribbling—as if the Spirit could not come through the Scriptures or the spoken word of the apostles, but the Spirit must come through their own writings and words. Why do they not abstain from their preaching and writing until the Spirit himself comes into the people apart from and in advance of their writings? After all, they boast that the Spirit has come into them without the preaching of the Scriptures. There is no time here to debate these matters more extensively. We have dealt with them sufficiently elsewhere.

For both those who believe prior to baptism and those who become believers in baptism have everything through the external Word that comes first. For example, adults who have reached the age of reason must have previously heard, "The one who believes and is baptized will be saved" [Mark 16:16], even though they were at first without faith and only after ten years received the Spirit and baptism. In Acts 10:1ff. Cornelius had long since heard from the Jews about a future Messiah, through whom he would be justified before God. His prayers and alms were acceptable in such faith (so Luke calls him "righteous and God-fearing" [Acts 10:2, 22]). Without such a preceding Word or hearing he could neither believe nor be righteous. However, St. Peter had to reveal to him that the Messiah now had come. (Up until then he had believed in him as the one who was to come.) His faith in the future Messiah did not hold him captive along with the other hardened, unbelieving Jews. He came to know that he had to be saved by the present Messiah and not, along with the Jews, deny or persecute him.

In short: Enthusiasm clings to Adam and his children from the beginning to the end of the world—fed and spread among them as poison by the old dragon. It is the source, power, and might of all the heresies, even that of the papacy and Mohammed. Therefore, we should and must insist that God does not want to deal with us human beings, except by means of his external Word and sacrament. Everything that boasts of being from the Spirit apart from such a Word and sacrament is of the devil. For God even desired to appear to Moses first in the burning bush and by means of the spoken word; no prophet—not even Elijah or Elisha—received the Spirit outside of or without the Ten Commandments; John the Baptizer was not conceived without Gabriel's preceding Word, nor did he leap in his mother's womb without Mary's voice; and St. Peter says: the prophets did not prophesy "by human will" but "by the Holy Spirit," indeed, as "holy people of God." However, without the external Word, they were not holy— much less would the Holy Spirit have moved them to speak while they were still unholy. Peter says they were holy because the Holy Spirit speaks through them.

Concerning Excommunication:

We maintain that the "great" excommunication, as the pope calls it, is a purely secular penalty and does not concern us who serve the church. However, the "small" (that is, the truly Christian) excommunication is that public, obstinate sinners should not be admitted to the sacrament or other fellowship in the church until they improve their behavior and avoid sin. The preachers should not mix civil punishments together with this spiritual penalty or excommunication.

Concerning Ordination and Vocation:

If the bishops wanted to be true bishops and to attend to the church and the gospel, then a person might—for the sake of love and unity but not out of necessity—give them leave to ordain and confirm us and our preachers, provided all the pretense and fraud of unchristian ceremony and pomp were set aside. However, they are not now and do not want to be true bishops. Rather, they are political lords and princes who do not want to preach, teach, baptize, commune, or perform any proper work or office of the church. In addition, they persecute and condemn those who do take up a call to such an office. Despite this, the church must not remain without servants on their account.

Therefore, as the ancient examples of the church and the Fathers teach us, we should and will ordain suitable persons to this office ourselves. They may not forbid or prevent us, even as their own canon laws say, because their laws say that those who are ordained even by heretics should also be regarded as ordained and remain ordained. Similarly, St. Jerome writes about the church at Alexandria that it had originally been ruled by the priests and preachers together, without bishops.

Concerning the Marriage of Priests:

They had neither the authority nor the right to forbid marriage and burden the divine estate of priests with perpetual celibacy. Instead, they acted like anti-Christian, tyrannical, wicked scoundrels and thus gave occasion for all kinds of horrible, abominable, and countless sins of sexual immorality. And they are still mired in them. Now, as little as the power has been given to them or to us to make a female out of a male or a male out of a female—or to abolish sexual distinctions altogether—so little did they have the power to separate such creatures of God or to forbid them from living together honestly in marriage. Therefore, we will not consent to their miserable celibacy and we will not tolerate it. We want marriage to be free, as God ordered and instituted it. We do not want to disrupt or inhibit God's work, for St. Paul says that would be "a teaching of demons."

Concerning the Church:

We do not concede to them that they are the church, and frankly they are not the church. We do not want to hear what they command or forbid in the name of the church, because, God be praised, a seven-year-old child knows what the church is: holy believers and "the little sheep who hear the voice of their shepherd." Therefore, children pray in this way, "I believe in one holy Christian church." This holiness does not consist of surplices, tonsures, long albs, or other ceremonies of theirs that they have invented over and above the Holy Scriptures. Its holiness exists in the Word of God and true faith.

How a Person Is Justified and Concerning Good Works:

I cannot change at all what I have consistently taught about this until now, namely, that "through faith" (as St. Peter says [Acts 15:9]) we receive a different, new, clean heart and that, for the sake of Christ our mediator, God will and does regard us as completely righteous and holy. Although sin in the flesh is still not completely gone or dead, God will nevertheless not count it or consider it.

Good works follow such faith. Renewal, forgiveness of sin, and whatever in these works is still sinful or imperfect should not even be counted as sin or imperfection, precisely because of this same Christ. Instead, the human creature should be called and should be completely righteous and holy—according to both the person and his or her works— by the pure grace and mercy that have been poured and spread over us in Christ. Therefore we cannot boast about the great merit of our works, where they are viewed apart from grace and mercy. Rather, as it is written, "Let the one who boasts, boast in the Lord" [1 Corinthians 1:31; 2 Corinthians 10:17]. That is, if one has a gracious God, then everything is good. Furthermore, we also say that if good works do not follow, then faith is false and not true.

Concerning Monastic Vows:

Because monastic vows are in direct conflict with the first and chief article, they should simply be done away with. It is about these that Christ spoke in Matthew 24:5 ("I am Christ . . ."). For those who vow to live a monastic life believe that they lead a better life than the ordinary Christian, and through their works they intend to help not only themselves but others get to heaven. This is known as denying Christ, etc. They boast, on the basis of their St. Thomas, that monastic vows are equal to baptism. This is blasphemy against God.

Concerning Human Regulations:

That the papists say human regulations help attain the forgiveness of sins or merit salvation is unchristian and damnable. Christ says in Matthew 15:9, "In vain do they worship me, teaching human precepts as doctrines." Also, the Letter to Titus 1:14 mentions "those who reject the truth." Furthermore, it is also not right when they say that it is a mortal sin to break such regulations.

These are the articles on which I must stand and on which I intend to stand, God willing, until my death. I can neither change nor concede anything in them. If anyone desires to do so, it is on that person's conscience.

Finally, there still remains the papal bag of tricks, filled with foolish, childish articles such as the consecration of churches, baptizing bells, baptizing altar stones, and inviting to the rites the "godparents" who give money for these things. This baptizing mocks and ridicules Holy Baptism and ought not be tolerated.

Moreover, there is the consecration of candles, palms, spices, oats, cakes, etc. In fact, these cannot be called consecration, nor are they. Rather, they are pure mockery and deception. As far as these innumerable magic tricks go— which we suggest their god and they themselves adore until they become tired of them—we do not wish to bother with these things.

Preface to Luther's German Writings:
The Wittenberg Edition (1539)

September 1539: Luther, without enthusiasm, lets his friends publish a collection of his German writings. He does not want his
books to distract readers from reading the Bible. After all, he had
only wanted to preach and teach God's Word—so, he seems to
say, go to the source itself. Yet, because they insist, he provides
this preface to orient readers to his life's work.

Interestingly, Luther ends with a humorous, and profound
point—sending readers (university students and would-be clergy)
off to study theology with a playful reminder not to take themselves too seriously.

DR. MARTIN LUTHER'S PREFACE[1]

I would rather have seen all my books hidden and then disappear than set this kind of example (and I shudder as I think
about it). You see, I understand how little the church has bene-
fited since it started to collect the innumerable works of the early
church, councils, and professors—establishing huge libraries for
them along the way. And the church did this above and beyond
the Holy Scriptures. By doing so, the church not only wasted
valuable time that could have been used to study the Scriptures,
it also lost true knowledge of God's Word. Eventually, the
church lost the Bible in the dust under the bench (as it happened
to Deuteronomy).[2]

Although it has been profitable and necessary that the writings of some church fathers and councils have remained, as witnesses and histories, nevertheless I think, "Moderation in all

things."[3] and we need not regret that the books of many fathers and councils have, by God's grace, disappeared. If they had all remained in existence, no room would be left for anything but books; and yet all of them together would not have improved on what one finds in the Holy Scriptures.

It was also our intention and hope, when we ourselves began to translate the Bible into German, that there should be less writing and more studying and reading of the Scriptures. Every other piece of writing is to lead the way into and point toward the Scriptures, as John the Baptizer did toward Christ, saying, "He must increase, but I must decrease,"[4] in order that everyone may drink of the fresh spring themselves, as all the patriarchs, who wanted to accomplish anything worthwhile, had to do.

Neither councils, fathers, nor we, in spite of the greatest and best success possible, will do as well as the Holy Scriptures, that is, as well as God himself has done. (We must, of course, also have the Holy Spirit, faith, godly speech, and works, if we are to be saved.) Therefore, it behooves us to let the prophets and apostles stand at the professor's lectern, while we, down below at their feet, listen to what they say. It is not they who must hear what we say.

I cannot, however, prevent them from wanting to collect and publish my works through the press (small honor to me), although it is not my will. I have no choice but to let them risk the labor and the expense of this project. My consolation is that, in time, my books will lie forgotten in the dust anyhow, especially if I (by God's grace) have written anything good. "I am not better than my ancestors."[5] He who comes second should indeed be the first one forgotten. Inasmuch as they have been capable of leaving the Bible itself lying under the bench, and have also forgotten the fathers and the councils—the better ones all the faster—accordingly there is a good hope, once the overzealousness of this time has abated, that my books also will not last long. There is especially good hope of this, because it has begun to rain and snow books and teachers, many of which already lie there forgotten and moldering. Even their names are not remembered anymore, despite their confident hope that they would eternally be on sale in the market and rule churches.

Very well, so let the undertaking proceed in the name of God, except that I make the friendly request of anyone who wishes to have my books at this time, not to let them on any account hinder him from studying the Scriptures themselves. Let him put them to use as I put the decraptals and excretals of the pope to use, and the books of the sophists. That is, if I occasionally wish to see what they have done, or if I wish to ponder the historical facts of the time, I use them. But I do not study in them or act in perfect accord with what they deemed good. I do not treat the books of the fathers and the councils much differently.

Herein I follow the example of St. Augustine,[6] who was, among other things, the first and almost the only one who determined to be subject to the Holy Scriptures alone, and independent of the books of all the fathers and saints. On account of that he got into a fierce fight with St. Jerome, who reproached him by pointing to the books of his forefathers; but he did not turn to them. And if the example of St. Augustine had been followed, the pope would not have become Antichrist, and that countless mass of books, which is like a crawling swarm of vermin, would not have found its way into the church, and the Bible would have remained on the pulpit.

Moreover, I want to point out to you a correct way of studying theology, for I have had practice in that. If you keep to it, you will become so learned that you yourself could (if it were necessary) write books just as good as those of the fathers and councils, even as I (in God) dare to presume and boast, without arrogance and lying, that in the matter of writing books I do not stand much behind some of the fathers. Of my life I can by no means make the same boast. This is the way taught by holy King David (and doubtless used also by all the patriarchs and prophets) in the 119th Psalm. There you will find three rules, amply presented throughout the whole Psalm. They are *Oratio, Meditatio, Tentatio*.[7]

Firstly, you should know that the Holy Scriptures constitute a book that turns the wisdom of all other books into foolishness, because not one teaches about eternal life except this one alone. Therefore you should straightaway despair of your reason and understanding. With them you will not attain eternal life, but, on the contrary, your presumptuousness will plunge you and others with you out of heaven (as happened to Lucifer) into the abyss of hell. But kneel down in your little room [Matthew 6:6] and earnestly ask God with real humility that he through his dear Son may give you his Holy Spirit, who will enlighten you, lead you, and give you true knowledge.

Thus you see how David keeps praying in the above-mentioned Psalm, "Teach me, Lord, instruct me, lead me, show me,"[8] and many more words like these. Although he well knew and daily heard and read the text of Moses and other books besides, still he wants to lay hold of the real teacher of the Scriptures himself, so that he may not seize upon them pell-mell with his reason and become his own teacher. For such practice gives rise to factious spirits who allow themselves to nurture the delusion that the Scriptures are subject to them and can be easily grasped with their reason, as if they were *Markolf*[9] or Aesop's Fables, for which no Holy Spirit and no prayers are needed.

Secondly, you should meditate, that is, not only in your heart, but also externally, by actually repeating and comparing oral speech and literal words of the book, reading and rereading them with diligent attention and reflection, so that you may see what the Holy Spirit means by them. And take care that you do not grow weary or think that you have done enough when you have read, heard, and spoken them once or twice, and that you then have complete understanding. You will never be a particularly good theologian if you do that, for you will be like untimely fruit which falls to the ground before it is half ripe.

Thus you see in this same Psalm how David constantly boasts that he will talk, meditate, speak, sing, hear, read, day and night and always, about nothing except God's Word and commandments. For God will not give you Spirit without the external Word; so take your cue from that. His command to write, preach, read, hear, sing, speak, etc., outwardly was not given in vain.

Third, there is *tentatio*. This is *the* lesson that teaches you not only to know and understand, but also to experience how God's Word is wisdom beyond all wisdom: true, sweet, delightful, strong, and full of comfort.

You can now see how David, in the Psalm mentioned, complains so often about all kinds of enemies, arrogant princes or tyrants, false spirits and factions, whom he must tolerate because he meditates, that is, because he is occupied with God's

Word (as has been said) in all manner of ways. For as soon as God's Word takes root and grows in you, the devil will attack you, and will make a real doctor of you, and by his assaults[10] will teach you to seek and love God's Word. I myself (if you will permit me, a mere mouse-dropping, hidden in the pepper) am deeply indebted to my papists that through the devil's raging they have beaten, oppressed, and distressed me so much. They have thus made a fairly good theologian of me, which I would not have become otherwise. And I heartily grant them what they have won in return for making this of me, honor, victory, and triumph, for that's the way they wanted it.

There now, with that you have David's rules. If you study hard in accord with his example, then you will also sing and boast with him in the Psalm, "The law of your mouth is better to me than thousands of gold and silver pieces" [Psalm 119:72]. Also, "Thy commandment makes me wiser than my enemies, for it is ever with me. I have more understanding than all my teachers, for your testimonies are my meditation. I understand more than the aged, for I keep your precepts," etc. [Psalm 119:98–100]. And it will be your experience that the books of the fathers will taste stale and putrid to you in comparison. You will not only despise the books written by adversaries, but the longer you write and teach the less you will be pleased with yourself. When you have reached this point, then do not be afraid to hope that you have begun to become a real theologian, who can teach not only the young and imperfect Christians, but also the maturing and perfect ones. For indeed, Christ's church has all kinds of Christians in it who are young, old, weak, sick, healthy, strong, energetic, lazy, simple, wise, etc. However, if you think you have made it and want to boost your own ego—flattering yourself with your own little books, doctrines, and writings, when you've done it beautifully and preached excellently; greatly pleased when someone praises you in the presence of others; if you perhaps look for praise, and would sulk or quit what you are doing if you did not get it—if you are like that, my friend, then take yourself by the ears, and if you do it right, will find a beautiful pair of big, long, shaggy donkey ears. Then do not spare any expense! Decorate them with golden bells, so that people will be able to hear you wherever you go, point their fingers at you, and say, "Look! Look! There goes that clever beast, who can write such exquisite books and preach so remarkably well." Then you will be blessed way beyond measure in the kingdom of heaven. Yes, in that heaven where hellfire is ready for the devil and his angels.

To summarize: Let us be proud and seek honor in the places where we can. But in this book the honor is God's alone, as it is said, "God opposes the proud, but gives grace to the humble" [1 Peter 5:5]; to whom be glory, world without end, Amen.[11]

Sermon at the Pleissenburg, Leipzig, on John 14:23–31 (1539)[1]

Luther preaches here on the eve of Pentecost, May 24, 1539, at festivities marking the official establishment of Lutheranism in Leipzig, Saxony. Though ill, the Reformer preached to a crowded chapel before Duke Henry, who had recently succeeded his Roman Catholic brother, George. In the polemical style of the day and with rhetorical references to the audience and the place where they gathered, Luther describes "the church." For Luther, the word of God, the apostolic witness to Jesus Christ, consitutes the church. Ecclesiastical structures are important, but they do not, in and of themselves, make the church the church. Therefore, Luther identifies the importance and role of the word of God as the issue at stake between Lutheran and Roman Catholic ecclesiologies. Ironically, twenty years before, Luther had famously debated John Eck in the same castle's great hall.

Because I'm so sick, I'm not sure my head will let me fully lay out our teaching in its entirety. So, I will follow, by God's grace, the text of the Gospel that will be read at worship tomorrow morning.

Our Lord Christ said, "If a person loves me, that person will keep my word, etc." [John 14:23], occasioned by the fact that shortly before this the Lord Christ had expressed himself in almost the same way: "He who has my commandments and keeps them, he it is who loves me . . . and I will love him and manifest myself to him" [John 14:21]. For this reason, the good Judas (not Iscariot) asked, "Lord, how is it that you will manifest your-self to us, and not to the world?" [John 14:22]. It is to this ques-tion that the Lord Christ is replying here. And here one sees the fleshly and Jewish notions which the apostles held; they were hoping for a worldly kingdom of the Lord Christ and they wanted to be the chief ones in that kingdom. Already they had disputed about who should be the greatest in that kingdom [Mark 9:34] and had divided it up into provinces. To this day the Jews have this same attitude and they hope for an earthly messiah.

Because the Lord Christ said here, "He who has my com-mandments and keeps them, him will I love and manifest myself to him" [John 14:21], Judas says: Are we to be the only ones? Is it to be such a meager revelation and manifestation? Will it not be manifest to the whole world, including the Jews and the Gen-tiles? What is it going to be? Are we to be the only ones to in-herit you, and the Gentiles know nothing? This false Jewish delusion was in the apostles and that is why this Gospel here de-scribes the kingdom of the Lord Christ and paints a far different picture of it for the disciples. It is as if he were saying: No, the world has a different kingdom, my dear Judas; that's why I say: If a person loves me, he will keep my word, and I will be with him along with my Father and the Holy Spirit and make our home with him. This home is God's dwelling, as Jerusalem was called the dwelling of God, which he himself chose as his own: Here is my hearth, my house and dwelling [Isaiah 31:9]; just as today the churches are called God's dwellings on account of the Word and sacraments. Here I think that Christ is pronouncing a severe judgment, here he is prophesying and forgetting the dwell-ing of Jerusalem, of which all the prophets said: Here will I dwell forever. This dwelling the Lord Christ pulls down and erects and builds a new dwelling, a new Jerusalem, not made of stones and wood, but rather: If a person loves me and keeps my Word, there shall be my castle, my chamber, my dwelling.

In saying this Christ gave the answer to the argument concern-ing the true church; for to this day you hear our papists boasting and saying: the church, the church! It is true that Christ wants to have his home where the Father and the Holy Spirit want to be and to dwell. The entire Trinity dwells in the true church; what the true church does and directs is done and directed by God. Now the new church is a different dwelling from that of Jerusalem; he tears down all the prophecies concerning Jerusalem, as if Jerusalem were nothing in his eyes, and he builds another dwelling, the Christian church. Here we agree with the papists that there is one Christian church; but Christ wants to be everywhere in the land. These are fine, heartwarming words—that God wants to come down to us, God wants to come to us and we do not need to clamber up to him, he wants to be with us to the end of the world: here dwells the Holy Spirit, effecting and creating everything in the Christian church.

But what is the point of disagreement between the papists and us? Answer: How we understand the nature of the true Christian church. Should one then be obedient to the Christian church? Yes, certainly, all believers owe this obedience; for St. Peter commands in the fourth chapter of his first Epistle: "Whoever speaks" should speak "as one who utters oracles of God" [1 Peter 4:11]. If anybody wants to preach, let him suppress his own words and let them prevail in worldly and domestic affairs; here in the church he should speak nothing but the Word of this rich Householder; otherwise it is not the true church. This is why it must always be said that it is God who is speaking. After all, this is the way it must be in this world; if a prince wants to rule, his voice must be heard in his country and his house. And if this happens in this miserable life, so much the more must we let God's Word resound in the church and in eternal life. All subjects and governments must be obedient to the Word of their Lord. This is called "stewardship."[2] Therefore a preacher conducts the household of God by virtue and on the strength of his commission and office, and he dare not say anything different from what God says and commands. And even though there may be a lot of talk which is not the Word of God, the church is not in all this talk, even though they begin to yell like mad. All they do is to shriek: church, church! Listen to the pope and the bishops!

But when they are asked: What is the Christian church? What does it say and do? they reply that the church looks to the pope, cardinals, and bishops. This is not true! Therefore, we must look to Christ and listen to him as he describes the true Christian church in contrast to their phony shrieking. For one should and one must rather believe Christ and the apostles, that one must speak God's Word and do as St. Peter and here the Lord Christ says: He who keeps my Word, there is my dwelling, there is the Builder, my Word must remain in it; otherwise it shall not be my house. Our papists want to improve on this, and therefore they may be in peril. Christ says: "We will make our home with them."[3] There the Holy Spirit will be at work. There must be a people that loves God and keeps his commandments. Quite bluntly, this is what he wants.

Here Christ is not speaking of how the church is built, as he spoke above concerning the dwelling. But when it has been built, then the Word must certainly be there, and a Christian should listen to nothing but God's Word. Elsewhere, in worldly affairs, he hears other things, how the wicked should be punished and the good protected, and about the economy. But here in the Christian church it should be a house in which only the Word of God resounds. Therefore, let them shriek themselves crazy with their bellowing: Church! Church! Without the Word of God, it amounts to nothing. My dear Christians are steadfast confessors of the Word, in life and in death. They will not forsake this dwelling, so dearly do they love this Prince. Whether in favor or not, for this they will leave country and people, body and life. Thus we read of a Roman centurion, a martyr, who, when he was stripped of everything, said, "This I know; they cannot take away from me my Lord Christ." Therefore a Christian says: This Christ I must have, though it cost me everything else; what I cannot take with me can go; Christ alone is enough for me. Therefore all Christians should stand strong and steadfast upon the Word alone, as St. Peter says, "by the strength which God supplies" [1 Peter 4:11].

Behold how it all happens in weakness. Look at baptism; it is water; where does the hallowing and the power come from? From the pope? No, it comes from God, who says, "He who believes and is baptized" [Mark 16:16]. For the pope puts trust in the consecrated water. Why, pope? Who gave you the power? The ecclesia, the church? Yes, indeed, where is it written? It's all smoke and mirrors![4] Therefore the consecrated water is Satan's goblin bath which cripples, blinds, and consecrates the people without the Word. But in the church one should teach and preach nothing besides or apart from the Word of God. For the pastor who does the baptizing says: It is not I who baptize you; I am only the instrument of the Father, Son, and Holy Spirit; this is not my work.

In the same way, the blessed sacrament is not simply administered by human beings, but by God's command. We only lend our hands to it. Do you think this is an insignificant meal, which feeds not only the soul but also the mortal body of a poor, condemned sinner for the forgiveness of sins in order that the body too may live? This is God's power, the Host's power, not ours.

So also in the absolution, when a distressed sinner is pardoned. By what authority and command is he pardoned? Not by human command, but by God's command. Behold, here by God's power I deliver you from the kingdom of the devil and transfer you to the kingdom of God [Colossians 1:13]. So it is too with our prayer, which gains all things from God, not through its own power, or because it is able to do this, but because it trusts in God's promise. In the world you see how hard it is to approach the Roman emperor and gain help; but a devout Christian can always come to God with a humble, believing prayer and be heard.

To summarize: The Word and the Holy Spirit (the One who prepares us for prayer) are under God's control. We believe the Word and this faith emboldens our hearts so that we would even call ourselves children of our Heavenly Father. What gives rise to this faith? The answer: God, who teaches us to pray in the Lord's Prayer and puts the Psalms into our hands. If we pray without faith, then we are doubly profane (at least that is what our disgusting holiness under the papacy taught us).

Wherever a believer's heart trusts the promise of God, it prays easily and unassumingly, "Our Father." And God hears that prayer. Outside of God's church, you can powerfully present your requests and petitions to majestic royalty and mighty rulers, but here you have no power to pray except in Christ Jesus. That way, we may not brag about our holiness like the papists do—even though they would object and contend it would be presumptuous to call oneself holy and acceptable in God's sight—teaching all the while that they can "prepare" themselves for prayer.

They also teach prayer with their choirs. Here they say, "We have prayed, even in our doubts, and it has not led us to give it up, as if we were poor sinners."

Oh, stop it would you?! It would be better to drop such praying altogether if you've lapsed into despair. Despair ruins everything, and if you go to baptism, prayer, and the sacrament without faith and in despair, then you are mocking God. What you should quickly say, however, is this: I am certain that my dear God has so commanded and that he has assured me of the forgiveness of sins; therefore, I will baptize, absolve, and pray. And immediately you will receive this treasure in your heart. It does not depend on our worth or unworthiness, because both of these can only make us despair. Therefore, do not allow yourself by any means to be driven to despair. For it is a mockery of God when we do not believe the words, "Go and baptize" [Matthew 28:19], that is, baptize those who repent and are sorry for their sins. Here you hear that this is not human work, but the work of God the Father; he is the Householder who wills to dwell here. But if we despair, then we should stay away from the sacrament and from prayer. First learn to say: "All right, it makes no difference that I am unworthy. God is truthful nevertheless, and he has most certainly promised and assured us. I will stake my life on this."

And this we did not know under the papacy. Indeed, I, Martin Luther, for a long time could not find my way out of this papal dream, because they were constantly blathering to me about my worthiness and unworthiness. Therefore, you youngsters, learn to know the church rightly.

Concerning penitence or penance we teach that it consists in the acknowledgment of sins and genuine trust in God, who forgives them all for Christ's sake. The pope, on the contrary, does nothing, but scolds and devises intolerable burdens. And besides, he knows nothing of grace and faith, much less does he teach what the Christian church really is.

But don't forget the main point here, namely, that God wants to make his dwelling here. Therefore, when the hand is laid upon your head and the forgiveness of sins is proclaimed to you in the words: "I absolve you from all your sins in the name of Christ," you should take hold of this Word with a sure faith and be strengthened out of the mouth of the preacher. And this is what Christ and St. Peter are saying: He, the Lord, wants to dwell in this church; the Word alone must resound in it.

In short, the church is a dwelling, in order that God may be loved and heard. Not wood or stones, not dumb animals, it should be people, who know, love, and praise God. And that you may be able to trust God with certainty in all things, including cross and suffering, you should know that it is the true church, even though it be made up of scarcely two believing persons. That's why Christ says: He who loves me keeps my Word; there I will dwell, there you have my church.

So now you must guard yourselves against the pope's church, bedaubed and bedizened with gold and pearls; for here Christ teaches us the opposite. To love God and keep his Word is not the pope's long robe and crown, nor even his decretals. There is a great difference between what God commands and what human beings command. Look how the pope brazenly announces—we should invoke the saints and conduct ourselves according to his human precepts. Does God's Word command this too? I still do not see it. But this I know very well, that God's Word says: I, Christ, go to the Father, and he who believes in me will be saved. Because I, I have suffered for him and I also give him the Holy Spirit from on high.

So the Lord Christ and the pope each have their own church— with a major difference. As Christ himself, the best teacher of all, describes it—telling us what it is and where it is: wherever his Word is purely preached. As a result, the place that you hear this Word, you may know that is the true church. Because where the Word of God is absent, there are also no truly faithful confessors of and martyrs for the faith. And if the Word of God were not present, then we would have been deceived by Christ and he would have indeed betrayed us!

If we could only allow it all to depend on Christ and mock and laugh at the pope, because Christ clearly says here, not "he who has my Word," but "he who keeps it, loves me and is also my disciple." Many of you have the Word, true enough, but do not keep it, and in time of trouble and trial fall away altogether and deny Christ.

It would, of course, be nice if we could always have both: the Word and our temporary possessions,[5] but "there's not much big game (i.e., peace) in heaven."[6] It is therefore something which must be recognized as a great blessing of God when there is mutual understanding and peace among temporal lords. But if not, then let them all go—goods, fame, wife, and child—if only this treasure would be left to us.

Nevertheless, I'm afraid that there will be among us many weathervanes, false brethren, and similar weeds. I am not going to be a prophet, because I must prophesy nothing but evil, and who would presume to be able to fathom it all? It will turn out all right, because now we have it. Now let us see to it that we hold on to it. But let us be valiant against Satan, who intends to sift us like wheat [cf. Luke 22:31]. For it may well be that you will have your bit of bread under a good government and then the devil will soon set a snare for you in your security and presumption, so that you will no longer trust and give place to the Word of God as much as you did before. That's why Christ says: My sheep not only hear me, they also obey and follow me [John 10:3–5]; they increase in faith daily through hearing the Word of God and the right and perfect use of the blessed sacraments. There is strengthening and comfort in this church. And it is also the true church, not cowls, tonsures, and long robes, of which the Word of God knows nothing, but rather wherever two or three are gathered together [Matthew 18:20], no matter whether it be on the ocean or in the depths of the earth, if only they have before them the Word of God and believe and trust in the same, there is most certainly the real, ancient, true, apostolic church.

But we were so blinded in the papacy that, even though St. Peter tells us that "we have the prophetic word made more sure" and that we "do well to pay attention to this as to a lamp shining in a dark place" [2 Peter 1:19], we still cannot see what a bright light we have in the gospel. Therefore, we must note here once again the description of the Christian church that Christ gives us, namely, that it is a group of people who not only have his Word but also love and keep it and forsake everything for the sake of love.

From this then you can answer the screamers and the spitters who can only spew, "Church, Church!" "Tell me, dear follower of the pope, what is the church?" Answer: "the pope and his cardinals." Oh, listen to that, you dimwit! Where is it written in God's Word that Father Pope and Brother Cardinal are the true church? Was it because that was what the fine parrot bird said to the black jackdaw?

But Christ tells you and me something far different. He says: My church is where my Word is preached purely and is unadulterated and kept. Therefore St. Paul warns that we should flee and avoid those who would lead us away from God's Word, for if anyone defiles God's temple, which we are, God will destroy him [1 Corinthians 3:17]. And St. Peter also says: Take heed, if you are going to preach, then you should preach nothing but God's Word [1 Peter 4:11], otherwise you will defile God's church.

Let us, therefore, carefully note how Christ has described his church for us. Because this description is a mighty thunderbolt against the miserable pope and his pronouncements, who has made a stinking toilet out of God's church.

If anybody wants to teach human precepts, let them do so in secular and domestic affairs and leave the church alone. After all, the papists are truly empty belchers and talkers, because Christ himself here says: He who hears my Word and keeps it, to him will I and my Father come and make our home with him. This is the end of Jerusalem and Moses; here there is to be a little band of Christ, who hear God's Word and keep the same and rely upon it in every misfortune. This is my church. This Lord we shall believe, even though the pope blows his top over it.

With these words, Christ also responds to the apostle Judas, who imagined that when Christ showed his power, he would become a great worldly emperor and that the apostles would become great princes. But he was dead wrong! Instead, Christ tells him bluntly that his kingdom is not of this world and they, with all believers, would themselves be the kingdom of heaven in which God, Father, Son, and Holy Spirit, dwells. God does not install angels, emperors, kings, princes, and lords in that church. God is the householder and the only one to speak and act: "There I will live," says God, "with every believer for eternity." But Judas, who was "good," could not understand this. The Holy Spirit, therefore, had to teach it to him.

Of this future and this ministry, dear Christians, you will hear tomorrow, God willing. If I cannot do it, then it will be done by others who can do it better than I, though they will not admit it.[7] Let this today serve as an introduction to tomorrow's sermon. May the Lord help us; I cannot go on further now.

Further Reading

BIOGRAPHIES OF LUTHER

Brecht, Martin. *Martin Luther*, 3 vols. Minneapolis: Fortress Press, 1985–93. The most thorough scholarly Luther biography of the twentieth century.

Hendrix, Scott. *Martin Luther: Visionary Reformer*. New Haven, Conn.: Yale University Press, 2015. An insightful account of Luther's life and thought, with particular focus on the Reformer's own Reformation ideals.

Lull, Timothy, and Derek Nelson. *The Resilient Reformer*. Minneapolis: Fortress Press, 2015. Presents Luther in the context of his struggles, both private and public.

Marty, Martin E. *Martin Luther: A Life*. New York: Penguin Books, 2004. An accessible account by the dean of scholars of religion in America.

Metaxas, Eric. *Martin Luther*. New York: Viking, 2017. A readable biography by a brilliant writer.

LUTHER'S THEOLOGY

Barth, Hans-Martin. *The Theology of Martin Luther: A Critical Assessment*. Minneapolis: Fortress Press, 2013. An honest, critical presentation of Luther's theology in the global context.

Bayer, Oswald. *Martin Luther's Theology*. Grand Rapids, Mich.: Eerdmans Publishing, 2008.

Forde, Gerhard. *On Being a Theologian of the Cross*. Grand Rapids, Mich.: Eerdmans Publishing, 1997. A close reading of the Heidelberg Disputation, interpreted for the present.

Ruge-Jones, Philip. *Cross in Tensions: Luther's Theology of the Cross as Theologico-Social Critique*. Princeton, N.J.: Pickwick Publications, Princeton Theological Monograph Series, 2008. Luther's

theology as critical engagement with theologies of glory, in both
the sixteenth and the twenty-first centuries.

Russell, William R. *Luther's Theological Testament: The Schmalkald
Articles*. Minneapolis: Fortress Press, 1995. Interprets Luther's ma-
ture theological priorities as the Reformer's bequest to posterity.

LUTHER STUDIES

Forell, George W. *Faith Active in Love*. Minneapolis: Augsburg Publishing House, 1954. A classic presentation of Luther's social ethics.

Gritsch, Eric. *Martin Luther's Anti-Semitism: Against His Better
Judgment*. Grand Rapids, Mich.: Eerdmans Publishing, 2012. Ar-
gues that Luther's anti-Jewish stance does not reflect his own, best
theological priorities.

Lindberg, Carter. *Beyond Charity: Reformation Initiatives for the
Poor*. Minneapolis: Fortress Press, 1993. Interprets Luther's service to the poor as an outgrowth of communal worship.

Oberman, Heiko. *The Roots of Anti-Semitism*. Philadelphia: Fortress
Press, 1984. Evaluates Luther's anti-Jewish writings in their
sixteenth-century context.

Glossary of Names

Abelard, Peter (1079–1142), French philosopher and theologian.

Albert, Archbishop of Mainz (1490–1545), Roman Catholic prelate who authorized the sale of indulgences in Saxony (as a thanks offering to the pope for elevating him to the archbishopric).

Ambrose (c. 340–97), bishop of Milan from 374, theologian and preacher. Mentor of Augustine. Ambrose was baptized eight days before he was ordained and consecrated bishop.

Amsdorf, Nicholas von (1483–1565), professor at Wittenberg and early collaborator with Luther. Lutheran bishop of Naumburg-Zeitz (1541–47).

Anthony (c. 251–356), Egyptian ascetic who lived as a hermit, generally seen as a forerunner of monasticism.

Anthony of Padua (1195-1231), Saint, Portuguese Catholic priest and friar of the Franciscan Order. Patron saint of lost and stolen articles.

Aquinas, Thomas (c. 1225–74), O.P., author of *The Summa of Theology*—exemplar of Scholasticism's use of classical Greek philosophy (particularly Aristotle and Plato) to explicate theological concepts.

Aristotle (c. 384–322 BC), Greek philosopher and profound influence on late medieval Scholastic thought.

Athanasius (c. 296–373), bishop of Alexandria from 328, whose advocacy for Trinitarian Christianity influenced the ecumenical, creedal formulations of the early church councils.

Augustine (354–430), bishop of Hippo Regius, North Africa, from 396, prolific writer and influential theologian in the West. Inspired the observant Augustinian Order that accepted Luther as a friar.

Aurogallus, Matthew (1490–1543), teacher of Hebrew at Wittenberg from 1521, was one of Luther's chief assistants in translating the Old Testament.

Bartholomew, St., one of the twelve Apostles. His feast day is usually observed on August 24.

Bernard (1090–1153), abbot of Clairvaux, prolific writer and interpreter of Scripture.

Biel, Gabriel (c. 1420–95), late Scholastic nominalist theologian.

Brenz, John (1499–1570), reformer in Württemberg, preacher in Schwäbisch Hall, and later provost in Stuttgart.

Bucer, Martin (1491–1551), reformer and preacher in Strasbourg, professor at Cambridge.

Cajetan, Thomas de Vio (1469–1534), Dominican cardinal, papal legate who examined Luther at the Diet of Augsburg in 1518.

Campeggio, Lorenzo (1474–1539), archbishop of Bologna, served as papal legate to England and the Holy Roman Empire.

Caraccioli, Marinus (1469–1538), papal legate, who promulgated the pope's excommunication of Luther in German lands outside of Saxony.

Charles V (1500–1558), Holy Roman Emperor from 1519 to 1556.

Cochlaeus, John (1479–1552), Roman Catholic controversialist and critic of Luther.

Cranach, Lucas, the Elder (1472–1553), German Renaissance artist from Wittenberg, a friend of Luther's; his workshop (with son Lucas the Younger) produced numerous images to accompany the efforts of Protestant reformers.

Cruciger, Caspar (1504–48), professor at Wittenberg and student of Philipp Melanchthon's.

Cyprian (c. 200–258), bishop of Carthage from 248 and early Latin theologian.

Dominic (1170–1221), founder of the monastic Order of Preachers (aka, the Dominicans).

Eck, John (1486–1543), theologian and professor from Ingolstadt, early opponent of Luther who debated Karlstadt and Luther at the Leipzig Disputation in 1519. Eck helped to write the papal bull of excommunication against Luther and then oversaw its promulgation in Saxony.

Emser, Jerome (1478–1527), secretary of Duke George of Saxony and early, frequent literary opponent of Luther.

Erasmus of Rotterdam, Desiderius (1469–1536), humanist scholar and opponent of Luther on the nature and speed of church reform. An influential Roman Catholic sixteenth-century thinker.

Eusebius (c. 260–c. 340), bishop of Caesarea Maritima who authored of the first history of the church.

Faber, John (1478–1541), a German humanist who opposed Luther in the early 1520s.

Francis of Assisi (1181/2–1226), founder of the Order of Friars Minor (Franciscans), noted for his generosity and simple faith. Canonized two years after his death by Pope Gregory IX.

Frederick III (1463–1525), elector-prince of Saxony from 1486, called "the Wise," he used his considerable power creatively to protect Luther during the complex early years of the Reformation. Succeeded by his brother, John the Steadfast.

Gerson, John (1363–1429), Scholastic theologian and spiritual writer.

Gregory I (c. 540–604), pope from 590, known as "St. Gregory the Great," noted teacher and writer.

Horace (65–8 BC), Roman poet and satirist.

Hus, John (c. 1372–1415), Bohemian reformer and preacher in Prague who was burned as a heretic at the Council of Constance.

Innocent III (1160–1216), pope from 1198 and defender of extreme papal power over civil affairs.

Jerome (c. 348–420), presbyter, Latin theologian and translator.

Joachim II (1505–71), elector of Brandenburg from 1535.

John (1483–1532), Elector-Prince of Saxony from 1525. Known as "the Steadfast" or "the Constant," he succeeded and maintained the policies of his older brother, Frederick III. Succeeded by his son, John-Frederick the Magnanimous.

John (1513–71), margrave of Brandenburg.

John Frederick (1503–54), the Magnanimous, prince (1532–46) of Saxony, son of John the Steadfast and nephew of Frederick III. A staunch supporter of Luther and leader of the Smalcald League of Protestants.

Jonas, Justus (1493–1555), collaborator with Luther, professor at Wittenberg and reformer of Halle. Original signer of Luther's SA.

Juvenal (c. 60–c. 140), Roman poet and satirist.

Karlstadt, Andreas Bodenstein von (c. 1480–1541), an early supporter of Luther and professor at Wittenberg until 1524. He came to disagree profoundly with Luther and left Wittenberg to seek a more congenial context for his ideas (deemed by Luther, "heretical") and methods (deemed by Luther, "fanatical").

Lang, John (1488–1548), supportive Augustinian brother of Luther in Erfurt, later leader of evangelical movement there.

Leo X (1475–1521), pope from 1513 who excommunicated Luther. Leo authorized the sale of indulgences by Archbishop Albert of Mainz.

Lombard, Peter (c. 1100–1160), compiled biblical and patristic texts into a book, *The Sentences*, on theological topics that became the basic theological text in medieval Europe.

Major, George (1502–74), professor at Wittenberg, student of Melanchthon.

Melanchthon, Philipp (1497–1560), professor at Wittenberg, evangelical theologian. Important and supportive colleague and friend to Luther. His work to reform education in Germany earned him the title the "Teacher of Germany" (*Praeceptor Germaniae*).

Mohammed (c. 570–632), Prophet of Islam.

Müntzer, Thomas (c. 1489–1525), German apocalyptic preacher; a leader of the 1525 Peasants' War, he was executed for insurrection.

Ovid (43 BC–c. AD 17), Latin poet.

Paul III (1468–1549), pope from 1534 and first convener of the Council of Trent.

Paul of Samosata (third century), heretical bishop of Antioch c. 260–68.

Pelagius (c. 350–420), opponent of Augustine who affirmed the necessary role of free will in Christian salvation. Pelagianism was condemned by the councils of Ephesus (431) and Orange (529).

Philip I (1504–76), landgrave of Hesse from 1519, supporter of Luther and founding member of the Smalcald League.

Plato (c. 427–347 BC), Greek philosopher.

Prierias, Silvester (1456–1523), papal theologian and opponent of Luther.

Scotus, John Duns (c. 1265–1308), late medieval Scholastic theologian/philosopher and proponent of nominalism.

Spalatin, George (1484–1545), secretary to Frederick the Wise and spokesman for the Lutheran Reformation at the electoral Saxon court.

Staupitz, John (1468?–1524), Vicar General of the Augustinian Order in Germany; knew Luther well and supported him.

Thomas, St., see Aquinas

William of Occam [Ockham], O.F.M. (c. 1285–1347), late medieval nominalist theologian and philosopher, known for "Occam's razor."

Wimpina, Konrad (c. 1459/60–1531), Scholastic theologian and defender of John Tetzel.

Zeno (fourth–third century BC), Greek Stoic philosopher.

Zwilling, Gabriel (c. 1487–1558), Augustinian monk and preacher during the 1522 Wittenberg disturbances, pastor in Torgau, Saxony.

Zwingli, Ulrich (1484–1531), Reformed theologian and preacher in Zurich who disagreed with Luther over the nature of the gospel, Christology, and its implications for understanding the sacraments.

Notes

PREFACE

1. David Whyte, *Consolations: The Solace, Nourishment and Underlying Meaning of Everyday Words* (Langley, Wash.: Many Rivers Press, 2015), Kindle Edition, Kindle Location 696.
2. See "The Smalcald Articles," Part II, Article 1, in this volume.
3. Jaroslav Pelikan and Helmut Lehmann, General Eds. (St. Louis and Minneapolis: Concordia Publishing House and Augsburg-Fortress Press), 1955–1986. Similarly, to my colleagues on the translation team for the latest edition of *The Book of Concord* (Minneapolis: Fortress Press, 2000), Robert Kolb and Timothy Wengert, General Editors, I express the same sort of indebtedness and confession to you.

INTRODUCTION

1. Katherine von Bora and Luther married in 1525. Although Luther was not a parish pastor, their family would serve as an enduring model for the Protestant parsonage. Katie (a former nun) served alongside her husband. She understood and supported his work. She managed their household and, when necessary, could match wits with him intellectually and interpersonally. When Luther died in 1546, he broke with the tradition of primogeniture and willed his entire estate to Katie—a sign of his enduring respect and love for her. They had six biological children, four of whom outlived Martin and Katie, raised four orphan children, and Katie had one miscarriage.
2. The Luthers regularly hosted guests for meals and conversations. As Martin talked, visitors took notes. Many of these notes have

been compiled in the famous "Table Talks" (*Tischreden*) in WATR, volumes 1–6. Selections have been translated in LW 54.

3. "Diet," here, is derived from the Latin word for day (as in *carpe diem*, "seize the day") and does not refer to what one eats. Rather, it describes a periodic meeting of the ruling European nobility convoked by the emperor, who had been elected from their ranks and presided over the business of the diet. Such assemblies were traditionally within a day's (i.e., "diet") journey for attendees and they would conduct their business during their days together.

4. The phrase "Diet of Worms" looks odd to most English-speakers. Worms's location (central to the empire, on the Rhine River) made it an advantageous place to meet.

5. Translation mine. Cf., also, "Luther at the Diet of Worms" (1521). LW 32, 112–113.

6. Andrew M. Greeley describes himself with this phrase in his memoir *Furthermore!: Memories of a Parish Priest* (New York: Tom Doherty Associates, 2011), Kindle edition, Kindle locations 266–67.

7. *Tomus primus omnium operum* [*Vorrede zum ersten Bande der Gesamtausgaben seiner lateinischen Schriften*, Wittenberg] (1545), WA 54:176–187. Cf. also LW 34:323–38.

8. Melanchthon first published the *Loci communes rerum theologicarum* in 1521, a sort of early evangelical "systematic theology." Philip was revising the *Loci* (something he did several times in his career) while assisting with the collection for which Luther wrote this foreword.

9. Luther's early duties in Wittenberg included preaching at the City Church. He received his doctorate in 1512.

10. This Imperial Diet began in midsummer and adjourned on September 22.

11. Although Luther arrived in Augsburg on October 7, his first audience with Cardinal Thomas Cajetan was not until October 12.

12. Luther uses a metaphor, *squamae* (literally, "scales"—of a fish or a skin disease).

13. The Papal Golden Rose, an award bestowed yearly by the pope on Europe's best, most faithful ruler. Frederick did not fall for this blatant manipulative papal flattery. He sent someone from his staff to receive the award on his behalf.

14. Juvenal, *Satires*, book VI.

15. *Confessions*, Migne 32:753.

16. As a lecturer of biblical theology, preacher in the City Church, and Augustinian monk, Luther was indeed immersed in the Scriptures.

17. 1 Peter 2:13. Luther misquotes from memory 1 Peter 3.

18. Roman Catholic tradition holds that the pope is the one who occupies the Chair of St. Peter.

19. Albert, archbishop of Mainz.

20. Virgil, *Georgics*, 2:484. The Internet Classics Archive by Daniel C. Stevenson, Web Atomics, World Wide Web presentation copyright © 1994–2009, classics.mit.edu/index.html, accessed May 1, 2016.

21. Exodus 16:8.

22. The relatively new Lutheran Studies Centre at Sabah Theological Seminary, Kota Kinabalu, Malaysia (Dr. Eric Trozzo, director) represents the church's commitment to interpret Luther in that context; www.stssabah.org.

23. www.lutheranworld.org/content/member-churches.

24. Paul Tillich, *The Courage to Be*, 2nd ed. (New Haven, Conn.: Yale University Press, 2000 [1st ed. 1952]), 41. Tillich self-consciously drew from Luther as a source of his reflections.

25. Sermon on Romans 11: 33–36 for Trinity Sunday. WA 508. Translation mine.

26. E.g., "That Jesus Christ Was Born a Jew" (1523) and "On the Jews and Their Lies" (1543).

27. Hitler's followers dredged up Luther's writings against the Jews and used them to help justify their anti-Semitic program. Cf. Heiko Oberman, *The Roots of Anti-Semitism* (Minneapolis: Fortress Press, 1984).

28. "Declaration of ELCA to Jewish Community," 1994, and the Lutheran World Federation document "A Shift in Jewish-Christian Relations?" (2003).

THE NINETY-FIVE THESES

1. "Disputatio pro Declaration Virtutis Indulgentiarum," in Wilfried Haerle, Johannes Schilling, and Guenther Wartenburg, eds., *Martin Luther: Lateinisch-Deutsche Studienausgabe*, vol. 2:

Christusglaube und Rechtfertigung (Leipzig: Evangelische Verlagsanstalt, 2006), 1–16. Cf., also, WA 1: 229–238.

2. Scott H. Hendrix, *Martin Luther: Visionary Reformer* (New Haven, Conn.: Yale University Press, 2015), Kindle edition, Kindle locations 1495–97.

3. Carter Lindberg, *The European Reformations* (Oxford, UK: Wiley-Blackwell, 2010).

4. Matthew 4:17, in the Latin Bible (Vulgate): *poenitentiam agite.* Luther translated this phrase "repent," or "be penitent," depending on context. As a noun, Luther preferred "repentance" or "penitence." Compare SA III:3.

5. Roman Catholic theology since Augustine (d. 430) had distinguished between the "guilt" of original sin, which was forgiven in baptism, and the "penalty" for sin, which remains until the believer enters eternal life.

6. Canon law, official pronouncements of the Roman Catholic Church, had legal status in medieval Europe. Luther refers here to "penitential canons." (See also theses 8 and 85.)

7. Matthew 13:25.

8. Thesis 6.

9. Matthew 20:16.

10. Crassus (d. 53 BC) supposedly owned most of the city of Rome when he died; symbolized extreme wealth and opulence.

11. Jeremiah 6:14.

12. Acts 14:22.

THE HEIDELBERG DISPUTATION

1. "Disputatio Heidelbergae Habita," in Michael Beyer and Wilfried Haerle, eds., *Martin Luther: Lateinisch-Deutsche Studienausgabe*, vol. 1: *Der Mensch vor Gott* (Leipzig: Evangelische Verlagsanstalt, 2006), 35–69. The proper name of this document is "Evidence for the theses discussed at the chapter meeting in Heidelberg, in May 1518." In preparation for the events in Heidelberg, Luther submitted forty theses, distinguishing between Theology (1–28) and Philosophy (29–40). Either at the meeting or shortly thereafter, he provided the textual evidence for his assertions.

2. This preface was part of the presentation to the German Augustinians at their meeting in April 1518.

3. The concept of "righteousness" or "justification" lay at the heart of Luther's reform proposal. The Latin *iustitia*," (like its Greek New Testament counterpart, δικαιοσυνη) can also mean "justice" or "justification." For Luther, believers are justified or made righteous by God's grace alone, apart from works of the law.

4. Theses 1–12: Sin and Good Works.

5. Romans 3:10–12.

6. Psalm 7:10.

7. Acts 15:9.

8. Psalm 143:2.

9. 2 Corinthians 6:9–10.

10. Luther here engages the late medieval doctrine of merit, as well as the distinction between "mortal sins" and "venial sins."

11. Proverbs 24:16.

12. Theses 7–12 relate, in various ways, to the concept of "the fear of God."

13. Psalm 143:2.

14. Matthew 6:12.

15. Ecclesiasticus (Sirach) 5:7 (one of the Apocryphal books of the Latin Vulgate).

16. Theses 13–18 discuss the topic of free will.

17. Peter Lombard compiled the *Four Books of Sentences* in the mid-twelfth century—a collection of biblical and patristic statements, or "sentences," on theological topics. Lombard's work became a basic text for theological instruction in medieval Europe.

18. 1 Peter 5:5.

19. Matthew 23:12.

20. Romans 8:20.

21. Mark 10:14, 16.

22. Theses 19–24: The Theologian of the Cross vs. the Theologian of the Glory.

23. *Posteriora*, the word the Vulgate uses in Exodus 33:23, when God said to Moses, "you shall see my 'back'; but my face shall not be seen."

24. John 14:9.

25. Romans 4:15.
26. Genesis 1:31.
27. Theses 25–28: God's Grace and Love.
28. Romans 1:17.
29. Romans 10:10.
30. Romans 3:28.
31. 1 Corinthians 1:30.
32. Ephesians 5:1.
33. Song of Solomon 1:4.
34. Song of Solomon 1:3.
35. Matthew 9:13.
36. Acts 20:35.
37. Luther originally presented an additional set of theses on philosophy (29–40) to the brothers at Heidelberg.

LETTER TO PHILIPP MELANCHTHON

1. WABR 2: 371–72.
2. That is, offering both bread and wine to all communicants during the mass. The laity in late medieval Europe were only allowed to receive the bread (wafer) of the mass. The wine was reserved for clergy.
3. Psalm 22:6.
4. The third request in the Lord's Prayer.
5. 2 Peter 3:13.

EIGHT SERMONS IN LENT

1. "Acht Sermon D.M. Luthers von ihm geprediget zu Wittemberg in der Fasten. Darin kürzlich begriffen von den Messen, Bildnüssen, beiderlei Gestalt des Sakraments, von den Speisen und heimlichen Beicht etc," in *Kirche und Schule: Schriften III*, Bearbeitet von Martin Luther, Thomas Kaufmann, Albrecht Beutel (Berlin: Verlag der Weltreligionen, 2015), 9–40. Cf. also WA 10 III:1–64; LW 51:70–100.
2. This series of sermons has also been known as Luther's "Invocavit Sermons."
3. Ephesians 2:3.
4. John 3:16.

5.   John 1:12.
6.   1 John 4:7, 11.
7.   James 2:26.
8.   Matthew 11:23.
9.   1 Corinthians 4:20.
10. James 1:22.
11. 1 Corinthians 13:12.
12. Romans 5:4.
13. Luther quotes 1 Corinthians 6:12 in Latin. His German translation of the New Testament would appear the following September.
14. Isaiah 46:3. Luther confuses Moses with Isaiah.
15. 1 Corinthians 3:2; Hebrews 5:12–13.
16. 1 Peter 2:2; Romans 14:1–3.
17. 1 Corinthians 8:7–13.
18. Luther refers to a series of violent demonstrations in Wittenberg that had occurred some six weeks earlier—forcing priests to celebrate Holy Communion in "both kinds" and without pastoral robes (and forcing parishioners to receive it), removing and destroying sculptures and paintings and relics from the City Church. This chaos prompted the Reformer to return from the Wartburg Castle and to preach these sermons. Andreas von Karlstadt (among others) had incited the populace to such action. Karlstadt and his followers were soon exiled from Wittenberg.
19. Ephesians 6:12.
20. Luther uses a technical German word here, the verb *bekennen*, which means to "confess the faith" (here translated as "agree with you"). This is not confessing one's sins in order to receive absolution. Luther and his followers would formally adopt particular statements of their core beliefs as "confessional writings," *Bekenntniss-schriften* (e.g., the Ecumenical Creeds, the Augsburg Confession, the Smalcald Articles). Lutherans would "confess" their common faith by publicly professing their adherence to such documents. The Latin word *confessio* is the root of the English word "confession," in this sense. Eventually, these "confessional writings" were collected into *The Book of Concord*.
21. "*Groben Kopfen.*" Note the double entendre: First, the phrase refers both to the distinctive head coverings of Roman Catholic hierarchs (e.g., the episcopal skullcap, the bishop's miter, monks'

shaved heads and nuns' head coverings, academic hoods, etc.). Second, it refers to the academic/impractical worlds of medieval academic theologians.

22. Matthew 15:13.

23. See Luther's 1520 writings *Address to the Christian Nobility of the German Nation* and *The Babylonian Captivity of the Church*.

24. Ecclesiasticus [aka Sirach] 33:13.

25. Acts 17:16–32.

26. Philipp Melanchthon and Nicholas von Amsdorf.

27. 1 Corinthians 7:18–24; Galatians 5:1.

28. 1 Corinthians 8:12.

29. Luther believed that God had established various "orders" in creation—marriage and family, government, economy/work, and church. Although God created these orders and they are "good" (Genesis 1), they now reflect the fallen, sinful character of creation. Nevertheless, they remain God-given structures through which human beings can live out their lives as God's creatures.

30. Karlstadt (d. 1541) and Gabriel Zwilling (d. 1558) were leaders of the disturbances in Wittenberg that prompted Luther to return from hiding (at the Wartburg Castle, near Eisenach) and to preach this series of sermons. Michael is, in the New Testament, an archangel, and Luther refers here to the Apostle Paul's comment in Galatians 1:8.

31. 1 Timothy 4:1–3.

32. Romans 8:4; 1 Corinthians 7:40.

33. Luther rather frequently refers to the Carthusians, one of the strictest monastic orders of his day.

34. "Images," here, refers to all manner of ecclesiastical art—both inside and outside of churches: stained glass, statuary, paintings, etc.

35. Luther refers here to the "Iconoclastic Controversy," which reached the highest levels of European power in the early eighth century, involving the Byzantine emperor Leo III and popes Gregory II and Gregory III, and was finally resolved in the papacy's favor in 843. Interestingly, the "Feast of Orthodoxy," in commemoration of the Seventh Ecumenical Council of 787's resolution of this question, was Invocavit Sunday.

36. Exodus 20:4.

37. Exodus 20:5.

38. Genesis 8:20; 12:7; 13:4; 13:18; 33:20.

39. Luther actually refers to Numbers 21:9.

40. Ecclesiasticus 19:2; 31:30.
41. Acts 16:3.
42. Matthew 26:26.
43. Matthew 27:34; Mark 15:23; Luke 23:36.
44. Luke 7:16.
45. Isaiah 52:12.
46. Ephesians 2:7.
47. Luther quotes St. Augustine of Hippo, *Enarratio in psalmos* XXI, Migne, 36:178.
48. 1 Corinthians 11:27–29. In the "Small Catechism" (1529), Luther develops this theme—that faith makes one worthy to receive the sacrament.
49. John 10:28, 29.
50. Matthew 26:21.
51. Luther quotes Genesis 18:19, in Latin: *Facite judicium et justitiara.*
52. Luther uses Latin: *Judicium facere est nos ipsos accusare et detonate; justitiam autem facere est fidere misericordiae Dei.*
53. Psalm 106:3.
54. Ephesians 6:11.

PREFACE TO ST. PAUL'S LETTER TO THE ROMANS

1. WADB VII:3–27.
2. Luther's famous question, sometimes translated "What does this mean?" in SC.
3. Romans 3:20.
4. In sixteenth-century style, Luther lampoons his opponents—specifically, he teases Scholastic theologians. Instead of *Schuldenker* ("Schoolmen") he calls them *Schulzänker* ("School-shrews")—"squeaky little mice."
5. Late Scholastic theologians (e.g., William of Occam, Gabriel Biel, et al.) taught that persons could freely "prepare" themselves to receive grace by the accumulation of merit. As Luther read Paul, however, attempts to keep the law and prepare oneself for grace did not merit salvation.
6. Romans 3:31.
7. Genesis 3.

8.   Genesis 3:15.

9.   Prior to 1539, the last two paragraphs here were reversed.

CONFESSION CONCERNING CHRIST'S SUPPER: PART III

1.   *Vom Abendmahl Christi. Bekenntnis*, WA 26:499–509; LW 37:-360–72.

2.   *Sacraments und tauffs schwermer*. Luther uses this pejorative construction simultaneously to distance himself from and to vilify those Protestant groups that do not interpret the sacraments as means of grace.

3.   Acts 2:15.

4.   This list represents various proposals, rejected by the early church, for understanding the mysteries of God, as revealed in the Scriptures. When the ecumenical councils defined the doctrines of the Holy Trinity and the Incarnation of God in Christ, they labeled the proposals of such groups "heretical." Various forms of their ideas, however, continued to arise throughout the history of the church. Luther had been labeled as a heretic and a teacher of ideas akin to some of these groups. Thus, he seeks to distance himself from them.

5.   Pelagius, in the early fifth century, taught that free will played a necessary role in one's salvation. St. Augustine of Hippo condemned Pelagianism, as did the councils of Ephesus (431) and Orange (529). Luther identified this heresy in the teachings of a number of his opponents (e.g., the Anabaptists, Erasmus, the Scholastics, Zwingli, etc.).

6.   Romans 6:23.

7.   1 Corinthians 15:56.

8.   Acts 4:12.

9.   Romans 3:25.

10.   1 Timothy 4:1.

11.   For Luther, the "orders of creation" (family, church, and government) are established by God and serve as basic social units of human community.

12.   Cf. the relevant sections in the "Small Catechism," in this volume.

13.   Cf. SA II, 1, 11ff.

14.   Cf. Thesis 83 of the *Ninety-Five Theses*, in this volume. A requiem (*Seelmesse*) is a mass celebrated on the anniversary of a

death. A vigil is a liturgy on the eve of the anniversary of the death being commemorated.

15. Cf. Thesis 15 of the *Ninety-Five Theses*.

16. Cf. Thesis 58 of the *Ninety-Five Theses*.

17. Cf. Luther's explanation of the third article of the Apostles' Creed in the "Small Catechism," in this volume.

18. These are the three traditional vows of monks and nuns. "Chastity," in this context, means celibacy.

19. Cf. Luther's "Eight Sermons in Lent," in this volume.

20. Origen in the third century taught that the devils would ultimately be converted. Though this view was condemned at the Second Council of Constantinople in 553, it was revived in the sixteenth century.

SMALL CATECHISM

1. *Enchiridion: Der Kleine Catechismus, Die Bekenntnisschriften der evangelisch-lutherischen Kirche* (Gütersloh: Gütersloher Verlagshaus, 1986), 481–578, vollständige Neuedition, ed. Irene Dingel et al. (Göttingen: Vandenhoeck und Ruprecht, 2014), 852–910.

2. Luther wrote a Latin word, *Enchiridion*, above the formal title, "Small Catechism." By doing so, he connects his work to St. Augustine (354-430), who had penned his *Enchiridion on Faith, Hope, and Love*, ca. 420, as a summary of Christian teaching for nonspecialists. Luther, then, places his catechism in a line of parish education resources that reaches back, at least, to the early fifth century (and perhaps even to the Apostle Paul). As an Augustinian brother in the monasteries at Erfurt and Wittenberg, Luther appreciated Augustine as a teacher of the church and not only uses the language of Augustine's *Enchiridion* but also uses Augustine's basic outline. \

3. 2 Timothy 1:2.

4. Medieval catechisms commonly explicated, in order, the Lord's Prayer, the Creed, and the Ten Commandments. Luther, as we shall see, reorders and reinterprets these three aspects of catechesis. By doing so, he builds into the catechism a law-gospel structure that identifies the core of his reform proposal—in both content and method. He intends to teach the basics of Christian theology in a practical way to uninformed or misinformed lay folks of all ages and socioeconomic groups, so that believers

might more clearly know and relate meaningfully to the loving God revealed in the Scriptures.

5. Luther here reflects the late medieval European context (i.e., "Christendom"). He refers to Christian freedom as the specific liberties that believers receive from Christ (e.g., freedom from sin, guilt, death, etc.). He also assumes that to be a citizen means to be a Christian. Cf. LC, "Shorter Preface," 2.

6. Cf. the opening lines of Luther's first Lenten sermon of 1522.

7. LC, "Shorter Preface," 2.

8. 1 Corinthians 11:25.

9. Luther rearranges biblical texts from Exodus 20 and Deuteronomy 5 in order to emphasize his understanding of unbelief and idolatry as the root of original sin.

10. Luther's use of Exodus 20:5–6 and Deuteronomy 5:9–10 returns to his opening discussion of idolatry and unbelief as the original sin.

11. Titus 3:8.

12. Luther's use of *Heiligung* (sanctification) emphasizes for his readers the work of the Holy Spirit (*Der Heiliger Geist*). The traditional translation into English, "sanctification," a Latin-based word, makes a similar connection with *Spiritus Sanctus*.

13. Luther uses a long-standing German translation of the Apostles' Creed, *christliche Kirche* (as German churches still do today) from the Latin *ecclesia catholica*.

14. The doxology, "for the kingdom, the power, and the glory are yours, now and forever," was not in the earliest versions of the catechism. Luther, as was his habit, consistently followed the medieval catechetical tradition and ended the Lord's Prayer, as he does here, with the "Amen."

15. Matthew 28:19.

16. Mark 16:16.

17. Titus 3:5–8.

18. Romans 6:4.

19. In 1531, Luther had inserted a short section on the practice of private confession and absolution between his discussions of the Sacraments.

20. Luther blends passages from 1 Corinthians 11:23–25; Matthew 26:26–28; Mark 14:22–24; Luke 22:19f.

ON TRANSLATING

1. Donkeys were symbols of stubbornness and stupidity.

2. Chickens symbolized ignorance and foolishness.

3. Cf. Wander (ed.), *Sprichwörter-Lexikon*, III:579, "*Meister*," no. 8; "The real Master Know-it-all is the one who can bridle the horse at the rear and ride it backward."

4. Jerome Emser had died November 8, 1527, after nearly a decade of polemics directed against Luther.

5. Emser had admitted that Luther's translation "was nicer and sounded better" than the old version, but added, "This is why the common folk prefer to read it, and amid the sweet words they swallow the hook before they know it." Arnold E. Berger, *Luthers Werke* (Leipzig: Bibliographisches Institut [no date]), III:172, n. 2.

6. The sixth satire of the Roman poet Juvenal (ca. 60–140). Luther used the quotation when he wanted to characterize the pope's outrageous claim to unlimited power.

7. The origin and precise meaning of this idiom remain obscure.

8. Luther refers to John Faber. The Reformer delivers a pun here: Per the fashion of the day, Faber had taken a surname other than his birth name. Luther, though, plays off Faber's original family name, *Schmied* or smith.

9. Rotzlöffel, literally, "Snot-spoon," a prerogative term for young, inexperienced, persons with an inflated idea of their own importance and abilities. Luther uses it here, to lampoon John Cochlaeus (1479–1552), one of his most enthusiastic detractors. Luther makes a pun, based on Cochlaeus' name, which means "spoon," in Latin. The English phrase, "snot-nosed-little-kid" retains something of this meaning.

10. Wander (ed.), *Sprichwörter-Lexikon*, III, 1334, "*Pflügen*," no. 5.

11. The proverb has reference to the silent amazement which unthinkingly gapes at something new. Wander (ed.), *Sprichwörter-Lexikon*, I:100, "*Ansehen*," no. 37.

12. Although text does not identify the woman who anointed Jesus's feet, tradition had assumed she was Mary Magdalene.

13. *Du holdselige* was Luther's rendering of the Vulgate *gratia plena*. WADB 6:210–11.

14. The German *Gott grusse dich, du liebe Maria*, literally, "God greet
     you, you dear Mary," has no exact equivalent in English. "God greet
     you," used as a greeting on arrival, is comparable to the English
     "God be with you" (contracted to "good-bye"), used as a parting
     salutation; in a sermon on the Annunciation, March 25, 1525, Luther
     held this same expression to be the equivalent of the Vulgate's *Domi-
     nus vobiscum* in Judges 6:12 and Ruth 2:4, i.e., an informal Hebrew
     greeting. WA 17 I:153, ll. 14–23. *Liebe* is frequently used quite for-
     mally in German modes of address without any connotations of the
     term's literal meaning of inner attachment, sympathy, and affection;
     it can be translated rather literally as "beloved," but also rather freely
     as "oh" or "my"—or left untranslated, with the tone of voice alone
     conveying the particular connotation intended. What Luther here in-
     tended as a rather literal term of endearment, his critics construed
     as a meaningless formal term of common familiarity. Cf. Grimm,
     Deutsches Wörterbuch, VI:896–98.

15. Luther refers to a 1527 translation of the Hebrew Prophets by
     anti-Trinitarian Anabaptists. He saw theological biases in their
     rendering of the Hebrew into German.

16. Thomas Münzer.

17. An oft-repeated technical phrase in papal bulls.

18. This is the major theme of Luther's 1520 treatise *The Babylonian
     Captivity of the Church*, LW 36:11–126.

SERMON ON LUKE 2:1–14, CHRISTMAS DAY

1.   Luther had already preached in Wittenberg's City Church that
     morning. WA 32:251–61.

2.   Gospel: the Christian message or "good news"; an early account
     of the life of Jesus.

3.   Psalms 73:25: "Whom have I in heaven but you? And there is
     nothing on earth that I desire other than you."

4.   Romans 8:31: "What then are we to say about these things? If
     God is for us, who is against us?"

5.   Merit: worthy of divine favor, reward, or retribution.

6.   At this point, Luther quotes the mixed Latin/German text of the
     fourteenth-century Christmas carol "In dulci Jubilo." Translation
     mine.

A REGULAR WAY TO PRAY (WRITTEN FOR A GOOD FRIEND)

1. Luther quotes 1 Thessalonians 5:17, although Jesus does affirm persistent prayer in Luke 11:9–13.
2. Matthew 5:18 (KJV).
3. These rhymes render Proverbs 10:2 as jingles.
4. In some early editions, Psalm 51 was inserted at this point.

ST. PAUL'S MAIN POINT IN HIS LETTER TO THE GALATIANS

1. WA 401:3–51. In "Epistolam S. Pauli ad Galatas Commentarius ex praelectione D. Martini Lutheri collectus. 1535," LW 26:3–11.
2. WATR 1:146.
3. 1 Peter 5:8.
4. The Latin phrase is *ex puris naturalibus;* cf. LW, 2:121, n. 37. On the meaning of the phrase in high Scholasticism cf. Thomas Aquinas, *Summa Theologica*, I–II, Q. 109, Art. 4.
5. These afflictions and terrors are *"Anfechtungen"* (Latin: *tentatio*).
6. A quotation from Bernard of Clairvaux, *Sermones in cantica*, Sermon XX, *Patrologia, Series Latina*, CLXXXIII:867; cf. also LW, 22:52, n. 42.

THE SMALCALD ARTICLES

1. Luther gave these articles this expansive title when he published them in the summer of 1538.
2. In 1538, when Luther wrote the Preface and published SA, the council had already been postponed twice and did not meet until December 1545 at Trent (Hubert Jedin, *A History of the Council of Trent* [London: Thomas Nelson & Sons, 1957], 1:313–54).
3. John 10:3. SA III:12, 2.
4. Genesis 19.
5. A reference to the distinctive haircut, the tonsure, sported by some medieval monastic orders.
6. Romans 8:26.
7. SC II:3, 4; Smith and Jacobs, *Luther's Correspondence* II:25–33.

8. Luther refers to Cardinal Lorenzo Campeggio, who represented the pope at the Diet of Augsburg in 1530.
9. This metaphor occurs in late medieval polemical literature, even depicted graphically in woodcuts and artwork.
10. Luther lists here some of the pious practices that arose from this understanding of the mass.
11. Luther critiques those groups who value personal experience or direct revelation of some kind over the Scriptures.

PREFACE TO LUTHER'S GERMAN WRITINGS

1. *Vorrede,* WA 50:(654), 657–61.
2. Cf. 2 Kings 22:8.
3. Horace, *Satires* I:1, 106. Luther quotes Horace in Latin, "*Est modus in rebus.*"
4. John 3:30.
5. 1 Kings 19:4. Luther actually cites the Latin Bible, "*Non ere melior Patribus meis.*"
6. *Epistola* 82, Migne 33, 277.
7. Prayer, meditation, Assaults. Tentatio is the Latin equivalent of *Anfechtung*—an attack by the devil, suffering *imposed by the devil on believers to test their faith.*
8. Psalm 119:26ff.
9. The very popular medieval legend of Solomon and Markolf was treated in a verse epic, chapbooks, dialogues, and farces. The figure of Markolf, a sly and unprincipled rogue, was known in Germany as early as the tenth century.
10. *Anfechtungen.*
11. The last two sentences are in Latin in the original text.

SERMON AT THE PLEISSENBURG, LEIPZIG

1. WA 47:772–79.
2. 1 Corinthians 4:1.
3. John 14:23.
4. Luther uses an idiom, *Im Rauchloch.*
5. *Zeitliche Partecke.*

6. *Es ist der liebe Wilpret (der Friede) im Himmelreich gar seltsam.*
   Luther is addressing nobility in this sermon—who, as a privileged
   class, had the means to hunt for sport. However, there is no wild
   game in heaven. What, then, would a prince do?

7. Luther preached in St. Thomas' Church on the next afternoon.
   Others of his party preached on Pentecost morning in various
   Leipzig congregations: e.g., Justus Jonas, Paul Lindenau, and
   Frederick Myconius.